WILLIAM WALKER ATKINSON

THE ARCANES
THE COMPLETE FOUR BOOKS

THE ARCANE TEACHING
THE ARCANE FORMULAS
VRIL: VITAL MAGNETISM
THE MYSTERY OF SEX

®2016 TIMELESS WISDOM COLLECTION

This book is part of a vast collection of the best classics, available both in print and ebooks. In TWC we strive for high quality books at affordable prices. Also, we look for uniformity in size, external presentation and font type, to allow you to create a beautifully organized library. For available titles please search AMAZON for "TIMELESS WISDOM COLLECTION" or join our newsletter at: TIMELESSWISDOMBOOKS@GMAIL.COM (and receive a free welcome ebook: your choice, from the collection).

This book is a product of its time, and it does not necessarily reflect the same views on race, gender, sexuality, ethnicity, and interpersonal relations as it would if it was written today.

CONTENTS

BOOK ONE THE ARCANE I. THE ARCANE TEACHING 1
PART I. FUNDAMENTAL PRINCIPLES. 1
   LESSON I. THE ARCANE TEACHING. 1
   LESSON II. ABSOLUTE LAW. 8
   LESSON III. INFINITY OF NOTHINGNESS. 16
PART II. THE COSMOS. 23
   LESSON IV. THE MANIFESTATION. 23
   LESSON V. THE COSMIC WILL. 30
   LESSON VI. INVOLUTION AND EVOLUTION. 38
PART III. THE LIFE OF THE EGO. 47
   LESSON VII. THE ONE AND THE MANY. 47
   LESSON VIII. METEMPSYCHOSIS. 55
   LESSON IX. SURVIVAL OF THE FITTEST. 62
PART IV. FATE OR FREEDOM? 71
   LESSON X. FATE AND DESTINY. 71
   LESSON XI. LAW, ORDER, AND SEQUENCE. 78
   LESSON XII. DOMINANT DESIRE; SOVEREIGN WILL. 85
PART V. THE ASTRAL PLANE. 94
   LESSON XIII. LOWER ASTRAL PLANES. 94
   LESSON XIV. ASTRAL "BLACK-KEYS." 101
   LESSON XV. HIGHER ASTRAL PLANES. 109
PART VI. OCCULT FORCES. 117
   LESSON XVI. PSYCHIC PHENOMENA. 117
   LESSON XVII. MENTALISM. 124
   LESSON XVIII. INVOCATION AND EVOCATION. 131
PART VII. ARCANE SECRETS. 140
   LESSON XIX. THE SECRET OF THE OPPOSITES. 140
   LESSON XX. THE SECRET OF RHYTHM. 147
   LESSON XXI. THE SECRET OF BALANCE. 154

BOOK TWO THE ARCANE II. THE ARCANE FORMULAS 162
- LESSON I. EGOHOOD. 162
- LESSON II. ESTABLISHING THE EGO I. 166
- LESSON III. ESTABLISHING THE EGO II. 170
- LESSON IV. ESTABLISHING THE EGO III. 174
- LESSON V. WILL-FOCALIZATION...179
- LESSON VI. THE EXCLUDED MIDDLE. 183
- LESSON VII. MASTERING THE OPPOSITES.....................................189
- LESSON VIII. NEUTRALIZING RHYTHM. 193
- LESSON IX. CYCLICITY AND BALANCE..197
- LESSON X. MENTALISM IN A NUTSHELL. 201

BOOK THREE THE ARCANE III. VRIL: VITAL MAGNETISM 216
- LESSON I. THE NATURE OF VRIL 217
- LESSON II. VRIL IN ORGANIC LIFE 222
- LESSON III. THE MECHANISM OF VRIL 226
- LES SON IV. VRIL IN PHYSICAL MANIFESTATION 234
- LESSON V. THE TRANSFORMATION OF VRIL 238
- LESSON VI. VRIL IN FOOD AND WATER 240
- LESSON VII. VRIL IN THE AIR 245
- LESSON VIII. VRIL AND THE BREATH 249
- LESSON IX. SECRET OF VRIL ABSORPTION 256
- LESSON X. APPLICATION OF VRIL-POWER....................................261
- LESSON XI. CONSERVING VRIL-POWER...266
- LESSON XII. THE PSYCHIC PHASE OF VRIL...................................271
- FINAL ADVICE 274

BOOK FOUR THE ARCANE IV. THE MYSTERY OF SEX OR SEX POLARITY 275
- I. THE UNIVERSALITY OF SEX..275
- II. THE LAW OF LOVE..279
- III. THE EVOLUTION OF SEX..284
- IV. SEX IN PLANT LIFE 289
- V. SEX IN ANIMAL LIFE 293
- VI. SEX IN HUMAN LIFE..299
- VII. THE PHYSICAL FUNCTION OF SEX 304
- VIII. SATYRISM 310
- IX. HIGHER PHASES OF SEX 315
- X. REGENERATION 320

THE TIMELESS WISDOM COLLECTION

Emerson once said: *"Consider what you have in the smallest chosen library. A company of the wisest and wittiest men that could be picked out of all civil countries in a thousand years, have set in best order the results of their learning and wisdom. The men themselves were hid and inaccessible, solitary, impatient of interruptions, fenced by etiquette; but the thought which they did not uncover to their bosom friend is here written out in transparent words to us, the strangers of another age."*

TWC is YOUR small library. Thousands of individual books and anthologies, the best of the best in fiction and non-fiction from the 19th and 20th Centuries, written by men and women whose lives were committed to enlighten the world with the wisdom of the ages.

Our fiction features names as Hemingway, Faulkner, Wells, Orwell, Huxley, Doyle, Twain, Burroughs, Chesterton, Alcott, C. S. Lewis, J. M. Barrie, Edgar Wallace, and hundreds more... Authors who have enriched our lives and forever enlarged our capacity to dream, to get enamoured by the characters, to suffer their pain, tragedies, and triumphs as if they were ours; as if they were true...

In self-development and positive-thinking, our authors include Napoleon Hill, Dale Carnegie, Charles Haanel, William Atkinson, Orison Swett Marden, Wallace Wattles, James Allen, Christian D. Larson, Florence Scovell-Shinn, Robert Collier and many more.

In Psychology, we have the works of Freud, Jung, Coué, Coriat, Adler and many others; and in philosophy, the works of Kant, Russell, Whitehead and Eucken, among others. In theosophy and mysticism, our authors include Blavatsky, Bulwer, Besant, Leadbeater, and Sinnet. We feature the works of scientists as Eddington, Darwin, and J.W.Dunne; successful industrialists as Henry Ford, Andrew Carnegie and Charles Schwab; and Economists as John Maynard Keynes...

Thousands of carefully selected masterpieces that have brilliantly captured the essence of life, are now being placed in your hands. *The results of the learning and wisdom of the greatest minds, set in best order,* as Emerson would say. Books for enlightenment, learning, illumination... that will provide the seeker –the one who is ready and is paying attention–, some of the deepest answers to life.

Mauricio Chaves-Mesén, Author of
12 Laws of Successful Entrepreneurs;
Think Success, and ***The Knights of Nostradamus***

ABOUT WILLIAM WALKER ATKINSON

Born in Maryland in 1862, he began working life at 15 in his parent's grocery store. He married at age 27, and became an attorney in Pennsylvania.

While he gained material success as a lawyer, the stress and overstrain brought him to a complete physical and mental breakdown that ended in a financial disaster. He looked for healing and in the late 1880's he found the principles of New Thought, and in applying them he restored his health, mental vigor and material prosperity.

Atkinson then began to write articles on the truths he felt he had discovered. His "A Mental Science Catechism," appeared in Charles Fillmore's *Modern Thought' in 1889.*

By the early 1890's Atkinson moved to Chicago, then a major centre for New Thought, and became an active promoter of the movement as an editor and author.

In 1900 he wrote his first book, *Thought-Force in Business and Everyday Life*, a series of lessons in personal magnetism, psychic influence, thought-force, concentration, will-power, and practical mental science. Soon after he met Sydney Flower, a well-known New Thought publisher and businessman, and in December 1901 he became editor of Flower's popular *New Thought* magazine (until 1905), and a very prolific writer of dozens of well appreciated articles in the magazine; and later on, he was a regular contributor to Elizabeth Towne's Magazine, Nautilus.

Throughout his subsequent career, Atkinson wrote and published over 100 different books, some under his own name and many under pseudonyms such as Yogi Ramacharaka, Theron Q. Dumont, Theodore Sheldon, Magus Incognito, Edward Walker, Three Initiates and Swami Bhakta Vishita.

Among the first to develop the concept of Law of Attraction, Atkinson is considered, together with Orison Swett Marden and Wallace Wattles, the masters of self-development and positive thinking, and the real promoters of New Thought, a movement that came very much to life again with the Millennium

He died November 22, 1932 in Los Angeles, California at the age of 69, after 50 years of successful career in business, writing, occultism, and the law, and a life surrounded by mysteries, including his own death.

BOOK ONE
THE ARCANE I.

THE ARCANE TEACHING

PART I. FUNDAMENTAL PRINCIPLES.

Lesson I. The Arcane Teaching.

The Arcane Teaching has come down to the present age through the corridors of time, from the dim ages of past eras, races, and schools of thought. Even those highest in the councils of "The Custodians of The Scroll," are unable to trace the Teaching, in an unbroken direct line, further back than the time of Pythagoras (about 500 b. c.), and a little later in Ancient Greece, although they find many references to, and extracts from, the teachings of ancient Egypt and Chaldea, which serve to show that the Pythagorean and Ancient Grecian Arcane Schools were founded on occult instruction still more remote, received in a direct line of succession of teachers and pupils extending over centuries. Investigators have found traces of the Arcane Teaching in the records of Persia and Medea, and it is believed that the inspiration for the original philosophical teaching (not the religion or the pessimism, however) of Gautama, the founder of Buddhism, was received from Arcane sources. Traces are also to be found in the Hebrew Esoteric Teachings of the "Kabbalah" and the "Zohar."

The Grecian Arcane Teaching was undoubtedly obtained directly from Egyptian sources through Pythagoras, the relation between the early Grecian teaching and philosophies, and the older school of old Egypt, being very close and intimate. Pythagoras is known to have received instruction from Egyptian and Persian hierophants. Besides the traditions of the Arcanes, there is to be found the closest resemblance between the ancient Grecian teachings, and those of the Egyptian Esoteric Fraternities. Some of the Teachers, however, hold that the Grecian and Egyptian schools, respectively, were but two separate off-shoots of an original and older Teaching which had its origin in the lost continent of Atlantis. There are many Arcane traditions connecting the Teaching with Atlantis, and it is possible that both Egypt and Greece received it from this common source, instead of Greece being indebted to Egypt for the line of transmission. But, be this as it may, it is a fact that all of the traces of teaching that the various occult schools gather from the traditions, scraps of doctrine, and legends regarding Atlantis can be reconciled with the Grecian Arcane Teaching.

And it is also a fact that the fragments of the Egyptian Esoteric Teachings, many of which are still preserved in an undoubted direct line of succession, are practically identical, in fundamental and basic points with the Grecian Arcane Teaching. And, as we have said, the Persian, Medean, and Chaldean legends and traditions, and scraps of teaching, show a common source of origin with that of ancient Greece.

We are speaking now of the historical view of the subject, alone. The traditions of the Arcanes hold that the Teaching, in some form, is as old as the race itself, and that it has been known to the advanced minds of every great civilization of the past, many of which disappeared thousands upon thousands of years ago, all traces of them having been lost to the present sub-race. The traditions hold that the Teaching was handed down from the Elder Brethren of the race—certain advanced souls who appeared in the earliest days, in order to plant the seeds of Truth, so that they would grow, blossom and bear fruit throughout the ages to follow. We do not ask you to accept this statement—it is not material—the Teaching bears the evidence of its own truth within itself, without needing the belief in any such authority. It agrees with the highest reason, and intuition of man, and to those who are ready to receive it, it shows itself as true. We mention the ancient traditions only that you may know what is accepted as truth by those high in authority among the Arcanes.

The word "Arcane" is derived from the Latin word, "*arcanus*," meaning "shut up, closed, hidden, away," being derived from "*arca*," meaning "a treasure chest." The English word means: "Hidden; concealed; secret; esoteric; mystic;" etc. So, the term "The Arcane Teaching." means "The Secret Doctrine."

The Arcanes are a loosely organized body of men, who have lived in all countries, in all times, since the days of the Ancient Greece, and probably for thousands of years before. They keep alive the old Teaching, traditions, legends, and instruction, and give the same to the few whom they meet who are deemed ready to receive the same. The *innermost* Teaching is never written or printed, and is passed from mouth to ear—from teacher to student—from hierophant to neophyte—as in the old days. Much of this inner Teaching is of a nature that renders it most advisable that it be reserved for the few, for it contains instruction of a nature that would cause it to be most dangerous were it to fall into unworthy hands. Even as it is, bits of it have leaked out, from time to time, and falling into the hands of unworthy persons have been used improperly. Every student of occultism is aware of the danger of which we speak. But the general principles of the Arcane Teachings have always been offered freely to those who felt attracted to them, and by them. Portions of them may be found in the various schools of the Hermetic Philosophy, and among the Rosicrucian and similar teachings. In Freemasonry, there are hints of the ancient teachings, carefully disguised and unrecognized by the ordinary members of the order.

The exception to the rule regarding written or printed Teaching, is to be found in what the Arcanes know as "The Arcane Scroll," which contains many Arcane Aphorisms, or statements of Teaching, and which are written and renewed from time to time. The authorized copies are in the hands of special persons, high in the Arcane councils, who are known as "The Custodians of The Scroll," and who are to be found in every country of the globe, unknown and working silently. These persons belong to all walks of life, and society, and carefully avoid notoriety or public attention, in order to escape the sensational exploitation of the press, and the idle curiosity of the "wonder-seekers" who are to be found everywhere. While many of these Arcane Aphorisms have to do with the special branches of the Teachings, and are not allowed to be printed and distributed generally, still the Custodians have always been willing that the fundamental Aphorisms be quoted from in writings and books on the subject. Accordingly we shall embody a number of the Arcane Aphorisms in this series of lessons, always quoting them as such, and printing them in darker type, that they may be distinguished from our own comments and explanations and personal interpretations. These Aphorisms contain the highest occult truths, and principles, and we are very glad to have been accorded the privilege of presenting them to our students.

The Arcane Teaching is based upon the fundamental principle of the existence of an Absolute Supreme Power, which is the Cause and Reason of the Cosmos and all the manifestations contained therein— all that men call "the universe." This Absolute Supreme Power is known in the Arcane Teaching as "The Law," and is represented in the symbols by the word "Lex."

The Law is regarded as an Abstract Principle of Power, impossible of being represented by words or even by symbols. It is not a Pantheistic Deity, or Being—It is an Absolute *Principle*, beyond definition or description. It does not manifest Itself in a universe of shapes and forms, by separating Itself into the Many as the Pantheistic Being is held to do in certain philosophies. Instead of this It *causes* Universal Being to proceed from Infinite Not-Being— *causes* the Cosmos to arise from Chaos—*causes* Manifestation to arise from the Unmanifest—*causes* Everything to arise from Infinite Nothing. The Law is not Being—but the Cause of Being. It cannot be said to "Be," in the ordinary sense— It *causes* the verb "To Be" to have a meaning.

The Arcane Teaching is not Pantheism, either expressed or implied—either frankly stated, or subtly concealed behind words. The Absolute can never become the Relative. The Law can never separate Itself into bits of "You and I." Nor is the Cosmos to be regarded as a nightmare dream; meditation; illusion; delusion; or imagination; of the Absolute, as some of the philosophical schools of India, and the pessimistic schools of the West, would have men believe, against all the natural intuition of the race. The Law does not dream, meditate, imagine, or "think"—neither is it deluded, or subject to illusion, delusion or "ignorance," as some have taught. These are but qualities belonging to *beings*—the Law is above beings, and even above Being. To hold otherwise is to degrade It, and to deny Its Absoluteness.

The Arcane Teaching holds that other than The Law there is but Infinity, which is Nothingness. The Teaching distinguishes between the Absolute Law and Infinity, in which it differs from the majority of other philosophies which holds them to be identical. But this daring conception is defended and proven to be logical by the Arcane Teachers, and in this teaching is to be found the only rational explanation of the Cause and Manifestation of the Cosmos. The Nothingness of Infinity, is not a condition of "Not-ness," but a condition or state of "No-Thingness." Infinity is an Infinite No-Thing, in which, however, sleeps the latency, possibility, potency, and promise, of Everything, past, present, and future. In its Infinite Nothingness, *no thing* is in actuality, but *every thing* is in latency and possibility, under The Law. The Arcane Teaching on the subject of the Infinity of Nothingness, is a startling revelation to those who have been searching for the

Truth in other philosophies, but who have found themselves wandering 'round and 'round in a mental circle—never arriving anywhere. The Infinity of Nothingness is capable of logical and rational proof. This doctrine flies squarely in the face of the current philosophical dogmas of "From Nothing, no thing comes," or "Ex Nihilo, nihil fit." On the contrary it boldly asserts "From Nothing, Everything comes," or "Ex Nihilo, Omnis fit." But, it must be remembered, that this Nothing contains within itself the possibility, latency, and promise of Everything. It is a No-Thing, instead of a "Not."

The Arcane Teachings hold that at the expiration of the great cycle of time—after æons of Cosmic Night, or Period of Infinite Nothingness, The Law moves over the emptiness of Infinity, and the first activities of a new Cosmic Day, or Manifest Cosmos, begin to show themselves. The first manifestation is the Cosmic Will, or Life Principle.

This Cosmic Will is the One Life of the Cosmos, which many philosophies mistakenly claim to be the Absolute Itself. It is the Universal Being, but it is *under* The Law, and *relative* to It, and is not *absolute*. From this Cosmic Will, Logos, Demiurge, World-Spirit, or Universal Life Principle, is manifested the Cosmos or Manifested Universe of life, shape and form. The Cosmos is *alive* in every part, and its real nature vests in the Cosmic Will, which is ever behind, under, and in, all manifestations of the universal activities, from lowest to highest. Here is the World Spirit, or Pantheistic One-All—*but it is under The Law!*

In the Cosmos is contained "The Three Principles"—of Substance, Motion, and Consciousness; respectively. From the Three Principles arise all the infinite variety of combinations of mind, energy and matter, which go to make up the varieties of manifestation in the universe. The Arcane Teaching includes the doctrine of Perpetual Evolution of Substance, Energy, and Consciousness, respectively, on all the various planes of activity. The Teaching is that there are infinite planes of evolution, in groups of seven, which are sub-divided in seven, and so on.

The Arcane Teaching holds that the Cosmos is regulated by "The Seven Laws," which are superimposed by The Law upon the Cosmic Will, and thus upon all that is manifested. These Seven Cosmic Laws are as follows:

I. *The Law of Orderly Trend.* Under this law there is always manifested law and order in the Cosmos, from suns to atoms; from highest to lowest; matter, energy, and mind. There is no Disorder, Inharmony, or Chance in the Cosmos.

II. *The Law of Analogy.* Under this law, there is found a correspondence and agreement between all of the various forms of manifestation. What is true of the atom, is true of the sun. What is true of the ameba is true of man, and beings above man. What is true of matter, is true of energy and mind. To know one is to know all. "As above, so below," as the Hermetists express it. "*Ex Uno disce Omnes*"—"From One know All," as the Arcane axiom says. This law is applied in studying the higher planes—they may be known by the lower, just as solar systems may be known by studying the atoms and molecules.

III. *The Law of Sequence.* Under this Law, there is included the activities of what is generally known as "Cause and Effect." Nothing happens by chance. Nothing happens without a precedent manifestation, and a subsequent manifestation. Everything has its "before and after" things. Nothing stands alone, and independent of what has gone before, nor can it escape from acting upon that which comes after. Everything proceeds from something, and is succeeded by something.

IV. *The Law of Rhythm.* Under this law falls a variety of phenomena, among which is the important phenomenon of Vibration. Everything is in constant vibration—everything material, mental or of energy. Upon this fact depends the variety, degrees, states and conditions of the manifestations of the Cosmos. All is in vibration—physical, mental and spiritual. Vibration is the key of relative power, and relative activities. To control Vibration is to control all forces in the universe. The control of Vibrations forms an important part of the Arcane formulas.

V. *The Law of Balance.* Under this law there is to be found an explanation for the universal equilibrium, compensation and balance, observed in all of the manifestations of the Cosmos. One thing balances another, in the physical, mental and spiritual. Everything has something set opposite it, to balance it. Everything has its compensation. Everything has its Cosmic price. In an understanding of the Law of Balance, there is to be found the Secret of Power and Poise. The Arcane Teaching contain formulas for Balance.

VI. *The Law of Cyclicity.* Under this law is found the cyclic, or circular trend of all things, physical, mental and spiritual. Everything moves in circles. The wise and strong convert the circles into spirals. Instead of traveling around in an eternal circle, the wise and strong rise in spirals to attainment and advancement. Worlds and atoms; Cosmos and Man; all are under this law, and move in accordance therewith. To convert the Circle into the Spiral, is one of the Arcane Secrets, conveyed in its formulas.

VII. *The Law of Opposites.* Under this law is to be found the explanation of that wonderful fact in nature—the fact that everything has its opposite; everything *is*, and *is not*, at the same time; everything has its other side; every truth is but a half-truth;

everything is a paradox; every thesis has its anti-thesis; every truth contains a bit of untruth, and every untruth a bit of truth; every male contains female—every female contains male. Also the fact that opposite things are alike, in the end; that extremes meet; the contradictions may be reconciled. In this great Cosmic law is found the fact that diametrically opposite things, physical, mental and spiritual, are in reality but the different poles of the same thing. In this law is found the Mystery of Polarity—in it vests the Secret of Sex-Generation and Regeneration—the Arcane Teaching embraces all these.

The Arcane Teaching, as presented in these Lessons, will include the Arcane Formulas whereby the Seven Laws may be applied under the mind and will of the individual, enabling him to take advantage of the flood-tide of Rhythm, and to neutralize the ebb-tide; to enable him to neutralize the Opposites; to find and hold the Balance and Poise; to convert the Cycles into Rising Spirals; to take advantage of the Law of Sequence—thus to Master Fate, instead of being her Slave; to conquer laws by laws; to oppose principle to principle; to acquire the Art of Mental Alchemy, or Transmutation of Mental States and Conditions. These and many other fields of occult knowledge will the Arcane Teaching open out to the earnest seeker. To those who are ready, this Teaching will appeal. Do you feel attracted to it—then follow the leading of your intuition. If not, pass it by for the present, for you are not prepared—instead call the attention of some person more ready, to it, and thus be an instrument of The Law.

Lesson II. Absolute Law.

The Arcane Scroll contains the following Aphorisms regarding this Supreme Power, which in the Arcane Teaching is known as "The Law."

Aphorism i. "The Law is."

Aphorism ii. "Beyond The Law there is Not. Higher than The Law there is Not. Elder than the Law there is Not."

Aphorism iii. "The Law is the Absolute. Existing beyond Time, and Space, and Change; transcending the Three Principles and the

Seven Laws; It ever hath been, ever is, and ever shall be. Ever Unique; Unconditioned; Immutable; Self-Existent; Self-Sufficient; Independent; Abstract; It dwelleth Unknowable, Unthinkable, Ineffable."

Aphorism iv. "The Law is the Efficient Reason of All-Things; and is the Supreme Power and Causer."

A consideration of the above four Aphorisms will throw light on the inner meanings contained within them. Let us now consider them in detail:

Aphorism i. "The Law Is." In this Aphorism the word "is" denotes "present, actual existence." It is as strong a term denoting actual existence as the English language supplies. But, in the ancient Arcane terminology its Grecian equivalent was used in a still stronger sense than the ordinary use of the word "is" indicates. In the English language, the word "is" is used as the third person singular of the verb "Be," in the indicative mood, present tense. But the words "is" and "be" have two entirely different original meanings, particularly when considered from the point of view of the ancient Arcane schools. To explain further: The word "Be" is derived from the Greek word "*phuo*," meaning: "to bring forth; to produce; to be born;" etc., the original meaning signifying beginning in time; existence of a preceding cause; relativity, etc. And, accordingly, the ancient Greek philosophers, especially those of the Arcane schools, used the term "be" and "being" to denote the relative existence of the phenomenal or manifested universe, and not in the sense of *absolute existence*. The word "is," on the contrary, is desired from the word, "*esti*," which in turn was derived from the Sanskrit word "*asti*," both of which denote "existence," in its *absolute* sense, without reference to birth, bringing forth, or production. In its true and Arcane significance the word "is" is analogous to "am," which had its origin in the Sanskrit "*asmi*," signifying *absolute existence*, which significance was also imparted to analogous words in the Hebrew, Egyptian and other Oriental languages. The word "Is" has the significance of the word "Am" in the following quotation from Exodus, iii. 14, in the Hebrew Sacred Books: "And God said unto Moses, 'I am That I am'; and he said, Thus shalt thou say unto the children of Israel: I am hath sent me unto you." This then is the sense in which the Arcane Aphorism employs the term "is"—in the sense of Absolute Existence. We have taken the pains to explain this to you at length, not for the purpose of verbal hair-splitting, but in order to bring out the true occult meaning of the term.

This, particularly, because we shall use the term "Being" in its relative sense in connection with the Cosmos, as we proceed. Remember that there is no "is-ness" other than that of The Law—all other "is-ness" is but "Being" which is relative, created, and phenomenal. In the true sense, there is no is other than the existence of The Law. For this reason we shall always print the word in capital letters when we use it in its Arcane significance.

Aphorism ii. "Beyond The Law there is Not. Higher than The Law there is Not. Elder than The Law there is Not." In these three sentences is taught the Absolute Omnipresence; the Absolute Supremacy; the Eternity; and the Self-Existence of The Law. There is naught *beyond* It, for there is no beyond; there is naught elder than It, for it is eternal and self-existent, there being nothing precedent to It to have caused or created It. We must here ask you to consider the fact that the Aphorism uses the term "Not," instead of "Nothing," for the reason that the Arcane meaning of the two terms is different. In the Arcane sense, the word "Not" means absolute negation—that is it denotes the absence of "is-ness," or "am-ness," and also the absence of even relative "being." "Not" means *absolute not-ness*—a condition of non-existence past, present, or future; absolute or relative. It is a positive denial of any existence whatsoever, of any kind, character, or degree, past, present or future. Further than this, language cannot go. But, the words: "Nothing," and "Nothingness," although generally used as meaning "not-ness" in the sense just mentioned, have an entirely different Arcane significance and meaning. In the Aphorisms, and in all of the Arcane Teaching these words are used in a relative sense, a capital "N" being employed to denote the said use of the word.

We shall consider this "'Nothingness," a little later on.

Aphorism iii. The first sentence is: "The Law is Absolute." In this sentence is stated the highest truth capable of being expressed in words. Let us examine the term and see what it really means. "Absolute" means, in its original and essential significance:

"Unbound; Free; Unfettered; Unrestrained." There are a number of derivative meanings, but the above definition gives the essential meaning of the term—and that meaning may be reduced to one word: "free." In other words, Absoluteness means Perfect Freedom—Sovereignty—Supremacy. There can be nothing *higher* than Absoluteness. There can be nothing *over* Absoluteness. There can be no Power *beyond* Absoluteness.

The "Law" of a thing, or things, is the sovereign power that exercises a control over it. And an Absolute Law is the supreme, highest and unqualified Power over all things. Therefore is the Absolute called Law—therefore is The Law called Absolute. The term, Absolute Law is the highest and most positive term in the language, expressing Power and Control. There can be nothing that can oppose such Power; or run contrary to It, or overrule It, or "break" It. It is Power Absolutely Supreme.

The Absolute Law must not only be Self-Governed and Uncontrolled, but must also be Self-Existent and Causeless, for if there were aught else to have created It, or to have caused It to exist, then that "other" would be the Absolute. The very meaning of the term precludes any outside Cause affecting It— It is Causeless; and It exists of, and *because* of, Itself. To speak of aught causing, governing, or binding the Absolute, is to utter words that have no meaning. And even if we postulate a Supreme Being, governed by the "laws of His own inner nature," then these "inner laws," rather than the Supreme Being are the Absolute. So, you see that at the last the Law and the Absolute must be the one and the same.

The Aphorism continues: Existing beyond, Time, and Space and Change transcending the Three Principles and the Seven Laws; It hath ever been, ever is, and ever shall be. The words: "Is, hath, ever been, and ever shall be," denotes the Eternality of The Law," for a Self-Existent, Causeless, Absolute, *must* be Eternal— for naught could have caused it, nor could aught ever terminate it. "Beyond Time and Space" expresses Its Omnipresence and Eternality—Time and Space belong to the Infinite Nothingness, which is subject to the Absolute Law. "Transcending the Three Principles and the Seven Laws"—by this is meant the Three

Principles of the Cosmos, and the Seven Laws by which The Law manifests Itself through the Cosmos, when the latter emerges in Manifestation from the Unmanifest, Infinity of Nothingness.

"Transcending," means, of course: "surpassing; surmounting; being above"; "being beyond"; etc. As the Three Principles are aspects of the Cosmos; and the Seven Laws are caused by The Absolute Law, it follows that the latter is superior and over them. "Ever Unique; Unconditioned; Immutable; Self-Existent; Self-Sufficient; Independent; and Abstract"—let us consider the meaning of each of the words composing this remarkable sentence:

Ever: "Always; forever; continually; without cessation."

Unique: "Without a like or equal; unmatched; Unparalleled; sole."

Unconditioned: "Not subject to conditions or limitations; hence, inconceivable; incognitable."

Immutable: "Unchangeable; invariable; changeless."

Self-Existent: "Free from Cause; existing independent of aught else."

Self-Sufficient: "Sufficient for self, without aid or co-operation."

Independent: "Not dependent; not subject to control; not relying on aught; not subordinate or coordinate."

Abstract: "Apart from aught else; separate from aught else; existing apart and in Itself"; etc.

The above definitions need no further explanation or comment—they tell their own tale, and convey the meaning of the Aphorism clearly, when thus defined. The Aphorism closes with the following words: "It dwelleth Unknowable; Unthinkable; Ineffable." These three words have the following meaning:

Unknowable: "That which cannot be known, being too difficult or subtle for the human intellect"; etc.

Unthinkable: "That which cannot be made an object of thought; incapable of being thought; incognitable; eluding the understanding"; etc.

Ineffable: "Incapable of being expressed in words; inexpressible; indescribable"; etc.

The combined idea of the three terms is well expressed by Herbert Spencer in his famous sentence; "By continually seeking to know, and being continually thrown back with a deepened conviction of the impossibility of knowing, we may keep alive the consciousness that it is alike our highest wisdom and our highest duty to regard that through which all things exist as The Unknowable." Or, as Edwin Arnold in his "Light of Asia" voices the beginning of the teachings of the Buddha: "

Om, Amitaya! measure not with words

The Immeasurable: nor sink the string of thought Into the

Fathomless, who asks doth err, Who answers, errs. Say naught!

Shall any gazer see with mortal eyes; Or any searcher know with mortal mind?

Veil after veil will lift—but there must be Veil upon veil behind."

But, it may be asked: If The Law is Unknowable, Unthinkable, and Ineffable, then why do you attempt to inform us regarding It; why do you attempt to teach us about It? The answer, O Neophyte, is this: We seek not to explain the unexplainable Law to you—we strive not to describe its nature to you, for that would be impossible, there being no words to express It, and no minds capable of understanding It were It explained. The Aphorism expresses this truth fully and emphatically. But we do desire to impress upon your minds and understanding, the fact that It is. Not only do we ask you to believe this because the Arcane Teaching is the repository of the reports of the highest minds of the race—the illumined of all ages—but also because the intellect and intuition of every advanced man reports to him this truth, and informs him that back of, beyond, over and under, and in All, there is the Supreme Law.

No matter what may be his religion, ancient or modern; or his lack of religion—no matter what may be his philosophy, metaphysics or theology, named or unnamed—no matter upon what lines he may have thought, if he has thought at all—Man must ever recognize the report of his reason, and his intuition, which informs him of the existence of a Supreme and Universal Law, governing all things. To deny this, is to deny reason. Faith is not required—reason suffices and fully informs that The Law is. And with that is-ness, the report ceases—the knowledge is then known, to low and high alike. While advanced beings on higher planes have reported great knowledge regarding the Cosmos, they state positively that they know no more regarding the nature of The Law than does the humble thinker on our own plane. But from the highest comes the same report as that which informs the mind of the lowest—The Law IS. Therefore in asking you to accept this report of the illumined, the highest of the race, including those whom we call the Elder Brethren, we ask you to accept only that which your own reason informs you to be a basic truth—The Law is.

It is true that the race has built around the conception of the Absolute Law, the varying conceptions of personal deities, and pantheistic beings, but analyze them all and you will find that the *reason* for the activities of these deities, personal or pantheistic, has been the desire; will; want; inclination or "inner-laws" which are supposed to actuate their manifestations, or incite their activities, either consciously, unconsciously; or according to some of the Hindu schools, because of ignorance, illusion, or self-deception. In short, all of these conceptions of deity are Beings who are actuated by motives, feelings, desires of "inner-laws," just as are men, and other manifested or created things. The anthropomorphic idea is evidenced not only in the crude conceptions of deity held by the savages, but also in the higher concepts; and even in the conceptions of a Pantheistic Being, or Absolute Being held by some of the philosophers and religious teachers of East and West. The pantheistic conception is utterly illogical, for as Schopenhauer says: "When we think of Nature as God, we show God to the door." And as the Arcane Teachers point out, even admitting any of these conceptions of Being, the mind must see that in the "inner law" that moves Being to activity—the Law of Itself—*there* alone is to be found the Absolute. In such case the Law not the Being, is the Absolute, for it is the causer, and controller, and mover, and *reason* of the universe.

It is true that some of the philosophers and teachers try to explain away this fact, by saying that "Being and Law" are One. But this is no solution, for even if that be admitted, then the Law *within* the Being is the Efficient Reason and Causer of Action, and the rest of the Being is controlled, acted upon and moved by the Law within it. The whole idea of *Being* must be discarded in considering the Absolute. The Absolute is, and can be, only Law. For in all conceptions, The Law is, and must be, seen to be the Ultimate Cause of all activity. The advocates of Absolute Being, object that they are unable to conceive of Law without a Law giving Being. But, considering this answer, we soon see that in order for the Law giving Being to proceed to *give* or *promulgate* Law, it must be *moved* by some inner law, desire, want, or will of its own nature—and that simply pushes back the question one step further. Try as we may, we cannot escape the conviction that Law is the First, and Last Cause—the Beginning and the Ending—the Efficient Reason of All-Things. Law is *not* a Being—*not* a Mind—*not* a Spirit—*not* a Thing—It is Law, and naught else. We must accept It as Absolute Power, and as the Aphorisms present It to us. Beyond this we cannot go. Examine the Aphorisms carefully, and you will find that they agree fully with the highest reports of your reason, and in no way run contrary to it.

Aphorism iv. The Law is the Efficient Reason of All-Things, and is the Supreme Power and Causer of the Cosmos.

In this Aphorism is stated plainly and clearly the truth that The Law is the Supreme Power of the Cosmos, and the Causer thereof. The term "Efficient Reason" conveys the entire truth regarding the creation of or evolution of the Cosmos. Let us consider the definition of the two words composing the term, in order to see the meaning still more clearly:

Efficient: "Causing or producing effects or results; acting as the cause of effects; a prime mover; actively operative; etc."

Reason: "An efficient cause; a final cause; explanation; that which explains or accounts for anything; motive of action; etc."

The Cosmos is explainable only by The Law. Without The Law there could be no Cosmos. The Law is the cause of the Cosmos, and of every manifestation within it. The very word "Cosmos" is derived from the Greek word meaning: "the universe as governed by law." Not only the Arcane Teaching, but modern science states as its first axiom: *"The Cosmos is Governed by Law."* To those who prefer the idea of an anthropomorphic Being, or a World-Spirit, as the Absolute, we have to say that, unfortunately for their idea, the facts of the Cosmos are all against them—Law is everywhere seen to be dominant and sovereign, even in its relative manifestations. We cannot escape it, and should not desire to; and will not desire to, when we understand its meaning. The explanation of this must wait until its proper place in these lessons is reached. Enough for the present to state that in all human ideas of Law there is to be found the correlated ideas of Justice and Equity. Know then that this relative idea, when transformed to the absolute plane, results in the identification of Absolute Justice and Absolute Equity, with the Absolute Law. Could mortal ask more? Has he ought to fear of Absolute Equity and Justice? Can he not postulate in the Absolute all the highest conceptions of Fair Play that he finds in himself? The Cosmos is Governed by Law!

Lesson III. Infinity of Nothingness.

We now invite you to consider the correlative principle of Truth, in which is set forth the Infinity of Nothingness—Chaos—the Unmanifest; from which, *under The Law*, emerges Everything—the Cosmos— the Manifest. We have informed you that The Law is not a Pantheistic Being, either breaking Itself into bits, or parts, in order to create Universes; neither does It imagine, mentally create, dream, or meditate into existence a false and fictitious Universe "all in its mind," as pseudo-occultism and pessimistic philosophies would have you believe. Listen to the Aphorism:

Aphorism v. "Other than The Law, there is but Infinity, which is Nothingness. But in that Infinity of Nothingness, there is Unmanifest, the Latency, Possibility, Futurity, Potentiality, and Promise of Manifest Everythingness. It is the Chaos from which, under The Law, emerges the Cosmos. It is the Womb of the Cosmos."

Postponing for the moment the consideration of the distinction between the Absolute and Infinity, which is uncommon in ordinary modern thought, we wish to call your attention to the fact that Infinity is not designated as "Not," or as partaking of "not-ness," but is spoken of as "Nothingness," which is a state of Nothing. In the Arcane Teaching the words: "Nothing" and "Nothingness," signify "No-Thing," and "No-Thingness," respectively. This may seem like metaphysical hair-splitting, but it is not. Not having common words to express uncommon ideas, philosophers must needs split common words into shades of meaning and significance, or else remain silent with their thoughts unexpressed. In order to understand "No-Thingness," and a "No-Thing," you must understand the meaning of the word "Thing" to which these words are opposed. A "Thing" is "whatever exists as a separate object of sense or thought," in the sense of *being* and having apparent qualities which can be thought of in terms of sense-perception, such as size, shape, form, etc.—something connected directly or indirectly with physical appearance—something of the relative universe—something having a correspondence in experience.

And No-thingness must be the opposite of Thingness.

Therefore the Aphorism practically says that Infinity is a "Latency" that is No-Thing in reality, but yet has an existence of some kind, at least potentially. It can contain naught actually apparent to the senses; naught that can be experienced; naught that can be sensed; naught that can be thought of by the intellect, nor pictured in the imagination—in short, nothing that is capable of inducing a mental image in your mind. And yet it *exists* (if the word can be used) as a state or condition in which all is in Latency, Possibility, Futurity, Potentiality, and Promise. In short, it is The Unmanifest containing All Manifestation within it in latency, possibility and futurity, awaiting the force of The Law to bid it conceive, produce, and bring forth Being. We shall learn about this Infinite Nothingness shortly, in connection with another Aphorism. Enough for the present to realize the words of the Aphorism before us, which informs us that other than The Law there is Not, with the exception of the Infinity of Nothingness which exists in latency. Other than The Law, there is Not in the absolute sense.

Philosophies and schools of metaphysics have generally confused the meaning of the two terms "absolute" and "relative," and have used them as identical in meaning. The Arcane Teaching makes a sharp distinction between the two terms, however—not a difference based upon a metaphysical hair-splitting tendency, but because there are two entirely different ideas which must be expressed in these two words, and, in spite of the customs of the metaphysicians the distinction must be made. We do not wish to lead you into an extended metaphysical discussion, but we think that you should be taught to make this important distinction in the true meaning of these terms.

The term "absolute," in its true sense and essential meaning, implies an *apartness; separation; independence; self-existence; self-sufficiency; supreme; unfettered; free.* The "essence of the essence" of its meaning is to be found in the words "free, independent, self-sufficient." And when used in connection with the word "law," it represents the Supreme Power, depending upon no other power; its own sovereign; and the ruler of all else, without restriction. This conception we have in The Absolute Law, which is the Independent, Free, Sovereign Lord of All.

The term "infinite" has an entirely different meaning, in its true sense, although the philosophers and metaphysicians often add to it the attributes of the Absolute, which is a mistake. The word "infinite" in its true sense and essential meaning, implies *a state of boundlessness; limitlessness; not circumscribed; as to time, space, variety, possibilities, combination, shape, form, etc.* Its essence may be understood by referring to the words from which it sprung, i. e., the Latin words *"in,"* meaning *"not"*; and *"finitus"* meaning *"finished."* In short, the word "infinite" means *"not finished; not complete; capable of unlimited manifestation, and possibilities."* So, you see, while the idea of "Absolute" means *fixed, complete independent* state or condition; "Infinite" means a state of endless and unlimited possibilities of manifestation and expression.

The true philosophical idea of Infinity, consists of the conception of any sort of mental object as having the quality of quantity which cannot be exhausted by any succession of experiences, however prolonged or extended, in time, space, variety, or number. By holding this idea in mind, you will never make the mistake of confounding infinity with absoluteness, hereafter. The chief cause of the confusion arises from the unauthorized use of the term "infinite" in relation to "power." *Power belongs to the Absolute, and is not one of the attributes of Infinity.* "Infinite Power" would mean an infinite possibility of the *manifestation* and *expression* of unlimited power; while Absolute Power means *all the Power there is,* fixed, independent and sovereign, unvarying and immutable, and not subject to changes of degree, etc. Absolute Law is *not* an infinite capacity for expression of power—It is *Power-in-Itself*.

All the great thinkers of all times, esoteric and exoteric, have agreed in this idea of the Infinite being the Unlimited Possibility.

The best of the ancient Greek philosophers, from Aristotle down, held to this idea. As Schopenhauer says: "It is already a doctrine of Aristotle, that Infinity can never be *actu* (actual, given, fixed) but only *potentia* (in possibility, latency, promise, potentiality)." And as Lewes says: "If Zero is the sign of a vanished quantity, the Infinite is the sign of continuity." We trust that you now see that the Absolute could never become Relative or Many—and that the Infinite alone is capable of endless changes in shape, form, variety, in time, space, and number; and contains within itself the *promise, possibility, latency, and potentiality of Everything*.

The Arcane Teachers, in the olden time, illustrated this to their pupils by the following symbols: The figure "1" standing for the Absolute, and being fixed, independent, sovereign, and alone. By itself, and in itself it is incapable of multiplying or dividing—multiply anything by "1"; or divide anything by "1," and the thing remains unchanged. Multiply or divide "1" by itself, and the answer still is "1," showing that the Absolute cannot be increased or divided, even by itself. Subtract "1" from itself, and the result is "0," showing that if the Absolute were subtracted from it would cease to exist, and there would be naught left but the Infinite Nothingness. Then the Teachers called the attention of the pupil to the Zero, or "Infinite Nothing" symbol, i. e., "0." In itself, "0" means Nothing. Multiply or divide anything by "0," and the answer is always "0." Multiply

"0" by itself, and "0" remains—the Infinite cannot increase itself, for in its circle it includes All Possibility. But divide "0" by itself— and lo! "0 into 0 goes 1 time": the answer is "1." showing that if the Infinite be divided by itself, the Absolute is found to be at its centre, undisturbed, independent, self-existent. The symbol of Infinity, in mathematics, however, is not "0" or Unmanifest Infinity, but ∞ which indicates Manifest Infinity, the symbol always indicating endless continuation of action.

Now the symbol of the Infinite Nothing, becoming Infinite Everything. Place a string of "0's," as follows: 000,000,000,000,000—you see that they still mean "Nothing."

Now place "1" (the symbol of the Absolute), before the string and we have 1,000,000,000,000,000, which we may enlarge to infinite number by the addition of "o's." Or place the Absolute "1," behind the string, and we have .000,000,000.000,000,1, a very small decimal, which may be carried to infinitesimal smallness by the addition of "o's." Thus we see, by symbols, that the action of the Absolute Law on the Infinite Nothingness produces Infinite Greatness, or Infinite Smallness.

Now that you understand that Infinity means the Infinite *Possibility* of Things, rather than an Infinite Manifest *Thing*, you may be able to see that the Infinity of Nothingness of the Arcane Teaching is not quite so irrational as it appeared at first sight. In order to realize the truth of the Aphorism still more forcibly, let us consider what Infinity (even in the ordinary use of the term) really is. You will find that all thought if analyzed, implies the Nothingness of Infinity.

Non-Being, or Nothingness, was always regarded by certain schools of the ancient Greek philosophy, as existent in a philosophical sense. Empty space was considered as truly existent as the atoms which afterward appeared in space. Plato regarded Empty Space as the matrix, or mould, in which the universe was formed. He held that there was possible an abstract realization of pure empty space, which is Nothing; the Void, which is the all-containing receptacle of creative energy, and in which being, first distinguished into geometrical figures, becomes the framework of the physical world. Scotus held that since Deity creates the world out of Nothing, then Nothing must exist as an emanation of Deity. Hegel distinguished between a *"nicht,"* or "Not"; and a *"nichts,"* or "Nothing." Theology has always held that Deity "created the universe from Nothing," thereby implying at least a quasi-existence of Infinite Nothingness. Spinoza recognized an "infinitely infinite" which is practically an Infinite Nothing. Plato said that "Space as a Thing is incredible, difficult of explanation, most difficult to comprehend." And Zeno, the Eleatic, said: "If Space is a Thing, it must be *in* Something, and so in Space; for everything that is, is *in* Something, and so in Space; and so on *ad infinitum*. Therefore, Space is *not* a Thing." So much for the philosophers. Let us see what our own reason informs us.

Let us first examine the idea of Space. Space is the mental symbol for Infinity. Consider yourself as standing at a fixed point in Space—then you must realize that there exists an infinite distance or extension in Space, from that point, in an infinite number of directions. Leaving out of consideration all objects in space—considering Pure Empty Space—and you must see that there is an *endless extension* possible, in innumerable directions—extension without end. Imagine a number of miles represented *in a row of figures extending from earth to the most distant star*; then multiply that number by itself; and then the product by itself; and so on, for a time equal to the number of years since the Cosmic Day began. Then you would have a number of miles, the written figures of which would fill all the space that your mind is able of even conceiving. Then think of a Being traveling to the extent of that measurement—would he then be near the end of space? No! the distance traveled by him would be as a mathematical "Nothing" or Zero, compared with Infinite Space. No mathematician could have figured out the infinitesimal smallness of the fraction denoting the comparison, were he to have worked continually since the dawn of the Cosmic day. The calculation would be endless, because the result would be infinitesimal, and at the end, he would have to place the sign of "infinity" back of it. Just think! *To be able to travel for all Eternity through Space without coming to an end!* You cannot come to an end of Space, even in thought or imagination—try it! You will find that think as *far* as you will into Space, there must always be Infinite Space *beyond* that imagined point. There is "no up or down" in Space. Space is something with its centre *everywhere*, and its circumference *nowhere*. At the last, philosophy and science are compelled to hold that "Space is merely the *possibility* of infinite extension; or the *infinite possibility* of extension"—to the Universal Ether. In the end, Ether is called the Great Mystery of Science. It must be considered as a Nothing that is a Something. A leading scientific lecturer said, and wrote, recently: "The Ether is unconditioned, an entity of *no properties but of all possibilities*, or, more exactly, not an entity at all, but *an infinite possibility*." And, so we find, even Matter and Things themselves, arising from and being resolved into an Infinite Nothingness that is also Infinite Possibility.

Now, for a moment, let us endeavor to imagine the condition or state of the Infinity of Nothingness—the Unmanifest Cosmos—

during the Cosmic Night, and before the faintest dawn of the new Cosmic Day. The Three Cosmic Principles are resolved into the condition of the Unmanifest, but are not destroyed—there are Nothing, but *not* "Not!" The Three Cosmic Principles are Substance; Motion; and Consciousness, respectively. Substance has assumed its most subtle form, infinitely rarer and finer than the finest ether—it is practically Nothing, but yet exists in latency, possibility, and promise. Motion has assumed a rate of vibration so high that it is practically at Rest, although not destroyed —it is still Motion in latency. Consciousness has assumed the condition of a deep unconsciousness—a profound dreamless sleep; a swoon following upon the infinite ecstasy of the Supreme Cosmic Consciousness of the previous Cosmic Day. It knows Nothing; is conscious of Nothing—for there is but Nothing of which it could be conscious, or could know, for all manifestation has ceased until the dawn of the new Cosmic Day. It is even unconscious of the presence and power of The Law, although The Law still reigns over it, and will awaken it once more, as it has many times before, in the Eternal Chain of Cosmic Days and Nights.

The Cosmos sleeps in the condition of Infinite Nothingness—the Unmanifest! The Abysmal Abyss—the Eternal Deep— the Face of the Waters—the Void—the Cosmic Womb! The Mother Sleeps! The Laws of Cyclic Rhythm have brought to Her the Rest of the Cosmic Night! But she will awaken and greet her Supreme Lord at the dawn of the Cosmic Day. From the Cosmic Womb will proceed The Cosmic Will, which will manifest the universe of universes; infinitudes of infinitudes of shape, form, and variety, of things, life, and beings. In her Existence is the Promise of all that Shall Be throughout the Ages and Aeons of Eternities of Eternities. The Mother sleeps, sleeps, sleeps! But, through the Night, as through the Day, The Law is, immutable, unchanged, Absolute.

PART II. THE COSMOS.

Lesson IV. The Manifestation.

This is the Arcane Teaching regarding the process whereby the Unmanifest becomes Manifest; the Latency becomes Activity; the Possibility becomes Actuality; the Potentiality becomes Reality; the Promise becomes Fulfillment. Listen to the Aphorism:

Aphorism vi. "During the aeons of the Cosmic Night, The Law dwells Alone, in solitude; The Cosmos remains resolved into its condition of the Unmanifest—the Infinity of Nothingness. Then comes the dawn, when The Law superimposes the Infinity of Nothingness, and causes the Unmanifest to become Manifest; the Nothing to become Everything; Latency to become Activity;

Potentiality to become Reality; Promise to become Fulfillment."

At the extreme swing of the pendulum of Rhythm—at the point of the Cycle in which End fades into Beginning—the climax of the Cosmic Night is reached in the form of Absolute Rest, extending over æons of time. Then after the æons of

Absolute Rest come the first activities of the future Cosmic Day. During the Cosmic Night, as the Aphorism states: "The Law dwells Alone, in solitude; The Cosmos remains resolved into its condition of the Unmanifest—the Infinity of Nothingness."

Then begin the first stirrings of the birth of the new Cosmic Day, which the Aphorism describes as follows: "Then comes the dawn, when The Law superimposes the Infinity of Nothingness, and causes the Unmanifest to become Manifest; the Nothing to become Everything; Latency to become Reality; Promise to become Fulfillment." Let us consider what is meant by the words of the Aphorism.

The first step of the new activities is indicated by the words:

"The Law superimposes the Infinity of Nothingness." These words, at first consideration, would seem to indicate a decided action of The Law in the direction of "superimposing" Infinity. But such is not the Arcane Teaching. The Teachers hold that The

Law exerts no different degree or kind of power at the period of dawn, than at the period of dusk; no more at the period of high-noon, than at the period of midnight. During the Cosmic Day and Cosmic Night, The Law is unchangeable and constant in its power and influence. The difference is caused by the Cyclic Swing, or Rhythmic Movement, in the Cosmos itself, Manifest or Unmanifest. The Law is *over and above* Rhythm or Cyclicity, or any of the Seven Laws, and is Changeless. The Cosmos, on the contrary is *under* the Seven Laws superimposed by The Law, and is Changeable—Constantly Changing. The difference in the degree of power received from The Law is due to the changing condition of the Cosmos, or Infinity.

In order to understand what has been said, let us imagine a mighty magnet, constant in its power, and invariable in its manifestations of magnetic force upon all within its magnetic field. Then let us imagine an Infinity of infinitesimal particles of steel-filings, separated from the magnet by a glass watch-cover. Let us suppose that owing to the operation of some unknown magnetic law, the *receptivity* of the steel particles changes in rhythmic periods, or in cyclic recurrence. In that case, it would follow that, although the power of the magnet were unchangeable and its manifestations invariable, still the action of the steel-particles would cause it to appear otherwise. For at times there would be a marked degree of power shown, and at other times a much less degree would be exhibited—*but the difference would be in the nature of the steel-particles, and not in that of the magnet.*

Or, suppose, that the Earth were to manifest varying degrees of receptivity to the Attraction of Gravitation of the Sun—then while it would seem to be a varying degree of power of the sun, the difference would really be caused by the changes in the Earth, the Sun remaining constant and invariable all the time. In these two examples, may be seen the nature of the action of The Law upon the Cosmos, or Infinity.

Some of the occult schools who have been influenced by the Arcane Teaching, hold that The Law is *attracted* by Infinity, or the Cosmos, just as the latter is by The Law. In other words, they hold that there is a *mutual* attraction and effect—an action and a reaction—a reciprocal action. But this is incorrect. The Law is *never* attracted or affected in any way by the Cosmos, or Infinity. It is Absolute and beyond mutual Relationship. Were the Cosmos and Infinity not to exist, The Law would not vary a particle in any way whatsoever. Its Absoluteness raises it above Relations. But while this is so, the fact of the constant outpouring of the Power of The Law causes the Cosmos to be affected by it, just as are the steel-filings by the Magnet. According to Rhythm, the degree of Power received by the Cosmos must vary—but

The Law changes not. In fact, the Seven Laws, themselves, which produce these changes in the Cosmos, are a part of the action and power of The Law, as experienced by the Cosmos—they are superimposed by The Law.

The Aphorism says: "The Law superimposes the Infinity of Nothingness." What is meant by "superimposes"? The word "*super*" means "over, or above"; and "*impose*" means "to lay or place upon." "Superimpose" means "to place upon from above," or as used in the Aphorism: "To influence from above." In other words, the Infinity of Nothingness, or Unmanifest Cosmos, owing to the influence of Rhythm and Cyclicity, begins once more to experience the active radiation of the Power of The Law, which serves to vitalize and energize it, and thus begins the dawn of the new Cosmic Day—and the beginnings of the new Universal Life, or Cosmic Will.

In order to understand this awakening, or stirring into activity of the Cosmos, which dwells latent within the Womb of the Infinity of Nothingness, let us consider the Three Principles of the Cosmos, from which all forms, shapes, combinations and varieties of manifestation arise. These "Three Principles" are as follows: (1) The Cosmic Principle of Substance; (2) the Cosmic Principle of Motion; (3) the Cosmic Principle of Consciousness. These Three Principles are Unmanifest during the Cosmic Night, but awaken into nascence and activity with the first thrill of the dawn of the new Cosmic Day. In the end, and at the last, these Three must be considered as phases of One. But that One, in itself, is but the reflection, so to speak, of The Law, although not by any means to be considered as being "qualities" or "phases" of The Law. The Law has no "qualities" or "phases"—it is over and above these things, which are but the aspects of Infinity, or the Cosmos. The Three Principles are fundamental in all manifestations of the Cosmos, from lowest to highest—from the simplest to the most complex. Wherever is found any manifestation of the Cosmos, there is and *must be* found the presence of the Three Principles in some degree of development or activity. If you prefer, you may think of the Cosmos as *consisting of* merely these Three Principles, manifest or unmanifest. These Three Principles we can never know of themselves—we know them only through and by their manifestations. Let us consider them in detail, by the light of the Arcane Teaching.

I. *The First Principle—Substance*. Substance, as the term is used in the Arcane Teaching, means the underlying "body" of things— their material quality. Everything that is manifested in the Cosmos has its "body" or material quality. Substance includes all that we may think of as Matter, in its various degrees of solidity, or lack of solidity—from the hardest steel or granite, to the most rarefied gas or vapor known to science. It includes all that science dares to think of as material body, even in the highest flights of its reason or imagination—and then all that lies beyond those conceptions. The field of substance recognized by science, as compared with the real extent of the Principle of Substance, is as no more than a hair-line drawn across a yard-stick. There are forms of matter as much more solid and dense than steel or granite, as the latter are more solid and dense than hydrogen gas. And at the other end of the scale there are forms of substance that could not be described in words, so near akin to Nothing are they. Between these two extremes there lies a bewildering number of degrees. That which science calls electricity and other subtle forms of energy, are not "energy" at all, but merely energy or motion manifesting through subtle forms of substance, which act as its body. There are forms of substance many times finer and rarer than even these. There are bodies worn by beings on higher planes which are finer and rarer than electricity. Even the ordinary Astral Bodies of beings on our own plane and stage of development, are far rarer and finer than is electricity, or the finest rays of light or magnetism. These bodies are just as real as is the piece of the hardest steel through which they may pass as easily as the X Ray passes through stone. The Universal Ether, which science assumes to be the extreme limit, and infinity, of subtle tenuity and fineness, is solid and compact when compared with many of the higher forms of substance. So much for Manifest Substance.

Unmanifest Substance is held by the Arcanes to be identical with Pure Space. In the preceding Lesson, you have seen that Pure Space is considered as Nothing. This Nothing is merely the extreme limit of the fineness or rareness of Substance. Space is not a mere idea—it is substance carried to its extreme highest limit. The Arcanes do not object to the term Abstract Substance, although they do not regard "abstract" as meaning "not." One of the old Egyptian Hierophants was once asked by the Ruler of Egypt: "What is that which would exist were there no universe; no gods; no anything?" His answer was "Space!" And this Pure Space is the Unmanifest Cosmos, in its aspect or principle of Substance.

II. *The Second Principle—Motion.* Motion, as the term is used in the Arcane Teaching, means the underlying "energy; force; or motive power" of things—their quality of action. Motion, in the Arcane Teaching is the Principle in which is gathered the cause of all that we know under the names of Energy; Force; Motive Power; Action; Activity; Attraction; Repulsion; of any and all kinds or degrees. Without Motion there could be no activities, energy or force of any kind. We are familiar with many manifestations of the Principle of Motion, such as Gravitation; Cohesion; Chemical Affinity; Electronic Attraction; Expansion; Contraction; Centrifugal and Centripetal Force; the Motive

Force or Energy of Light, Heat, Electricity, Magnetism; the Energy of the Ultra-Electric Rays; etc. But these are only a very small fraction of the forms and varieties of energy and force known to the advanced students of the Arcane Teachings, not to speak of the Masters, or those on higher planes of life. There are Finer Forces not dreamt of by even the most daring scientist. Motion, like Substance, is found in each and every manifestation of the Cosmos. Wherever there is Substance there is Motion. In its highest form of manifestation Motion manifests in vibrations of such exceedingly high degree and effect that there seems to be a condition of Absolute Rest. This condition is the one existing before the first stirrings of the dawn of the new Cosmic Day. Motion is then Motionless, to all intents and purposes,—but it has not perished or been destroyed. It is Motion in Latency.

There is no such thing as Absolute Rest in the *Manifest* Cosmos, but in the *Unmanifest* Cosmos there is Motion of so high a degree that it seems motionless and at rest. Thus do extremes meet, in Infinity. When the Cosmos becomes manifest, Motion decreases its rate of action or vibration, and manifestation is really a lowering in the scale of Motion; just as manifestation is a lowering in the scale of Substance. There must first be Involution before there is Evolution, of both Substance and Motion.

III. *The Third Principle—Consciousness.* Consciousness as the term is used in the Arcane Teaching, means the principle of "awareness" or "mind action" of things—their quality of mentalizing or consciousing, or becoming "aware" of other things, inner and outer. We are familiar with the form and degree of consciousness manifested in ourselves and other human beings, and we recognize different shades and degrees in this. We know a little about consciousness in the lower animals, in varying degrees. And some of us know of the degrees of consciousness in plants, in varying degrees. And, those who have studied along occult lines have become aware of the existence of mind and consciousness in so-called inanimate objects—the minerals, metals, etc., and even in the atoms—and finally in the Ether. Everything in the Manifest Cosmos has *some* degree of Consciousness. But there are many other higher and lower degrees of Consciousness, than those just mentioned. From the Unconscious-Consciousness of the Cosmic Night, when the Cosmos is conscious of Nothing, because there is but Nothing of which to be conscious; to the moment of the High Noon of the Cosmic Day, when the Cosmos is fully conscious of itself as a whole— the extreme of Cosmic Consciousness; there is a scale impossible for man to grasp by reason or imagination. There are degrees and planes of Consciousness awaiting the Advancing Ego, which transcend any possible dream or picture. The race has just begun to manifest Consciousness worthy of the name.

It is just beginning to enter into the glorious possibilities of Cosmic Consciousness—it is just "beginning to begin."

And, so, when "The Law superimposes the Infinity of Nothingness," the stirrings of Manifestation are felt by the Unmanifest. The Three Principles of the Cosmos are awakened into activity—Substance, Motion, and Consciousness begin to combine and become active. There is manifested an unrest and tendency to stir into activity the latent possibilities of the Cosmos. Consciousness begins to awaken from its slumber of ages, *and strives to know itself, and to realize its being*. This imparts activity to Motion, which lowers its vibrations in its effort to manifest itself. This bestirs Substance into changing degrees of being. Thus do the first indications of the Cosmic Day begin to manifest themselves. From thence onward, throughout the Cosmic Day, until its close, there is constant change of form, shape and degree of Substance; constant change in manifestation of Motion; constant change in manifestation of Consciousness.

This first stirring of Cosmic activity has been symbolized by the first stirring of the embryo within its temporary home, in which it has lain quietly since its conception. It is the first signs of the sprouting of the tiny seed of the plant. It is the peculiar, weird and mysterious light which precedes the first actual glimmer of the rising sun. Creation is beginning. The Cosmic Will or Universal Life Principle is becoming active. The birth of the new Cosmos is approaching. The One Life is arousing itself. Infinity is preparing to become Manifest. The "o" is evolving into the ∞.

In the Manifestation of the Cosmos there is exhibited an infinitude of variety, degrees, shapes, form, and combinations of the Three Principles. It almost staggers the imagination to think of the fact that in the entire Cosmos there is never a single instance of exact duplication—*there are never two things precisely alike*. In view of this fact does it not seem folly to endeavor to make human beings adhere to a common standard—to fit into a common mould—to be cut from a common pattern?

And yet through the entire Cosmos there is ever manifest the Law of Analogy—that law which ever manifests a correspondence and agreement between all things on all planes. So true is this that if we discover certain fixed principles in one thing we may reason by analogy regarding other things, and thus discover the unknown "×" quality. "From One Know All," says the Arcane axiom. "As Above, So Below," adds the Hermetist.

And through the entire Cosmos there is ever manifest the Law of Orderly Trend. Everything proceeds according to Law and Order. There is no Chance or Disorder in the Cosmos. The Universe is governed by Law. And all things are under the Laws of the Cosmos.

And throughout the entire Cosmos is ever manifest the Law of Sequence. Events proceed in a continuous stream, ever flowing onward. No event is separate or isolated. Every event has its precedent, also its subsequent and consequent. Everything has its cause and its effect. Events compose a continuous and unbroken stream.

And throughout the entire Cosmos there is ever manifest the Law of Rhythm. Everything vibrates. Everything moves from one pole to the other—from one extreme to the opposite. Everything has its vibratory rate. Everything has its pendulum-like swing between its poles. Day is always followed by Night; Summer by Winter; Heat by Cold; Action by Reaction.

And throughout the entire Cosmos there is ever manifest the Law of Balance. There is universal equilibrium, compensation and balance. Everything has something balancing and counter-balancing it. Everything has its price. Everything has its compensation. Nature always maintains its balance. And man finds the Law of Balance always operative under the phase of the Law of Compensation. We must pay our price for everything—we cannot have our penny and our cake at the same time. We must ever pay, pay, pay. We can never get Something for Nothing.

And throughout the entire Cosmos there is ever manifest the Law of Cyclicity. Everything moves in Circles or Cycles, or Spirals. Worlds, nations, peoples, and individuals travel in cycles—the strong convert the cycles into Spirals.

And throughout the entire Cosmos there is ever manifest the Law of Opposites. Everything has its opposite pole. Everything has its other side. Everything is a paradox. Everything "is and isn't" at the same time. The Law of Polarity is one phase of this Law. In it is locked many Arcane Secrets.

Lesson V. The Cosmic Will.

This is The Arcane Teaching regarding the World-Spirit; the One-Life; the Life-Principle; the Logos; the Demiurge, or that Something which men have called by still other names, but which in Truth is but the Cosmic Will from which arises all life, and action, and shape and form, and change, and appearance, and variety, and manifestation—in fact, all that we include in the term "The Cosmos." Listen to the Aphorism.

Aphorism vii. "From the bosom of the Unmanifest, arises that which men call the World-Spirit; the One-Life; the Universal Being; the Life-Principle; the Logos; the Demiurge; but which in

Truth is but the Cosmic Will from which arises all life, and action, and shape and form, and change, and appearance, and variety, and manifestation. The Cosmic Will is the One which becomes Many—the Unity in which is Diversity—the First-Born from the Womb of Infinity,—the Cosmic Egg from which hatches the Universe. But this too, is under The Law."

By the term "The Cosmic Will" the Arcane Teaching designates the One Universal Living Creative Principle which has been recognized in all the great philosophies of all times and places. From the earliest dawn of philosophical thought, the great thinkers of the race have postulated the existence of a One Great Universal Living Creative Principle from which proceeded the Many. In some cases the One was held to be an Universal Being—even a Personal Being or Deity—while in others it was regarded simply as a Principle. But the underlying conception was the same—a One Living Creative Something from which the Many emerged—a Unity from which proceeded Diversity. This Universal Living Creative Principle was often confounded with The Absolute, although others held that it was subordinate. The Atlantean traditions show that those ancient people held to this fundamental idea; the Egyptians held to the existence of an Universal Life-Principle; the Chaldeans likewise; the Hindus held to the existence of the principle of Brahman, or the Universal-Life-Being, and the ancient Greek philosophers held firmly to the existence of the One Life Principle.

The Atlanteans, Chaldeans, and Egyptians held that this Universal Life Principle subdivided itself into the many forms of life and things, in obedience to an *inner law* of its being. The ancient Hindus held that the One manifested as the Many, the various schools giving different "reasons" for the manifestation as follows: one school held that Brahman manifested as the Many, in order to enjoy objective existence; another school held that *Prakriti*, the Universal Principle of Substance, was acted upon by the *Purushas*, or

Soul-Principles, which it had attracted to itself, and manifestations arose by reason thereof; another school held that Brahman was merely a subordinate creative principle, which was caused to create universes by the power of Para-Brahm; another school held that all manifestation was merely an illusory dream of *Maya* (the Creative Principle), in the mind of The Supreme Being; the Buddhists held that manifestation was caused by *tanha* or "thirst," in the Universal Will-to-Live which arose from the Void of Nothingness; other schools held ideas akin to those mentioned, or variations or combinations of them.

The Greeks always held to the existence of the Universal Life Principle, calling it by various names. The very term, "The Cosmos," was used by the Stoics and others to represent the idea of the *anima mundi* or "world-soul." Heraclitus held to the "world-spirit" which he symbolized as flame. Pythagoras, in his exoteric or popular teachings taught the doctrine of the Life Principle, symbolizing it as light or flame. Other schools recognized the existence of this One Life Principle calling it "Being," a term which has persisted in modern philosophy.

By some schools, notably the Platonian, the Universal Life Principle was called "The Demiurge," the term literally meaning the "universal worker." The Demiurge was held to be an exalted and mysterious agent, by and through whom The Absolute was supposed to have created the Universe—the life of the Demiurge flowed out into manifold forms, and became the Many. This idea was adhered to by the Gnostics of the early Christian church.

The term "The Logos" was also applied by some of the schools to this Universal Life Principle. The Logos was held to be the Creative Principle of Nature, objective in the world, giving order and regularity to the universe of shapes and forms which it had manifested. This idea of The Logos was inherent in many ancient religions, and permeated even early Christianity. Ueberweg, in his History of Philosophy, says: "The Logos was a being intermediate between God and the world....The Logos does not exist from eternity like God, and yet its genesis is not like our own and that of all other created beings; it is the first begotten son of God, and is for us, who are imperfect, a god....

Through the agency of The Logos, God created the world, and has revealed Himself to it."

In the early Christian Church there was much dispute about The Logos, but the revolution in the Church, effected by Constantine, drove it from its place of importance in the Christian theology. But, nevertheless, the idea has persisted, as witness Cudworth, the eminent English theologian and philosopher (1617–1688) who held to the existence of a "Plastic

Nature," of which he claimed: "It may well be concluded that there is a Plastic Nature, under God, which, as an inferior and subordinate instrument, doth grudgingly execute that part of his providence which consists in the orderly and regular motion of matter;" Cudworth held that this idea of Plastic Nature was reasonable in view of the fact that "the slow and gradual process in the generation of things would be a vain and idle pomp, or a trifling formality, if the moving power were omnipotent; as also may be noted those errors and bungles which are committed where the matter is inept and contumacious; which argues that the moving power is not irresistible, and that Nature is not altogether incapable of being sometimes frustrated and disappointed by the indisposition of matter. An Omnipotent Moving Power, being able to dispatch its work in a moment, would always act infallibly and irresistibly, as no ineptitude and stubbornness of matter would be able to hinder such a one, or to make Him fumble or bungle in anything." The Plastic Nature of Cudworth, and his followers, was but the old Demiurge, or Logos, of the Gnostics—but another name for the Universal Living Creative Principle, subordinate to the Higher Law.

Modern philosophers and thinkers have held to this idea of the Creative Principle, regarding it rather as a Life Principle than as a Being, however. Bruno held the existence of an *anima mundi*, or world-soul-principle; others have held to the Principle of "Nature"; Schopenhauer held to the existence of an Universal Will-to-Live, which manifested its life the universe of shape and form and variety; von Hartman held that there existed an "Unconscious," or Creative Principle, similar to that of Schopenhauer's "Will"; Wundt held to the existence of an "Universal Will"; Crusius held to an Universal Dominating Will; Balzac held to a "Universal Something, akin to Will"; Nietsche held to a "World-Will"; Maeterlinck holds to a Life

Principle; Bernard Shaw postulates the existence of a Universal Creative Energy which he calls, "The Life Forces."

The Naturalistic school of philosophy postulates the existence of a composite something which it calls "Nature," which acts as the Universal Creative Energy; other thinkers speak of "Nature" in its metonymic sense, as "The agent, producer, or creator of things; the powers which carry on the processes of creation; the powers concerned to produce existing phenomena, whether in sum or in detail; the personified sum and order of cause and effect." Spencer postulates the existence of an "infinite and eternal energy, from which all things proceed,... which transcends our reason and even our imagination." In short, this Universal Living Creative Principle or Life-Principle, is found, under one name or another, in nearly all of the leading philosophies or schools of thought, ancient or modern. The highest reports of the human reason agree in this conception and postulate.

But the true philosophic conception must be distinguished from that of Pantheism, which at first thought seems to be the same. Pantheism claims that this Creative Principle is Deity; God; or The Absolute—that Deity and Nature are identical— that the Universe is God, and God is the Universe. Herein lies a great error, which true philosophers and true occultists vigorously oppose. The idea of an Absolute—of an Omnipotent, Omniscient (all-powerful; all-wise) Being—being compelled to work Its way up gradually, haltingly, with mistakes and stumbles, is absurd. Cudworth (quoted a moment ago) makes this point clear. And to claim that an Absolute Being is trying to "gain experience" in this way, is ridiculous. The idea that the Absolute is "trying to accomplish something" by the universal manifestation, is illogical—*for if It has not been able to reach its goal in all the past of Eternity, It cannot reach it in all the future of Eternity, for the one is equal to the other*. Moreover, the Absolute must of necessity be self-sufficient, and can want nothing to perfect Itself. In short any attempt to postulate The Absolute; God; Deity or other Supreme Thing as being the struggling, striving, evolving Creative Energy, must end in failure or an illogical conclusion. It is only when it is assumed that this Creative Energy is subordinate to and ruled by an Absolute Sovereign Power, that it becomes logically thinkable. Pantheism, actual or implied, is illogical—even the idea of a Personal Deity is far more logical than is pure Pantheism. The Absolute and Nature can never be the same, try as men may to make it appear possible. Nature must always be relative, and subordinate to a superior and sovereign Power or Law, and *the latter must be The Absolute.*

Pantheism wears many masks and disguises, and is the underlying idea of many modern systems bearing high-sounding names. Any system which is based upon the idea of an Absolute which manifests as a relative—or of a Supreme Being which manifests as Nature, and natural things, is but Pantheism, though perhaps subtly disguised. Beware of this insidious error of thought. Apply these test-questions to any system, to puncture the bubble of Pantheism, if such is contained within it: (1) *Why* does your Absolute Being depart from Its absolute nature, and become relative, manifold, and divisible? (2) *How* can The Absolute lose its absolute nature and become relative? (3) *What becomes of* the absolute nature of The Absolute, when the latter transforms Itself into the relative? (4) How can the *Unconditioned* take on conditions and limitations? (5) How can the *Immutable and Changeless* manifest change? (6) How can the Indivisible divide and separate itself into parts? And if the teaching in question postulates in Absolute *Being*, the quality of Omniscience or Absolute Wisdom, ask also this question: (7) *How can the Omniscient All-Wise Absolute Being lose Its wisdom, and display the comparative ignorance of the relative forms?*

There are but two possible logical explanations of the Absolute and Relative, as follows: (I) That the Cosmos *has no existence except in the imagination* of The Absolute Being— either as a dream, meditation, reverie, or deliberate dramatic representation, lacking all reality; or (II) that the Universal Creative Principle or Energy is *not* Absolute, but is subordinate to a Sovereign Law. The first is the answer of certain Idealistic schools of Philosophy—the second is the answer of the Arcane Teachers of Atlantis, Chaldea, Egypt and Ancient Greece. Take your choice! But if you choose the former, then you must admit that The Absolute *deliberately and willfully* creates the illusion *for no reason except its own pleasure* (for no real result or gain is thinkable in such case), for it is ridiculous to hold that The Absolute could be *subject* to Illusion, Ignorance, or Maya, for if such were so it would no longer be the Absolute. In either case Pantheism is "escorted to the frontier." Do not be deluded by Pantheistic subtleties, or casuistic false reasoning. Pantheism at best is but a half-truth—the other half lies in the recognition of the Absolute Law.

The Arcane Teaching holds that the Cosmic Will—the first-born of the Womb of Infinity—the Cosmic Egg from which hatches the Universe—is in its last analysis, Spirit. By "Spirit" is meant "Essence"—remember this definition. "Essence" is a term derived from the Latin word, "*esse*," meaning "to be." Therefore Essence (or Spirit) means the "beingness" of Being. Spirit is the *essence of* the *Cosmos*. Spirit is that which is the first-born of the Infinity of Nothingness—the first *thing* to be. And from Spirit all the Cosmos proceeds—and at the last the

Cosmos is all Spirit. Back of Spirit there is naught by the Infinity of Nothingness. And over and above Spirit there is naught but The Law. Spirit is Being; and Being is Spirit.

The Arcane Teaching uses the term "Cosmic Will" to indicate the creative activities of Spirit. Spirit is the essence of the Cosmic Will—the Cosmic Will is the outward activities of Spirit. But Spirit and the Cosmic Will are the same thing—in its the inner and outer aspects. By "Will" is not meant that human quality called "will"—this latter is but the mental quality *which calls forth Will*. Will is the principle of all activity—it is activity *in itself*. Life is one of the manifestations of the Cosmic Will. Will is the "lifeness" of Life. Will is the outward aspect of Spirit.

In the Cosmic Will are inherent the "Three Principles," *viz.*, Substance; Motion; and Consciousness. In the infinitude of manifestation of these Three Principles by the Cosmic Will is found the explanation of the Cosmos or Universe. In their play, and interplay, is found the secret of shape, form, variety and degrees of Substance, Motion, and Consciousness. And from these arise Life. Therefore, in considering the Cosmos, in its activities and manifestations, we may now forget the deeper and more subtle metaphysical and philosophical terms which we have been compelled to consider—and, instead, let us see in universal operation and manifestation, a Living Universe or Cosmic Life Principle, ever moving, changing, flowing, evolving, proceeding, desiring, attaining, seeking, accomplishing. This is The Cosmic Will of the Arcane

Teaching—possessing all the attributes and qualities of the Universal Being of the Pantheists, except that of Absoluteness; for greater than the human imagination can conceive it though it be, yet it is subordinate to, and ever under, The Law In this teaching regarding the Cosmic Will, the Arcane Teaching gives us an intelligible explanation of that most perplexing idea of the One Life, or Universal Life, which has appeared in various guises and under various names in the philosophies of all times and peoples. That all Life, in the end, is One—that the individual lives are but manifestations of, and centres in, One Universal Life, has been the Truth taught by some of the greatest teachers of the race—the illumined of all ages. The majority of the schools make the fatal error of ascribing to the One Life the nature of The Absolute. The moment this is done the thinker is confronted with the paradox of the Absolute becoming Relative—a logical impossibility.

The best modern thought is fast coming to an agreement with the original Arcane principle that the Universal Life is *not* Absolute—*not* Independent and Self Governed—*not* Sovereign Power—*not* God, in the highest sense of the word; but instead is

Relative, Subordinate, and *under The Law*. The Arcane Teaching that the Universal Life is *not its own law*, but is under Law and governed by Laws, is the only explanation consistent with the highest report of the reason—the highest form of Logic—and the experience of science, based upon observed facts.

One of the greatest and most glaring of the fallacies of Pantheism or allied systems of thought, is that which assumes that The Absolute or Deity is "trying to" accomplish something—either in the direction of "gaining experience," or "building up" some great universe by continual progression. The idea of an Absolute, which must be Perfect, *desiring* anything other than it has is illogical. The idea of an Absolute Pantheistic Deity who must be All-Wise, trying to "gain experience" or *learn something* by playing the game of Many Parts, is childlike and ridiculous—surely an unworthy role to attribute to an Omniscient Deity. The idea of an Absolute or Omnipotent Deity "trying to," or *endeavoring* to build up universes by slow and arduous labor belongs to the category of child-thought. To think of such a Being doing "day work" is ridiculous—and then *what could He gain by it*, this Perfect and Self-Sufficient Being? And the fact remains that if all past Time has not been sufficient to accomplish perfect results, then all future Time will fail to accomplish them—for just as future Time has no ending, past Time has no beginning, *and existed forever*. And then, what did this Creative Being do in all the Eternity before Creation, if it be held that Creation had its beginning in time?

At the last analysis, the report of the illumined of the race will be found to agree with the highest report of the human reason—the report that the Universal Life can be but Relative; governed by a Sovereign Absolute Law; and subject to the Laws of Rhythm and Cyclicity—having its Ebb and Flow; its Action and Reaction; its Rise and Fall; its Days and Nights; its Periods of Creative Activity, and Creative Rest. And the Arcane Teaching squares fully with these requirements—for it is founded on Cosmic Truth.

Lesson VI. Involution And Evolution.

In order to understand the Arcane Teaching regarding the processes whereby the Cosmic Will manifests in the universe of life and action; shape and form; change, appearance, and variety; let us seek the wisdom of the Aphorisms. Listen to the Aphorisms:

Aphorism viii. By the Law of Analogy the Manifest Cosmos may be known. "Ex Uno disce Omnes"—From One know All. Like unto a World-Brain is the Cosmos. Its brain-substance is the Substance-Principle; its thought-energy is the Motion-Principle; its Mind is the Consciousness-Principle. Its will is the Cosmic Will. Its spirit is the Cosmic Spirit. Its laws are the Seven Laws. Its Sovereign is The Law.

Many philosophies have held that the universe is *mental*, in its last analysis, and that the Universal Mind is the reality behind the appearances. Others have held that the universe is merely an imagination, illusion, or dramatization, in the mind of a Supreme Being. But all of these conceptions use the terms "mind" or "mental" as something having no connection with material substance, the latter being an illusion. But the Arcane Teaching recognizes Substance as being as real and actual as Mind or Motion—the three being but aspects of the same thing—the Three Principles which are really One. And in giving to Substance and Motion equal places with Mind, the conception is seen to be rather more like a "World-*Brain*" than a "World-*Mind*," for like the brain it contains the principles of Substance, Motion and Consciousness. Thought is the product of these three—the action of Consciousness upon Substance, by means of the vibrations of Motion. As in the human brain, so in the Cosmic Brain—"as above, so below; as below, so above." From One know All. Substance and Motion are not illusions— they are co-equal with Mind, in reality and actuality. There can be no Mind without Substance and Motion; there can be no Substance without Mind and Motion; there can be no Motion without Mind and Substance. The "Three Principles" are always found together—in Everything the Three are found. There is no separateness in the Three Principles—there are, and must be, always in combination. And this combination in the Cosmos, gives us that which may be called the World-Brain.

Aphorism ix. In the World-Brain of the Cosmos arises and is manifested all natural phenomena. All natural phenomena is but the perpetual action and reaction; combination and re-combination; distribution and redistribution; of the Three Principles, in the World-Brain, by the Cosmic Will. As in the human brain material changes of form, shape, combination, character, and degree, result from mental activities—organic structural changes accompany mental states—states of consciousness are embodied in forms of material brain substance—so in the World-Brain, by the Cosmic Will, do Thoughts become Things; Desires take on Material Form; Ideas become Manifested; Mental Images become reproduced in the Material and Physical Forms, Shapes, and Appearances. Mental States precede Material Form—Mental Images precede Materialization.

In this Aphorism is contained a marvelous scientific truth, little suspected by the majority of thinkers. Every mental state produces a corresponding material change in the structure and substance of the brain—the brain-cells respond to the faintest mental state. The Arcane Teaching informs us that the Cosmos, being a great World-Brain, is governed by the same laws—"as below, so above." This being so, we may see how the Cosmos *while still being mental* may yet manifest in actual material and physical forms and phenomena, under the direction of the Mind. There is Mind back of every material and physical form and appearance. Here is the reconciliation between mentalism and materialism—idealism and naturalism. Read the above Aphorism carefully, a number of times—it contains the key of the material Cosmos, and the secret of Mentalism. Read between its lines. It informs you *why* and *how* Thoughts become Things—Mental States produce Material Forms—Mental Images cause Materialization. Here is the Key to unlock many Occult Doors. Can you use it?

Aphorism x. What men call "Matter" is but the countless centres produced by Will in the Substance Principle, through the action of the Motion Principle. What men call "Force and Energy" is but the action of the Motion-Principle upon the Substance-Principle, induced by the Will. What men call "Thought" is but the action of the Will upon the Consciousness-Principle, employing the Substance and

Motion-Principles in the operation. In every action of the Cosmic Will all Three Principles are employed and involved, in varying degrees and combinations. The Will is the Motive Power behind all manifestation in the World-Brain of the Cosmos.

The above Aphorism states that which some of the more advanced of modern scientists and philosophers now hold to be a proven fact. Science and Philosophy is fast approaching a meeting point, where they will see that behind the activities and phenomena of the universe there is to be found a Cosmic Will manifesting in the multitudinous variety of shape and form; life and action. Science and the Arcane Teaching agree upon this point. As a celebrated philosopher-scientist said:

"The material universe is but the outer wrapper behind which is hidden a spiritual creative activity; a striving, feeling, sensing, like that which we experience in ourselves." Conation (the voluntary power impelling to effort) is held by Wundt to be the fundamental essence of this activity. Thus Wundt postulates the existing of a Cosmic Will, similar to that of the Arcane Teaching. A recent paper by an English scientist says: "There is but one substance, and that is Spirit. Matter, so-called, is nothing but *rigid places in spirit*." Matter is now known to be but combinations of the *ions* or electrons, which are held to be little more than "centres of force" in the ether. Thought without *thinking-substance and motion* is held to be unthinkable. Likewise science now holds that there is life and mind in all material substance, from atom to protoplasm. Science like the Arcane Teachers, finds the Three Principles, Substance, Motion and Consciousness in everything. And science is beginning to see in "energy and force" the evidences of "something akin to conation." "Conation" is "the voluntary power impelling to effort; the faculty of voluntary agency," etc.; or as Mill said:

"Conation, in other words, is Desire or Will." So that science is meeting the Arcane Teaching face to face, on level ground. The symbol of the "World-Brain" is sure to come into general use in the science of the future.

And now for the inevitable question—the question which punctures the philosophical and metaphysical bubble of the Pantheists: "*Why* does this Cosmic Will manifest this energy, activity, desire, longing, striving, seeking and evolution?—what is the *necessity* of it all?—what is the end sought for? As difficult as this question may be—and though it has repeatedly been styled "unanswerable"—the Arcane Teaching does not shrink from its consideration; but gives the logical and only answer, *for the answer exists*. Listen to the Aphorism!

Aphorism xi. The Cosmic Will, as the World-Brain, seeking Consciousness through its appropriate Principle, manifests the natural phenomena of the universe. From a state of Unconsciousness, through many stages of Semi-Consciousness—through many degrees of Simple Consciousness; Self-Consciousness; Super-Consciousness; and states still higher in the scale, undreamt by mortal mind, on toward the highest states of Cosmic Consciousness—Spirit conscious of Itself; the Cosmic Will proceeds. Consciousness, in all of its phases, proceeds through Change—Consciousness depends upon Constant Change. Consciousness always produces Activity, and manifests Motion. Consciousness always manifests objectively in Change and Motion in Substance—in substantial shape and form. In this, then, is to be found the explanation of the phenomena of the involution and evolution of the Cosmos, with all the incidents thereof—in this is found the answer to the Ultimate "Why."

The above is one of the most important of the Basic Aphorisms—the one which explains the "Why" of the Manifest Evolving Cosmos. The answer is understandable only through the symbol of the "World-Brain." The Cosmic Spirit or Will, awakening from its sleep of Unconsciousness, during the Cosmic Night in the Infinity of Nothingness, seeks Consciousness. Consciousness is the "livingness" of Life—therefore *the Cosmos seeks Life itself. The Cosmos manifests in order to gain Conscious Life.* Like the mortal awakening from a profound sleep, almost death-like in its intensity, the Cosmos begins its task of *regaining* Consciousness, which is the "livingness" of its Life. And as to the mortal sleeper, such Consciousness comes to it slowly.

In order to fully appreciate the meaning of the Aphorism, we must regard the nature and meaning of "Consciousness." Consciousness means "awareness," and, of course, is purely mental in principle. The Aphorism says: "Consciousness in all of its phases, proceeds from Change—Consciousness depends upon constant Change." Is this borne out by modern psychology— let us see! The best authorities in modern psychology agree to this statement. To them, Consciousness is a stream of changing mental states, with their corresponding physical changes. The text-books say: "Every act of consciousness involves a change from a past state to a present." A leading authority says:

"Consciousness is in constant change"; also : "No state once gone can recur and be identical with what it was before"; also: "Consciousness does not appear to itself chopped into bits....It is nothing jointed; it flows. A 'river' or a 'stream' are the metaphors by which it is most naturally described. In talking of it, let us call it the stream of consciousness."

Another authority says: "Consciousness results from perpetual change. It is impossible to maintain a uniform conscious state. A uniform sensation of pressure becomes quickly unnoticeable—the pressure must perpetually vary or the sensation will cease, and this is true of all conscious states whatsoever." All the best authorities agree in the above position. The Cosmic Will which is embodied in the Cosmic Substance, just as is the will of man embodied in his brain-substance, must constantly manifest changes within that substance in order that it may be Conscious. It must do this constantly and perpetually, else it becomes Unconscious. When it is remembered that states of consciousness are always accompanied by corresponding material and physical changes—that thoughts become brain-things—then we can see the explanation of the constant change in the physical world, which we call natural phenomena.

The Aphorism also says: "Consciousness always produces Activity, and manifests Motion." Modern psychology also bears out this statement. Prof. William James has brought out this point most forcibly in his works. He says, among much else on the same subject: "All Consciousness is Motor"; also: "Using sweeping terms and ignoring exceptions, we might say that *every possible feeling produces a movement,* and that the movement is a movement of the entire organism, and of each and all its parts....In short, a process set up in the centres reverberates everywhere, and in some way or other affects the organism throughout, making its activities either greater or less." Is it not plain that, granted the existence of the Cosmic Will in its aspect of a World-Brain, then *every state of consciousness within it must produce activity and motion* within it; and *must also manifest the corresponding physical and material changes in its substance and organic structure?* Does not this, coupled with the fact that *consciousness depends upon constant change,* give us, in the words of the Aphorism, "the explanation of the phenomena of the involution and evolution of the Cosmos, with all the incident! thereof? Does not this explain to us the workings of the Law of Sequence?

This then is the cause behind the involution and evolution of the Cosmos as told by Modern Science. In awakening into Consciousness the World-Brain creates centres of material shape and form within itself. Then by slow degrees more complex form, and combinations appear. Upon the created worlds appear the material appropriate for the manifestation of organic life. Then Life, as we know it, appears. Then higher forms come. Then man. Then, as on certain of the worlds, being much higher in the scale than man, appear. And then on, and on, and on, ever in an ascending scale of Life and Being; shape and form; combination and degree.

In the World-Brain, there are many planes of consciousness, just as there are in your own brain-mind. There are the instinctive planes, and those still below—the sub-conscious, and those above—and the super-conscious, and other stages of which man does not as yet dream. Just as the various brain-cells perform their several functions, varying in the degree of importance and function—so do the various centres in the World-Brain play theirs, in the same varying importance and degree. Each is a part of the All. And there is a relationship and interdependence between all. None is alone and separate. Separateness is an illusion. All is One. The part played by Man— by You—in this great Cosmic Drama, will be considered in the succeeding parts of this series of lessons. Therein will be taught the lesson of "Man, Know Thyself!"

In considering the World-Brain, do not make the mistake of the average student, in thinking merely of this speck of dust called the Earth, as being all that is included in the Cosmos. In the Cosmos are contained an infinitude of infinitudes of universes; of suns, and planets. Space itself must be exhausted before the universes are exhausted. Number itself must be exhausted, before their number is exhausted. Remember, they are the products of Infinity, and consequently *their number, degrees, and variety is infinite in extent and possibility*.

Nor, should you make the mistake of explaining of the Cosmos in the terms of Time, except as a convenience in thinking. Conceptions of finite time or space have no place in the consideration of the Cosmos—that is, the mind is unable to think of a period of time sufficiently great to cover even one phase of the Cosmic Process. The Cosmic Day is unthinkable in figures. The highest figures possible to the mind of man would not represent the year-periods involved in a single second of the Cosmic Day. We are still in the Dawn of the Day, and yet that which men would call an Eternity has passed in the present Cosmic Day. Thought fails us. We are dealing in terms of Infinity. The Symbol is ∞.

In this lesson we have heard the answer to the Ultimate Question of the "Why" of the Cosmos. We have seen that that Answer is "Necessity and Law." It is the Law of the Cosmos that the Cosmic Will should *desire and will to live*; and, that in order to live, Consciousness (the "livingness of Life") is necessary; and that in order to gain consciousness, continual and constant change is *an actual necessity*. And this constant change produces the phenomena of the Manifest Cosmos. In a nutshell: *The Cosmos manifests in order to Live—and it Lives because Life is a Necessity of its nature under the Laws, and subordinate to The Law.* This is the Arcane

Answer to the "Unanswerable Question" of the philosophers of the schools. And in the Arcane conception of the World-Brain of the Cosmos, we have another great fundamental truth stated in simple terms, and by a familiar symbol. The human-brain has its analogy in the World-Brain. In this Arcane Teaching we may understand the principles of the embodiment of mind in matter, and the action of mind upon matter by means of energy. Compare this Teaching of the World-Brain with the teachings of science, in its phases of Inorganic Evolution, and Organic Evolution, and see how the Teaching throws light on the whole process. See how there is ever a mental action preceding the physical manifestation. Desire ever precedes function, shape and form. Mind is always embodied in substance. Substance always contains mind. The building of the crystal; the growth of the animal form from the single cell; the evolution of the chicken from the creative cell in the egg; all these are manifestations of physical action, structural change, and substance moving in response to mental inner causes. From One, know All. The Law of Analogy is ever manifest in the Cosmos—"As Above, so Below; as Below, so Above."

The conception of the Cosmic World-Brain also throws much light upon many phases of mental, psychic, and occult phenomena, in which the world is now taking such a decided interest. If Thoughts become Things in the Cosmic Brain, then following the Law of Analogy it is possible for Thoughts to materialize in Things on other planes of activity. The same principle is involved—the principle of mental creative activity. This is the Secret of Mentalism. This is the Key to Psychic Phenomena. This is the Explanation of Occultism. With a Cosmos, *mental in its nature*, with energy and substance; matter and motion; all receptive, responsive, and plastic and obedient to Mind—what cannot be accomplished by those who understand the Laws of Mentalism? With Will as the great creative power in the Cosmos—what is not possible to him who understands the Art of Willing. With Desire as the great Creative Energy, can we not see why Desire should be harnessed, controlled, directed, guided, mastered and employed in our lives, careers and destinies?

Apply these various conceptions of the Arcane Teaching to the various philosophical and metaphysical problems which have puzzled you—and see how many tangles it straightens out; how many inharmonies it reconciles; how it brings order out of the chaos of conflicting theories, dogmas and teachings.

The Arcane Teaching is a Disturber of teachings—but it is also the great Reconciler. It is the Chemical of Truth, which clears the waters of Thought.

PART III. THE LIFE OF THE EGO.

Lesson VII. The One And The Many.

We now invite you to consider the important philosophical problem of The One and The Many, as explained by the Arcane Teaching. In the philosophies which hold that The One Life is the Absolute, this problem is unexplainable, for it is impossible to conceive of the Absolute, which is immutable and indivisible, changing and dividing itself into parts, or apparently doing so. With the recognition of the fact that the Cosmic One Life is not the Absolute, but is under Law, then the difficulty vanishes. Let us listen to the Aphorism:

Aphorism xii. Know ye, that in Truth, there is but One Life and not many lives. Separateness is but relative and partial— illusory— the creative fiction of the Cosmos. Who teaches otherwise, errs. In the Cosmic Will there is the One Life in which, and by which, is manifested the Many.

In the previous lessons we have seen that the Cosmic Will is the "lifeness" of all Life, just as Consciousness is its "livingness." Back of, and under, all manifestations of Life, there is always the Cosmic Will. But the Cosmic Will precedes the particular manifestation that we call "Life," for it existed before Life appeared in the Cosmos. The great Cosmic energies and activities which manifested in world-building in all its phases, were but manifestations of the Cosmic Will bestirring itself.

The fundamental activities show but little evidence of what we call Life—there seems to be but little Life in the mineral kingdom— but still the Will is seen in operation there, building up and tearing down; arranging and rearranging; combining and recombining. The attraction and repulsion of the atoms (and of the particles composing the atoms) shows us that the Will is present and in operation in these lowly manifestations. In Gravitation, we see a wonderful evidence of the operation of the Cosmic Will. In Chemical Affinity and Molecular Cohesion we have similar evidences. In all the great Natural Laws, in evidence throughout the Cosmos, we may see the operation of the Cosmic Will, always. The laws of Physics demonstrate clearly the existence of some great Conative power, animating, energizing, and manifesting in every part and particle of creation. One must indeed be a blind materialist to fail to see ever at work that "Something Within" manifesting as the "Something Without." The building up of the crystal, from liquid to regular and exact geometrical form, should be sufficient to convince anyone that there is a "Something at work" in it. Even the materialist is forced to recognize these facts—and he *does* recognize it, and calls that Something by the name of "Nature." We have no quarrel with names—if the term "Nature" suits you, use it by all means. But if you think clearly, you must recognize that your "Nature" is Conative, and acts and manifests as a Cosmic Will.

These fundamental activities and manifestations of the Cosmic Will or One Life, are akin to the activities and manifestations of our own lives. Stop to consider that your body was built up from a single cell by your Live Forces—not only your fleshy parts, but your hair, nails, teeth, and even the hardest bones which form your framework. And, likewise, the flint-like shell of the clam, oyster, and other hard-shell animals were so built up; not to speak of the harder geometrical crystal forms of the diamond and other minerals, which are but "built-up" shapes and forms.

The diamond is composed of carbon, which is but a gaseous substance which becomes solid under certain conditions. The hard ivory of the elephant's tusk was built up from cells, by the Life Forces within the animal itself. So you see that Life can build up *hard substances* as well as soft ones. And the same force that builds up these hard substances, builds up the rocks and hills, and mountains, and minerals that form *the body of Nature*. Just as certain functions of the animal or human brain manifest in building up the body of the Cosmos.

The Cosmic Will from the beginning has sought to *embody* itself in objective form, in order to manifest Consciousness, which is the "livingness" of Life, as we have explained in a previous lesson. Like the Life Forces in any being, it first concerned itself in providing *a body* for itself, in order that it would have a substantial foundation for further and higher manifestation of its Life. In the Cosmos the material plane of activity is the one first operated upon. Then comes the slowing down of the vibrations of Motion, and the Principle of Substance produces the elementary particles which, combining, form matter. Then matter begins to evolve into higher forms, until at last there is produced the combination in which is possible the manifestation that we call Organic Life. From the lowly living cell-like creatures in the slimy depths of the primeval ocean-beds, arise step by step, slowly, tediously, painfully, arduously, and haltingly, but surely and steadily, form after form of higher and still higher living organisms. The modern scientific theory of Evolution—which, however, was antedated some twenty-five hundred years by the Ancient Greek Philosophers—tells us a true tale of the slow rise and development of life forms.

At last Man—a poor, weak, brutal creature with wonderful possibilities, was evolved by the One Life in its urge toward Conscious Life. And this poor creature has advanced wonderfully. And Evolution does not stop here—for Man is but an intermediate step. On other worlds in the Cosmos, there are beings as much higher than Man, as man is higher than the earthworm. Our planet is but one of millions upon millions of millions of worlds, in which Evolution is at work. We are away down low in the scale of worlds and being. There are beings as great as man's conceptions of the gods of old, dwelling on some of these planets and worlds. Some of us have dwelt on these brighter spheres, but have been sent back a grade or two in order to complete tasks left undone; or to gain experiences necessary; or because the fires of material desire had not yet died out in us, and we needed to "get enough of it" once more, in order to be free of the dross. There are planes of Life so transcendentally grand and exalted, that Man's wildest imagination cannot conceive of them. And, on the other hand, there are worlds lower in the scale so sunken in materiality and foulness, that the orthodox hell would be preferable to them. Man goes where his desires take him. He travels the road of his desires and thoughts. He makes his own route—he guides his own vessel. Man is his own Destiny.

The Many Lives are but Centres of Life in the great One Life. Separateness is but the "creative fiction" of the Cosmos— illusory and relative. All Life is but One, in its fundamental nature. The entire

Cosmos is but One Life, in which we are parts or centres—in its Being we "live and move and have our being."

The One Life is not far away, but is all around us, and immanent within us. While one phase of the Cosmic Paradox shows the individual to be but an infinitesimal unit in a stupendous whole, the other phase shows the individual to be identical with the Whole— connected with all by spiritual bonds and links—and sharing the infinite possibilities of the All. The life of the individual is not bounded by his personal limitations, but includes the life of the All. In this understanding and recognition there is found the reconciliation, unity and agreement between the contradictory phases of life and the universe. True spiritual advancement depends upon the increasing recognition and identification of the individual with the All.

An important point in the Arcane Teaching is that which holds that *the Cosmos is, and can be, conscious only through and by means of the various centres of consciousness within itself*. Without these centres of consciousness within itself— the consciousness of You and I and all the rest—the One Life would be unconscious. Just as the individual can be conscious only through his stream of units of consciousness, so can the One Life be conscious only through its stream of centres of consciousness. Destroy these centres of consciousness, and the Cosmos once more is resolved into its condition of Unconscious

Nothingness. And, moreover, the One Life can *live* only through its centres of Life—the centres called You and I, and the rest. Will is the "lifeness" of Life—Consciousness is the "livingness" of Life—and the individual is the centre of both Will and Consciousness, and therefore of Life. As the Cosmos advances in the Cosmic Day, there is manifested a constantly increasing blending or unification of the various centres of Life—a constantly increasing identification of the individual with the

All. And, thus is accomplished the approach to the Cosmic High Noon, when the One Life, *as one life and consciousness*, lives, wills and is conscious. Before that time comes, the illusion of Separateness is manifested—the "creative fiction" of the Cosmos operates in working out the approach to Cosmic Consciousness.

Thus it is seen that the Cosmos, or One Life, does not manifest as separate units of life in order to amuse itself, or to try experiments, or any of the various "explanations" hazarded by philosophy, metaphysics, or theology. It manifests through the centres, *because it must do so in order to live and be conscious*. Creation and the Universe is not a matter of whim, unreasoning desire, or arbitrary fiat of the One Life of the Cosmos. Far from that. It is the Cosmic Necessity. Just as you must *live* in order to be alive so must the Cosmos manifest Life in order to *live* and be conscious. Just as you find the imperative demand for life within yourself; so does the Cosmic Life find the imperative demand for Life within itself. The One Life is under the Law, just as you are under the Laws. The urge of "Must" is ever impelling it forward. It is not Free—it is under the Law and The Laws. The Law is ever over and above it—the Seven Laws are constantly in operation within it. The One Life is not a cruel, arbitrary master or ruler. It is your Greater Self, and subject to the same laws which govern you. *It is doing the best it can*, for itself, and therefore for you. When the individual realizes this fact— the fact that the One Life is doing the best it can; is bound by the Laws as much as is the individual; that there is no manifestation of arbitrary desire, or unreasoning whim in the Cosmic machinery; that One is All, and All is One; then there appears a *reason* and explanation for much in life which has hitherto defied explanation or reason; or theory of justice and equity. Then is there seen an explanation of that apparently arbitrary, despotic manifestation of power, which caused old Omar Khayyam to utter his rebellious protests, and cry aloud:

> "*Into this Universe, and 'Why' not knowing,*
> *Nor 'Whence,' like Water willy-nilly flowing;*
> *And out of it, as Wind along the Waste,*
> *I know not 'Whither,' willy-nilly blowing.*
> "*What, without asking, hither hurried 'Whence'?*
> *And, without asking, 'Whither' hurried hence!*
> *Oh, many a cup of this forbidden Wine*
> *Must drown the memory of that insolence!*
> "*A moment guessed—then back behind the Fold*
> *Immerst of Darkness round the Drama rolled,*

Which for the pastime of Eternity
He doth himself contrive, enact, behold.
"We are no other than a moving row
Of Magic Shadow-shapes that come and go
Round with the Sun-illumined Lantern held
In midnight by the Master of the Show.
"But helpless Pieces of the Game He plays
Upon His Chequer-board of Nights and Days;
Hither and Thither moves, and checks, and slays,
And one by one back in the Closet lays.
"The Ball no question makes of Ayes and Noes,
But Here or There as strikes the Player goes;
And He that tossed you down into the Field,
He knows about it all—He knows—He knows."

Many daring thinkers who setting aside "the bribe of heaven and threat of hell" have dared to look Life in the face, have been overcome by a sense of impotent subjection to an arbitrary Being who, *being able* to remedy conditions, and *knowing of* the pains of mortal life in the universe, nevertheless has deliberately imposed such conditions upon living things. Such thinkers find it impossible to reconcile the claimed qualities of Love and Good in such a Being, with the manifestations of apparent injustice, inequity, pain and suffering which made pessimists of great souls like Buddha, Lao-tze, and the writer of the Koheleth or Ecclesiastes. Indeed, viewing Life from this viewpoint, one finds it hard to escape the conviction which inspired the bitter words of old Omar, when he cried:

"What! out of senseless Nothing to provoke
A conscious Something to resent the yoke
Of unpermitted Pleasure, under pain
Of everlasting Penalties, if broke!
"What! from his helpless Creature be repaid
    Pure Gold for what he lent him dross-allay'd;
    Sue for a debt we never did contract
And cannot answer—Oh, the sorry trade!

> "O Thou who didst with pitfall and with gin Beset
> the Road I was to wander in,
>
> Thou wilt not with Predestined Evil round Enmesh,
> and then impute my fall to Sin!
>
> "O Thou who Man of baser Earth didst make, And
> ev'n with Paradise devise the Snake:
>
> For all the Sin wherewith the Face of Man
>
> Is blackened—Man's forgiveness give—and take!"

But with the dawning knowledge that the One Life, or World-Spirit, is *not* The Absolute, but is under Law and Laws superimposed upon it, then we have a picture of an Universal Being which suffers with us and through us; rises with us and through us; strives with us and through us; attains with us and through us; rejoices with us and through us; conquers with us and through us—and whose Life is composed of our lives; whose consciousness is composed of our consciousness. Such a Being is seen to be, at the last, *one with ourselves*, instead of an outside power—and consequently, such a Being is seen to be eternally making for Good-making for *our* good, for we are one with itself. Such a Being is seen to be but the Composite Self of all the individual selves of the Cosmos—the Real Self. And in the recognition of all this, our bitterness must die away, and a great feeling of compassion, sympathy, understanding and love must be manifested by us—and felt by us. Then must come that sense of Oneness with the All which is the great reconciler—which harmonizes the Opposites, and establishes the Cosmic Balance.

This One Life is You—and You are it. Centres of Life, apparently separate are we now—but steadily growing toward that time, phase and state of Cosmic Consciousness, in which the All shall know itself as One—and the One know itself as All.

As the Ego progresses through the stages of Spiritual Evolution, its consciousness enlarges and expands, including more and more of the Cosmos within it as the Self, until the stages of Cosmic Consciousness are reached in which the Ego finds itself blending into the Whole, and the All blending into the Self. This is what is meant by Cosmic Consciousness; Spiritual Consciousness; Transcendental Consciousness; the Higher Consciousness; the *Moksha*, of the Brahmans; the *Nirvana*, of the Buddhists; the Union with God, of the Mystics; the Divine Marriage, of the Sufis; the Brahmic Splendor, of the Oriental poets—of all those transcendental states of Consciousness, in which the Self blends into the All, in varying degrees according to the development of the soul. This is the Secret of the Mystics of all times and lands—this the Mystery of Buddha—this the Divine Bliss of the Brahmans—this the "Wine" of the Sufi symbology, Even old Omar, in his bitter complaint, was true to his Sufi instincts, and recognized the One:

"Whose secret Presence, through Creation's veins

Running Quicksilver-like eludes your pains; Taking all shapes from Mah to Mahi; and

They change and perish all—but He remains."

And this was the thought that inspired these striking lines from an unknown poet:

"Thou great Eternal Infinite! Thou great Unbounded Whole!

Thy body is the Universe! Thy spirit is its soul!

If Thou dost fill Immensity—If Thou art All-in-All—
Then I'm in Thee, and Thou in Me, or I'm not here at all!

How can I be outside of Thee, when Thou fill Earth and Air?

There surely is no place for Me outside of Everywhere!

If Thou art ALL, and Thou dost fill Immensity of Space,

Then in Thy Being do I dwell, or else I have no place.

And if I have no place at all—what am doing Here?

Beyond the All I cannot Be—outside of Everywhere!

Then truly in Thy Self am I—and Thou must be in Me;

Or else there is no All-in-All—no Me, nor Thee, to Be!"

This One is the great Cosmic Spirit—Cosmic Will—Life Principle—One Life of The Cosmos—in which the Arcane Teachers find the Real Self and Universal Being. This is the great Principle of Life and Being, in which "we live, and move, and have *our* being." This is the great Cosmic Life which awakens in the Dawn of the Cosmic Day, and thence proceeds gradually to evolve into the Cosmic Consciousness of High Noon; thence on to rest in the ecstatic state of transcendental Bliss, Consciousness, and Being—*sat-chit-ananda*, the Hindus call it—the Kingdom of Heaven, other mystics have called it—

during the Afternoon of the Cosmic day, which state extends over countless æons of time; thence passing into the dream-like slumber of the Twilight of the Cosmic Day; thence on toward the resolution into the state of Unconsciousness in the Infinity of Nothingness of the Cosmic Midnight; thence on to the Re-awakening at the first glimpses of the Dawn of the new Cosmic Day. As Above, so Below; as Below, so Above! From One, Know All!

Thus is the Great Cycle of the Cosmos—thus the Working of the Laws. And, ever over all dwells The Law, unchanged, peaceful, undisturbed—ever the same—Alone—Absolute.

Lesson VIII. Metempsychosis.

It is not our purpose to enter into a discussion of the world-old and world-wide doctrine of Metempsychosis, Re-Birth, Reincarnation, or Re-embodiment, or by whatever other name it may be known. The modern world has awakened to a new knowledge of this ancient doctrine and truth, but in learning it is has absorbed much error with the principle of truth. We shall not attempt to *prove* the doctrine of Metempsychosis. All true occultists know that every soul which ever has experienced re-embodiment or rebirth *has an intuitional assurance of the truth of having lived before, some time, somewhere*—an assurance perhaps dim, but still persistent. Those who have not this inner assurance in some degree have never experienced rebirth, although they may have rebirth awaiting them after the present earth life. To those who have not this inner assurance, it is folly to attempt to *prove* Metempsychosis— at the best they will receive it merely as one of a number of idle speculations on the unknowable hereafter. To those who have the inner assurance, in some degree, no other *proof* is necessary, although explanation and teaching regarding the same is eagerly sought after. In this, and the following lesson, we shall ask you to consider the Arcane Teaching regarding the details of Metempsychosis, Reincarnation, and Re-birth. Many of the points of the Teaching may seem strange and startling to those who have studied other teachings—but careful study and comparison will show the Truth in spite of the contradictions from without. For the first point, listen to the Aphorism:

Aphorism xiii. Know ye this first Truth of Metempsychosis: The Ego is evolved from the Personal Self. Every living thing possesses a Personal Self, but even among men, many fail to reach Egohood. Egohood is earned, not bestowed as an universal natural gift. Many personalities are born, but few Egos are evolved. Personality perishes in the Astral World, after the death of the physical body—Egohood persists in Re-embodiment and Rebirth.

This startling truth, embodied in the Aphorism, IS one of the fundamental principles of the Arcane Teaching. The majority of religions and philosophies have held to the idea of the universality of immortality, although there have been some notable exceptions to the rule. The Arcane Teaching however has always held that Egohood (with survival and re-birth) is conditional and exceptional. It has held that there must be earned and evolved an Ego, before that Ego may persist in Re-embodiment and Re-birth. Many of the ordinary teachings regarding Reincarnation hold that there is a continuous chain of Rebirth or Reincarnations from the lowest form of animal life (and often still lower) to that of advanced Man and beyond.

This is *not* so held in the Arcane Teaching. The Arcane Teaching holds that there is Physical Evolution from the very lowest life forms to the highest (up to a certain advanced stage to be noted hereafter), but that Spiritual Evolution begins only when the Ego is evolved from the Personal Self of some creature on the plane of humanity, or some plane equal to it in other worlds. From thence on there is Spiritual Evolution, and Metempsychosis, Re-birth or Re-embodiment, which latter continues until the Ego passes through that stage and thenceforth pursues its Spiritual Evolution without the necessity of Rebirth. Most positively does the Arcane Teaching deny that You, the Ego, as a soul, have arisen by steps of Spiritual Evolution from the various soul-stages of the animals. The Arcane Teachings also hold that the majority of human beings on earth to-day have not developed Egohood, and are therefore not likely to be reborn or re-embodied, but will, after a period of life in the Astral World, in their astral bodies, again die and fade away, being resolved into their original elements in the Cosmos.

All living things have Personality, and are able to distinguish between "Me and Not-Me"—between their personal selves and the things of the outside world. But only a portion of the human race have developed the phase called by psychologists, "Self-Consciousness," or "The Sense of Individuality," in which they are able to distinguish between the "I" and the "Me." By the "Me" is meant the things of personality-the body, the mental states, the feelings, the desires, the characteristics of personality, etc. By the "I" is meant that transcendental Something in oneself which is able to stand aside and apart *and view the "Me" as from outside*—that something which enables one to feel, "I Am"—that Something which enables one to know that he is superior to the body, or the personality, and that he will always be "I Am" no matter in what part of the Cosmos he may be, or after how many æons of time he may say it. It is most difficult to describe this phase of consciousness, but those who have it will recognize it, and those who have it not will likewise realize the lack. Some may not recognize it under the term Ego or the "I Am," but will understand when we say it is that which may be called "Soul Consciousness"—that is, a consciousness that You *are* a Soul, inhabiting a body and using a mind—a Something over and above personality and mortal life—a Something destined to live on, and on, and on-a Something which *feels and knows* that it is. A great many people do not recognize this Something Within them, but instead *believe* that they *have* a soul, or *will have* one at least—their idea of "soul" being something that will emerge *from them* after death. The true Soul recognizes itself as being *Now*—it can say "I Am the Soul— Here and Now!" This is Egohood in its early stages.

The Cosmic Will, or One Life, begins its work of physical evolution, working from lowly forms to higher and higher, the benefits of acquired conscious experience being transmitted through the laws of Sequence or Heredity. In this way the lower animals advanced in the scale of evolution, and Man appeared. But Man was, and in many cases is now, but a higher form of the lower animals—his soul life comes later. As Man advanced in the scale, there were evolved personalities which experienced the pangs of soul-birth. They felt the struggles of the developing Something Within, and began to realize that they were individuals—the "I Am" began to manifest itself.

These individuals were not always "good" people—both poles of the opposites manifested here as elsewhere—they were simply stronger and more soulful people—people who felt the Real Self within them. Thus were the Egos evolved.

When physical death overcame these individuals, after spending their allotted and usual time in the Astral World, and sinking into the astral slumber preceding the usual astral dissolution and final death, these Egos awoke to a new life in new bodies—Metempsychosis in its earlier stages. Each Ego was reborn into a new body, along the lines of its general character and desires, although it preserved but a faint memory of its past life. The Ego preserved its Character, however, although its Personality had slipped away from it. Thenceforth these Egos proceeded along the lines of Spiritual Evolution, in connection with Physical Evolution—and thereby the One Cosmic Life was enabled to evolve and progress *along two lines* of Evolution, instead of one as before—the Cosmic Will doubled its resources. In order to see the "why" and "how" of this process of re-embodiment, or re-birth, let us listen to the Aphorism:

Aphorism xiv. Know ye this second Truth of Metempsychosis: Persistence in Egohood in Rebirth or Re-embodiment, is but the Recollection or the Memory of the Cosmic Will, in the World-Brain. As the mortal brain recollects (and thus embodies) an idea, or thing—so does the World-Brain recollect (and thus embodies) the Egos. This is the Truth of Metempsychosis, and the phases of Life beyond Metempsychosis.

To those who have deemed incapable of solution the "how" of Re-embodiment, the Truth contained in the above Aphorism will come like a flash of lightning illumining the darkness of midnight. The analogy is seen at once by those familiar with the laws of the mind and the phenomena of the brain. An idea or thing, the impression of which is in the memory (occultists claim the memory to be largely astral in its nature) is recalled or recollected, and immediately passes into the field of consciousness. And to pass into the conscious field *it must be embodied* in the brain substance or cells—it must be given an appropriate body. The Cosmic Will remembers the Ego in the Astral World, and in the World-Brain it again embodies it in material form. We urge you to study this carefully and thoroughly, before proceeding further, in order that you may make this great Truth your own for all time. Consider this: To be remembered by the Cosmic Will in the World-Brain, is to persist in Being—*for whatever is so remembered cannot perish so long as the World-Brain persists and exists*.

And now listen to the Aphorism, telling the third truth of Metempsychosis: Aphorism xv. Know ye this third Truth of Metempsychosis: In recognizing and knowing the "I," the individual recognizes and knows the Cosmic Will—and the Cosmic Will knows and recognizes the individual. Egohood is mutual conscious recognition—all below this phase belongs to the sub-conscious plane of the World-Brain.

In this Aphorism is contained another remarkable Truth. It informs us that the "I Am," or "I," or "Soul" recognized by the individual, even faintly, is the conscious recognition of the Cosmic Will or One Life which is our Real Self. And, likewise, such recognition is mutual, for in it also is comprised the recognition of the individual by the One Life. When we know, recognize and realize the "One" within us; then the "One" recognizes us within itself. And thenceforth it remembers us, and our Spiritual Evolution begins. As the Aphorism says: "Egohood is mutual recognition—mutual recognition between the Individual and the All." The Aphorism also informs us that below the plane of Ego, all the life activities of the World-Brain are along sub-conscious lines—below the plane of Consciousness. In other words, the Being *in whom we are*, knows and is conscious of us, only when we are conscious of Being *within us*. The recognition is mutual in consciousness. And, correspondingly, as we advance in the great scale of Consciousness, we come into a closer recognition and consciousness of the One, and the One comes into a closer recognition and consciousness of us. Finally, at the High Noon of Cosmic Consciousness, we come to know that we *are* the One—and the One comes to know that *it is us*. And toward this is the aim and goal of Spiritual Evolution.

But not all the Egos reach this stage—many fall by the wayside, or sink into the mire. We shall speak of this in the succeeding lesson, and we mention it here merely to prevent a misapprehension.

The Arcane Teaching does not hold that Re-Birth is imposed arbitrarily upon the Ego, or by reason of punishment or reward for deeds "good and evil" of the physical life; but, on the contrary, that it proceeds in accordance with the operation of the Seven Laws following the general path of the Desire and Character of the

Individual. In other words, the "character" of the individual, which is composed of the sum of his experience and his desires, follows the line of the general Expression of his Desires in deciding his future embodiments and life. Desire is the strong motive force of Life, as we shall explain in a future lesson, and its urge toward expression leads him into certain channels of Re-birth. An understanding of Desire and the Will enables the individual to regulate his character so that he may practically map out his future lives instead of allowing them to be determined by Blind Desire as is the case with the majority of the race.

Nor does the Arcane Teaching hold that Metempsychosis shall always continue along *unconscious* lines. The advanced soul reaches the plane of Conscious Re-birth, after a certain stage is passed—and accompanying this comes the Memory of the Past Lives, so that Life becomes continuous in consciousness and memory, after a certain stage of progress is attained. At present, the average Ego is undergoing a stage of spiritual evolution akin to the mental stage of a child of a few years of age. The child remembers but little of its past— the happenings of a few months ago are forgotten—even the affairs of yesterday seem dim to-day. But as the child advances in years it has a better and still better remembrance of the past. And, in the same way the advancing soul develops a clearer and still clearer recollection of its past lives. The dim memories, and flashes of remembrance of the past, which many of us now have, will be succeeded eventually by a full remembrance of the details of our past lives.

Moreover, the Arcane Teaching does not hold that Metempsychosis is the final stage of spiritual Evolution. On the contrary, it holds that eventually the evolving Ego will reach the stage in which Re-embodiment is no longer necessary— and thenceforth the Ego will be able to actually *create* its own bodily vehicle of life from the Principle of Substance in which it is immersed.

The Arcane Teaching also hold that Re-embodiment on this one planet continues only so long as the Ego is attracted by Earth things—when it passes beyond the attractions of Earth it rises to meet the attractions of worlds higher in the plane, and so on and on. Or, likewise, it may become so gross that it may sink to a lower level of worlds beneath our own in development. Many of us now abiding on this planet, have been drawn here by reason of having fallen from the higher estate of higher worlds by reason of our material longings. This accounts for the feeling possessed by many that they are "far from home," accompanied by dim and bitter flashes of remembrance of a brighter, happier and more glorious life on some higher plane in the past. But the lesson will be heeded, and these "lost souls" who are "strangers far from home" will follow the "kindly light" which will lead them on to home once more.

The Arcane Teaching holds that the dual-nature in individuals—the "two natures struggling for supremacy"—arise from the struggle between the "I" which is the reincarnated Ego, and the "Me" which is the Personality received along the lines of heredity, ancestral race, thought, etc. The "I" is the Real Self-the

"Me" is the personality which has been inherited. The "character of the individual arises from the balance struck between the two. The weak soul allows the "Me" to bear down the balance in its own direction; while the strong soul asserts the "I," and seats itself upon the throne of Individuality.

The very fact of the existence of such a struggle between the "Me" and the "I" of the individual, shows that there must be an "I" or Ego superior to and in a measure independent of the inherited and acquired "Me." And the fact that the individual experiences this dual-nature is his proof that he has attained at least some degree of Egohood, for those of the race who lack Egohood are like the lower animals and simply follow inherited and racial desire. The only "conflict" in the minds of those lacking Egohood is the conflict between opposing desires of this kind-there is no "I" to set aside desire, or to master it by Will. The strong Ego is able to master Desire by Will-able not only to desire to will, but to *will* to will. Desire and Will are the two poles of the manifestation of "Will." Desire rules the individual, unless he masters it by Will. The Ego may assert its will over the inherited desires of the "Me" or False-Self.

Personality is connected with the physical body and its psychical inheritances, and acquired tendencies. Individuality is connected with the Ego, or Real Self, which is over and above Personality, or the things of personality. Personality is bound and tied by the relative things and persons connected with one's personal present incarnation. Individuality is free from those bonds, ties, and limitations, and soars above them in its Cosmic flight. Personality says "I am John Doe, of Akron, grocer, aged 48"; or "Mary Roe, spinster, aged 45"; as the case may be. Individuality says "I am that which I Am"—above names, and forms, and personal sheaths or vehicles.

Each Ego has been embodied in numerous personalities during the Spiritual Evolution. Old Atlantis; Chaldea; Egypt; Greece; and other ancient lands have known us. Rome, Tyre, Carthage, Babylon, Troy, and other cities of the past have been ours. We have worshipped Jove; Isis; Thor; Wodin; Baal; Pan; and many other strange gods. We have learned many lessons— we have had many defeats and many victories. And we are now emerging into a *conscious* realization of what it all means. We have reached the point where we shall have "some say in the matter." We are facing the Cosmic Adventure with open eyes, and bold hearts—we are going on, and on, and on! The dawn of the Cosmic Knowing is upon us. The light is rising over the hills, bidding us awake to the tasks of the day. Let neither Time nor Space terrify us. Let nations vanish, and worlds disappear— what is that to us? The Cosmos is our Home—all parts of Space our own—all Time ours to live in and employ. All the Time there is—all the Space there is—all the Knowledge there is—is ours to have and to hold. All this is the heritage of him who can say, and feel, "I Am!"

Lesson IX. Survival of the Fittest.

Of all the various points of the Arcane Teaching, that of the law of Spiritual Survival of the Fittest is one of the most startling, when contrasted with the ordinary teachings on the subject. Many thinkers who freely admit the existence in Nature of the law of Physical Survival of the Fittest, seem to find an idea of injustice in the correlated doctrine of the Spiritual Survival of the Fittest, although the two are but correspondences on two several planes, following the Law of Analogy. When the Teaching is examined in detail, it will be seen that not only does it conform to other manifestations of Nature, but also is in strict accordance with the fullest equity and justice. Particularly is the absolute equity and justice of the law seen, when it is perceived that the failure to survive of the Personality of those lacking Egohood is not the result of arbitrary fiat or dicta, but *is the result solely of the desire and will of the entity or "personality" itself*. The entity perishes and dissolves, *not in spite of its desires and will, but because of them.*

The lowest forms of life perish almost immediately after the moment of physical death. It is true that even the very lowest creatures have an Astral Body which survives the death of the Physical Body, but as all the desires of such creatures are bound up in their physical lives they have nothing to live for after the physical body is destroyed. Such "life" persists for a very short time in its Astral covering, for Desire fading away, the Astral Body dissolves into its original elements, and the entity perishes. As the scale of Life is ascended, there is a longer survival of the Astral Body of the creature, for its desires die more slowly, being more complex and tenacious. The Astral forms of the higher animals often persist for quite a time after their physical bodies have perished, but after a time their desires burn out and the Astral form dissolves and the entity perishes. In the case of domestic animals who have become strongly attached to their human friends, and who have absorbed "something" from the latters' love for and interest in them, the Astral form often persists for years finding great pleasure in being in the proximity of the human friends, although unseen. In this case the desire for survival is strong, and almost reaches the phase of Will.

When the scale of Man was reached by Evolution, there was but little change in the manifestation of Spiritual Survival of the Fittest, for primitive Man was but a little more than an intelligent beast. When his Astral form passed out of the physical body, it was like that of the beast—it found but little pleasure or satisfaction in life apart from the physical, for its desires were altogether along physical lines. It soon found that it "had nothing to live for," and became filled with weariness, *ennui*, and dissatisfaction, and soon found comfort in the Astral sleep which precedes Astral death. After a few years, the entity perished—*because it had no desire to live without a physical body*. And, as surprising as the fact may be to many, it is true that the majority of persons to-day have advanced but comparatively little beyond the spiritual plane of the savage. Such people are so tied to physical manifestation and sensual gratification, that life outside of the physical body soon wearies them and fills them with dissatisfaction. They set into motion the "reversal of desire"—the negative pole of the "Will-to-Live," and accordingly there begins a slow process of Astral weakening and loss of vitality, which results in dissolution and the final death of the entity. A writer reports such an entity as saying (in a communication from the Astral Plane): "The disembodied learn that the Hades of immortality is the lack of physical body." Lacking desire to continue disembodied life, and *lacking the*

Will of Egohood to demand Rebirth—the entity passes away gradually. Just as people in the physical body die for lack of interest, and because they have nothing left to live for—so do disembodied entities on the Astral plane likewise die because they have nothing to live for. Having failed to develop Egohood during physical life, *they have nothing left to survive* after the dying away of the Body of Desire. It is true that in rare cases, extreme love for, and by, some person possessing Egohood may develop the seeds of Egohood in a disembodied entity, on the Astral Plane and cause it to seek Rebirth. And likewise some entities develop Egohood in the Astral World, through instruction from others more advanced than themselves.

There is a great difference between the Will-to-Live of the strong-willed Ego, and the Desire to live again in the same Personality which is the only desire possible to these people who have not developed Egohood or Individuality. When one realizes the "I Am," over and above Personality, then the things of Personality are left behind, and the desire and will is simply to BE. The entity in the bonds of Personality, however, simply desires *to be and remain what he was*—his Personality of "John Doe, grocer, aged 48," being his idea of his Self. This Personality having perished, such an entity cannot find anything in itself to arouse the desire or will to persist as an "I" independent of the old Personality. There is no "I" in such a person—it is all "Me," and the "Me" is the old Personality. Try to grasp this distinction, before proceeding further—it gives the key to the situation.

It must not be understood that there is no "future life" awaiting these Egoless people, after they have passed out of the physical body. On the contrary they have a more or less extended term of life on the Astral Plane, which yields them more or less satisfaction, but which must die out in time because all the old desires have been lived-out and outlived on the psychical plane (see future lessons on the Astral Plane) *and there is nothing left to live for*. Rebirth is not known to them— they cannot conceive of it for they would think that they would in that case "be some other person," and their love of their own Personality shivers and shrinks at the thought of losing their beloved "self" (?), and so they repel all idea or desires in that direction. As we have said, they are all "Me," with no "I." The "Me" always perishes, sooner or later, the "I" alone being the Real Self. Where the "I" has not been evolved or "born," it cannot exist to persist after the dissolution of the "Me," of course.

There is seen to be no injustice or inequity in this failure to grant Rebirth to these Egoless entities. It is all a matter of their own nature and desires resulting from the same. They have no "I" which desires and wills to be reborn—consequently that which *is not* cannot suffer or be injured or deprived of anything. It is like accusing one of depriving an unconceived child of life—a meaningless statement. The "Me" of the Egoless entities passes many years—often many hundred years—on the Astral Plane, and exhausts every possibility of its nature, good and bad (see future lessons on the Astral Plane). It lives out to the utmost its possibilities—and then having *out-lived* them, it has no desire for life, or reason for continued life—*there is nothing to live*.

Therefore the Spiritual Survival of the Fittest is in perfect accord with exact equity and justice. Each gets that which his nature demands and desires. One cannot be robbed of that which is not his, and which he has not and never will have.

All through Nature you may see correspondences on the physical plane of the truth that "many are called, but few are chosen." Countless life-forms are created, but few survive. The fish lays millions of eggs, but only a few fish reach maturity. Countless seeds are cast forth by the plant, but only one or two take root. This is a law of Nature, and in its operation the inequity is only apparent. The Law of Balance is preserved. One cannot be robbed of what he has not. If one has not desires, he cannot be hurt by not having the result of desires. Place the savage in a palace, and he dies broken-hearted—restore him to his jungle and he is happy. Place the hungry wild-beast in a cage and feed him well, and you break his heart. Each craves his own. There is Compensation and Balance manifested on all planes of life.

And now for a consideration of those who have attained Egohood. Is their Destiny and Progress assured? you ask. Not at all! They have simply begun to climb the ladder of Spiritual Evolution. They will mount as far as their desire and will—not a step further. They may tire of the climbing and begin a retreat.

The law of Spiritual Survival of the Fittest has many phases; many planes; many stages—it is operative from first to last during the life of the Ego.

Let us suppose the case of an Ego which has not as yet reached the plane of *conscious* Rebirth. The Ego dwells for many years on the Astral Plane (see future lessons) and lives out its personal desires, and profits by its experience in so doing, for the "I" is there to learn and remember—for it has the faculty of Egohood, that of "standing aside and looking on at one's self." Gradually the personal desires and ideas are outlived, and the essence of the experience is retained by the Ego, the latter then feeling a sense of "age" and a need for rest. This is followed by the Astral Sleep, which sooner or later comes to all entities on the Astral Plane, but from which the Egoless fail to emerge, and from which they are resolved into Nothingness. But the Ego, having an "I" above Personality, *has something to survive*, and accordingly it is drawn into the channels of Rebirth, according to the currents of attraction, and again finds a physical body, this time suited as nearly as possible to the requirements of its "character." Then begins its new life on the physical, which may be long or short. Sometimes the new body is not found fully adapted to the growing requirements of the Ego—sometimes sickness or accidents cut short the new life—and sometimes the needed experience is gained quickly—and the Ego again passes to the Astral Plane, there to enjoy a period of rest and spiritual growth and assimilation, which will be manifested in a new birth later on.

But if the new life persists beyond childhood, the Ego must progress in order to attain further stages of Spiritual Evolution. If it simply lives its old life over again, without reaching forward to greater attainment and knowledge, then it is dangerously near falling into the attraction of the "descending path" which will take it down the ladder, step by step; life after life; and which, unless the Ego learns the lesson and again steps forward, will eventually cause it to lose its Egohood and become Egoless, which means eventually dissolution. But these downward steps are not in the nature of *punishment*—they are simply stages of the law of Sequence or Cause and Effect, proceeding along the lines of Desire and Will. These descending Egos follow their desires, just as much as do the ascending ones. It is *not* Reward or Punishment, in either case—it is simply Cause and Effect, and the Path of Desire. Desire is the great motive force. There are cases known of Egos descending the scale to such an extent, drawn by their material, physical and animal desires, that they have even descended to the scale of animals and eventually perished as entities, unless rescued by the love and affection of human friends who aroused in them the last flickering spark of Spirit, and thus set them again upon the upward path. These cases, however, are very rare.

It must not be supposed, however, that all persisting Egos are "good." On the contrary, there are many persisting Egos who are giants of "evil," possessed of the sense of the "I," but filled with personal desires of material aggrandizement and selfish attainment which makes them stand out above the crowd. But such, sooner or later, are taught their lesson and either change their natures or else sink to annihilation, for all real progress must lead toward the life of the One, not in the direction of selfish personal attainment and Separateness. The error of Separateness is often brought to the minds and understanding of these Egos, by their desires finally leading them to a place where they are actually *separated* from their kind, and thus they experience that hunger for human companionship, sympathy and love which results in a change in their entire nature. One has but to look at the inner lives of some of the selfish "great men" of our own and past ages, in order to see examples of this stage of experience.

And, so the evolving Ego rises in the scale—if he be Fit— and reaches higher and higher planes of life. He passes on to other worlds and universes, when he is fitted for them. He may fall back, again and again, but there is always a chance for him to regain his lost steps. Many in this Earth-world of ours have fallen back from higher planes, and suffer soul-hunger for their lost states—these will regain their lost estates, if they will but look upward and onward and live the Life. There are glories ahead of the persistent Egos which cannot be described in human words. We do not become "God" as the Pantheists hold—*but we become as gods*. There are infinite possibilities ahead for us—there is no limit to our greatness and attainment, if we are true to the Inner Light and our Real Self. Finally we reach the stages of the highest Cosmic Consciousness, in which the Cosmic Will experiences the consciousness of Itself as Itself—then do we know that We are It, and It is Us. The Cosmos becomes conscious only through the consciousness of its Centres of Consciousness—and we are those Centres. This is what Spiritual Evolution means—this is what it is for. This is why the law of the Spiritual Survival of the Fittest is operative—the Cosmos is endeavoring to develop itself to its utmost degree and stage of Consciousness. Just as do we endeavor to retain in our consciousness our best and highest thoughts, ideas, and knowledge, so does the Cosmos endeavor to remember and preserve its noblest, highest, and fullest creations. The Success of the Cosmos depends upon this—its Progress is dependent upon it—its Conscious Life renders it necessary. This is the End, Aim, and Goal of the Cosmic Evolution. And it is a worthy end and reason for all that is. The more one enters into the spirit of the understanding of the Universal Life, the more does he identify himself with that One Life, and the dimmer and smaller does mere Personality seem. And in the end, he finds himself willing and desirous of living his life, in, through and by that One Life of the Real Self—the Cosmic Self—the "I" of the All.

To those who think sadly of the personalities which disappear during the course of Spiritual Evolution, we would say that careful thought will show that even *they have lost nothing*. Not only is their dissolution caused by their own desires and lack of will; but moreover, nothing is really lost. Personality is nothing but the "creative fiction" at the best—all that was *real* in those entities who dropped by the wayside is *preserved*. The One Life is all that was real in them—and that One Life persisted and survived. It was but a changing of form in the One Life. *It was not the destruction of a real thing*. It was but the discarding of a poorly fitting suit of clothes, worn by the One Life and Real

Self. No one is injured—nothing is lost. The All remains the All. Personality is but the mask worn by the One. The One discards its mask, but remains Itself. Justice and Equity are not violated even in the faintest degree. The Wise see this and smile—the Unwise see it not and weep. The reflection of the sun in the falling raindrop disappears when the drop falls into the stream— but the stream remains, and the Sun still shines and is reflected in its running waters. All that Is, remains—though the shapes, and forms, and illusory appearances vanish.

The wise and thoughtful of all ages, and races, have recognized the Illusion of Personality and Separateness. Men have endeavored to escape it in many ways. The Buddhists and the German Pessimists have deemed Personal Life evil, and have devised plans to escape from the same. The Buddhists would escape by beating a Retreat and endeavoring to escape Rebirth by attaining Nothingness or *Para-Nirvana*—a Return to the Nothingness from which all came. The German Pessimists advocate a killing out of the Will-to-Live—a Cosmic suicide, so to speak. But the Arcane Teachers scorn the Retreat—they bid their students to look ahead—they sound the bugle call of

"Forward-Advance-Charge!" They press forward to the Cosmic Adventure. They urge all to go on, and on, and on—until the mists of Personality disappear before the sun of the One, and the individuals find themselves at One with the All. Surely this is a more glorious way to reach the goal! It is true that in the end, the One falls again into the Sleep of Nothingness, only to reawaken after the æons have passed—but what of that? Is it not better to advance, than to Retreat? Is it not better to be Brave than a Coward? Not to speak of the infinite glories ahead of the advancing soul, is it not "worthwhile" to attain Conscious Oneship with the All, rather than to deliberately choose the path of Retreat into Unconsciousness?

But to him who falls by the wayside—as well as to him who persists and survives—there is meted out an equitable reward. There is "no bribe of heaven or threat of hell" to those who Know. It is all Cause and Effect—each gets that for which he pays— each pays his price. And, finally to all comes that Peace which passeth all Understanding. There are no Lost Souls. There are None outside of the All. There is no Outside. All are included Within the One. Yea, even the last, least, and most unworthy.

For there *is* but One!

PART IV. FATE OR FREEDOM?

Lesson X. Fate and Destiny.

From the earliest days of philosophical reasoning, metaphysical speculation, and theological dogmatism, the great questions regarding Fate or Freedom have formed an important feature of controversy. In many forms, and in manifold guises, has this great question presented itself for consideration by the human mind. Backward and forward has this tennis-ball of thought been tossed, victory being claimed by all parties engaging in the game of discussion. Early philosophy was concerned with the question of Fate and Destiny vs. Freedom, and able thinkers arrayed themselves on the respective sides of the question. Metaphysics joined in the controversy with subtle and hair-splitting definitions, theories, explanations, and conceptions. Theology took an active interest in the fray, its particular tennis-ball being called Predestination, Foreordination, or Predetermination. Modern

Science has now entered the field and her advanced thinkers insist upon the truth of the principle of Determination (but not *pre*-Determination) by Natural Laws, which applies to all branches of science, and is seen in operation in all the fields of universal activity, physical and psychical.

The Arcane Teaching holds as Truth the idea that everything and all things—every event and all events—are governed by Law. That everything and every event is under Law, Order, and Sequence. That there is no such thing as Chance. That every event is a link in the Cosmic Sequence of events. That everything is a part of, and not apart from, the Whole Thing. That every event is a part of, and not apart from, the Whole Event.

That nothing "happens" without precedent causal events proceeding regularly and in logical sequence. That there are no "accidents," or events outside of the regular order. Hearing these statements, the student will feel impelled to ask the inevitable question: "Is this Reign of Law, Order, and Sequence, but another name for the old fetish of Fate, Destiny, or Predestination? Are we then ruled by arbitrary Fate—governed by the decree of Destiny? Are all events Preordained, Predetermined, and Predestined ?" And this question must be met—and shall be met—not ignored and evaded as is customary in so many of the teachings, philosophies, and theologies. Let us consider the matter in the light of the Arcane Teachings. Listen to the Aphorism:

Aphorism xvi. Know ye, that Fate is but the distorted image of Law, Order, and Sequence. The wise know that Fate, if existent, would be an exception to Law—a twin-error to Chance. Law there is; Order there is; Sequence there is—but Fate there is not.

Fate, Destiny, and Predestination would imply the existence of Decree and Foreknowledge in the Cosmic Mind. There is no such Decree; no such Foreknowledge. When the Cosmic Mind "knows" a thing or event, it knows according to Law, and the knowing and the manifestation are simultaneous. Fate, Destiny, and Predestination, are but names for half-truths—imperfect visions of Law, Order, and Sequence.

Although to the average mind there appears to be but slight connection between the idea of Fate or Destiny and that of the foreknowledge and decree of Deity, still the former ideas have had their birth in the latter. Back of the fundamental conception of Fate or Destiny one always finds the shadowy form of some Supernatural Being who *decrees* the Fate or Destiny. In the old mythologies the gods decreed the fate and destinies of mortals, and all cosmic happenings, the details and working out of the plan being left in the hands of minor supernatural beings, such as the Parcæ, Fates, or Destinies, who were goddesses believed to preside over the birth, life, and fortunes of men. In the Grecian and Roman mythologies these Fates were three in number, *Clotho* who held the spindle, *Lachesis* who drew out the thread of men's destiny, and *Atropos* who cut it off. The Supernatural Being, or beings, always promulgated the decree of Fate or Destiny. *Fate was never a matter of natural law and order, but always the working out of an arbitrary decree, or divine fiat.* This idea is seen to be correct by reference to the definitions of the terms as given by the best authorities. Consider the following definitions:

Destiny: "The power which presides over the lot or fortune of men; the fate, lot, doom, or fortune appointed, allotted, or predetermined for each person or thing; the ultimate fate of a person; etc."

Fate: "The decree of God by which the course of events is fixed; a fixed destiny depending upon a superior cause, and uncontrollable by man; appointed lot; doom; inevitable destiny; etc."

Fatalism: "The doctrine that all things are ordered for men by the arbitrary decrees of God....It is carried out to its most pitilessly logical extreme among the Mohammedans, where everything that can happen is 'kismet', or Fate....in theology it has given birth to theories of Predestination." (By some writers the term is used also as synonymous with "Determinism," which is the scientific doctrine of causation, continuity, etc., *from natural causes*. This usage of the term is misleading, and is historically incorrect.)

Predestination: "The act of appointing beforehand by irreversible decree or unchangeable purpose; the act of foreordaining, decreeing, beforehand, or predetermining events; the purpose of God from eternity respecting all events;" as, "God's infallible providence and predestination" (Joyce); and,

"If God pre sees events, he must have predetermined them" (Hale); also, as "By the decree of God for the manifestation of his glory, some men and angels are *predestined* unto everlasting life, and others *foreordained* to everlasting death. These angels and men are *predestinated* and *foreordained*." (Westminster Confession of Faith.)

So, it may be seen, that the decree of a Supernatural Being is always back of, under, and in, all true conceptions of Fate, Destiny, Predestination, etc. These ideas cannot be divorced— they stand and fall together.

One of the main points of difference between the opposing conceptions of Law, Order, and Sequence, and of Fate, Destiny and Predestination, is seen to be in the assumption and denial of the Divine foreknowledge, and decree. Fatalism holds that some Supernatural Being has foreknowledge, and exercises arbitrary decrees determining all events, including the fate or destiny of mankind, as a race and individually. The theory of Law, Order and Sequence, on the contrary discards the idea of foreknowledge, and denies the arbitrary decree and fore determination. Instead, it holds that the Cosmic Activities, and the incidental events, proceed regularly, orderly, and in sequence, from and by reason of the operation of Natural Laws. The Arcane Teachings hold that these Natural Laws are superimposed by, and are reflections of, The Absolute Law— the Efficient Reason of the Cosmos. The modern scientific schools of Determinism agree with the Arcane Teaching so far as the idea of determination by Natural Laws is concerned, but differ from it by holding that The Law is but a name which may be applied to the sum total of Natural Laws.

Another great point of difference between Fatalism and the Arcane Teaching is, that Fatalism insists upon *arbitrary happenings and events*, unrelated to, and in spite of, natural law and order. Fatalism denies that preceding events have any relation to the "fated happening," and holds that the latter would have happened *in spite of any precedent event*. In short, Fatalism makes the "fated happening a thing standing apart from the Chain of Sequence— something resulting from arbitrary and independent decree. Thus, Fatalism holds that one's death, for instance, is "fated" (decreed) to happen in a certain way, at a certain time, and at a certain place, irrespective of the Law and Order of the Cosmos. Fatalism carried to an extreme shows the fallacy of the idea, as for instance the Mohammedan who refuses to allow his wound to be treated for the reason that if he is fated to die of the wound he *will* die, and if fated to live then he will recover without treatment. Or, the fanatics who refuse to run from a wild beast, on the same grounds. Or those who refuse to rescue a drowning man, lest they interfere with Fate.

The following quotation from the article on Fatalism, contained in the New International Encyclopædia, will show the distinctive points between the teachings of Fatalism and those of the scientific school of Determinism, which latter agrees in many important essentials with the Arcane Teaching. The writer of the article says, in part: Fatalism is "the doctrine that the course of events is so determined that what an individual wills can have no great effect on that course. Fatalism must be carefully distinguished from Determinism, as the confusion of these two conceptions has been responsible for much of the popular prejudice existing against Determinism. Fatalism, as has been said, denies that Will has efficacy in shaping events. Determinism maintains that this causally efficient will is itself to be casually accounted for; this is entirely different from the fatalistic assertion that Will counts for nothing. In fact Determinism and Fatalism are fundamentally antagonistic. *Determinism asserts that events are determined by some of the events that immediately precede them; that if the latter were different the former would be different.* Fatalism *denies* that immediately preceding events have anything to do with the origination of events immediately following: *It asserts that the latter would occur even if the former were changed.*...To say that one's death is fixed by Fate is to deny that it takes place by natural law. Or, more accurately, it is to say that however much one varies the cause, one cannot vary the effect....The fatalist's position is that the *end* is predetermined, but not the *means*; the determinist's position is that the events now occurring lead by causality to other events, which are thus fixed because their causes are actually existent. Or, to put it still another way, for the fatalist what actually determines the event is not another event immediately preceding, but *some mysterious decree issued by some mysterious agent ages before the event*. This enables us to see that Fatalism gives no scope to the will. But Determinism, which merely asserts that every event has its determining conditions in its immediate antecedents, includes among the antecedents the human Will....Thus Determinism is consistent with a belief in the efficiency of Will, and Fatalism is not."

In short, Determination holds that events are *Determined*— Fatalism holds that they are *Predetermined*. The one recognizes Natural Laws as the determining power—the other holds that Supernatural Decree predetermines and foreordains.

Predestination is Fatalism carried to its logical conclusion; Predestination holds that God appoints and determines beforehand by irreversible decree or unchangeable purpose— arbitrarily and irrevocably predetermines—the events of the universe, first and last, great and small, in general and in detail. Not only the universe as it is at present, but as it must have been forever through all eternity, and as it will be forever through all eternity. If the Divine Fiat has so gone forth, then everything is predetermined, and the Eternal Universe is but an automaton registering the Divine Decree, down to the minutest detail. In this case, everything, indeed, is caused by "the Will of God."

Theologians endeavor to escape from the above conclusion by a flow of words—like the cuttle-fish they darken the waters of thought by the flow of dark, unintelligible words, and thus make their logical escape. But a plain consideration of the facts of the proposition, laying aside theological subtleties—a consideration in the light of Common Sense—shows us that admitting a Personal Deity, possessing All-Wisdom and All-Power, then Predestination must be a logical result. Let us examine the statement.

If Deity be All-Wise, (Omniscient), then he must *know* all things, absolutely, truly, infallibly—*all things*, past, present, and future. He must know the subsequent results of all actions— the subsequent effects of all causes, the operation of all laws. He would not be able to make mistakes of judgment, or errors of foresight. There could be no necessity for any changing of his mind, if his wisdom is absolute. He must possess perfect and infallible Foresight, Foreknowledge, and Prescience, which means: "The quality of having knowledge of, or foresight into, events before they take place." And if he so *knows* what will take place, and his knowledge be *true, perfect and infallible* (and it must be so to be *absolute*) then these foreseen, and foreknown, events *must* take place and occur. As Hale well says: "If God pre-sees events, he must have predetermined them." If this be not so, then the absolute qualities attributed to Deity are false and non-existent, or the terms are meaningless.

Moreover, if the All-Wise *knows* what will happen (and this he must know if he be All-Wise) then even his All-Power cannot change the things that he *knows to a certainty*. Some theologians, wishing to escape from this dilemma, have held that his All-Power may overcome his All-Knowing, and thus take away his infallible Foresight, Foreknowledge, and Prescience—but this is childish, for Absolute Knowledge could not be destroyed, impaired, inhibited, or changed. Deity must be held to be either absolute or not absolute. If he *is* absolute, the above facts must be assumed to be correct—if he *is not*, then we must go behind and beyond him for the *true* Absolute.

Moreover, if such a Deity exists, he must have *made* the laws of the universe, for there could have been nothing else to have made them, and if they existed without his making, then such a Deity would not be absolute. If he made them, then he must have set them in motion, and kept them in motion ever since. And, if so, then he must be held responsible for all that happens, or can possibly happen, under them—they are his own creation, and he is their Cause, and the Cause of all that proceeds from them. Moreover his All-Knowing must have made him *fully aware* of all the possibilities and certain effects of the operation of these laws. There is no escape from this conclusion. No wonder that old Omar raised his voice in indignant protest against this conception when accompanied by the "bribe of heaven and threat of hell" as a reward or punishment for doing that which must be inevitable because it has been predestined by Deity.

The conception of a Personal Deity, or Personal Supreme Being, absolute in nature, who created the universe and its laws, must carry with it as a logical accompaniment the conceptions of Foresight, Foreknowledge, and Predestination—which are but newer names for the old fetish of Fate and Destiny. In this is found the paradox of theology, from which it can never escape, and which it has never been able to reconcile. But the Arcane Teaching does not hold to Decree and Foreknowledge, either in a Personal Deity or in the Cosmic Mind. Its Aphorism denies the "existence of Decree and Foreknowledge in the Cosmic Mind." It says that "When the Cosmic Mind 'knows' a thing or event, it knows according to Law, and the knowing and the manifestation are simultaneous." For when the Cosmic Brain "thinks" or "knows" a thing or event—then the "thought" *becomes* a thing or event, and is actually manifested. The Cosmic Mind knows only what is existent, for what it knows is manifested because of the knowing. And what it knows, it knows because of the manifestation. In the Cosmic Mind, knowing and manifestation are identical— simultaneous—one. The Cosmos is the only Being that exists and can know the Cosmic Activities. Other than itself there is naught but The Law, which is above Being, and above Knowing, and above Action, as we know those terms. Any attempt to attribute to The Absolute the qualities, attributes, and properties of Man, inevitably results in postulating a Personal Deity, whose All-Knowledge is the Predestination of the Universe—whose will, decree, and fiat, is Fate. And in that case upon that Deity must be placed the responsibility *for everything that happens* in the universe. In that event, then indeed we may say with the poet: *"His the credit; His the blame; His the glory; His the shame."*

In the place of Fatalism, Destiny, and Predestination, the Arcane Teaching offers the Orderly Trend under Cosmic Laws inherent within the Cosmos, proceeding as Law, Order and Sequence. Not the result of arbitrary fiat or decree, but the result of natural laws proceeding in regular order, as the Cosmos evolves toward Cosmic Consciousness and All-Knowledge. When the Cosmos is resolved into Infinite Nothingness, then we find naught existent but The Law. And The Law is the only thing left upon which to fix the Final Blame—if blame there be. Fix it so, if you will. If it belong to The Law—give to It Its own. But The Law is no Person—no Being—It is Absolute Law—constant, unchanging, invariable, eternal. In Law we find the only refuge in our highest flights of thought, reason, or imagination. It is not a Law Giver—it is Law in Itself.

Lesson XI. Law, Order, and Sequence.

We live in a Cosmos governed by Laws existent by reason of the very being of the Cosmos and the existence of The Law. There is no blind Chance, nor Arbitrary Decree in the Cosmos. There is no place or room for these for Law fills the whole field of Cosmic Activity. There is no Disorder, or Inharmony. Everything is in Balance. Chaos does not exist. From The Law proceeds the Seven Cosmic Laws, which in turn are subdivided into seven; and these into seven; and so on, the septenary division and sub-division extending into the Infinitesimal. But in large and in small—and both are alike—there is ever Law and Order, Continuity and Sequence, Manifesting and in full operation.

And, over all is The Law of Laws—Absolute—Alone!

As the mists of the morning disappear before the rays of the rising sun, so will the superstitions, fables, and dogmas be dissipated by the knowledge of universal natural law and order. In a universe governed by eternal laws and Cosmic order there is no place for the Fates; the Destinies; the Arbitrary Decrees; of the fables, folk-lore and legends, even though they be covered by the robes of philosophy or theology. Before the light of Reason, these things must melt away, when the Truth is seen, the half-truths disappear. Fate,

Predestination, and Chance— Threefold Error—flee before the conception of Law and Order in the Cosmos. Listen to the Aphorism:

Aphorism xvii. Know ye that, under The Law, the Cosmos is governed by Law. Each and every thing, and all things, proceed in Orderly Trend. In the Cosmos there is no Chance; no Disorder; no Inharmony. The Three Principles—Substance, Motion, and Consciousness-are equally under Law. Those who teach otherwise, err.

This statement agrees with the report of the reason of the most advanced minds of the race, past and present. Every intelligent conception of the Cosmos must of necessity include the conception of Law. Without this inherent indwelling Law, the Cosmos could not exist—the Cosmos would be Chaos. The very origin of the term "Cosmos" shows the underlying thought in the minds of the ancient Greek philosophers who first used it. The word itself is derived from the archaic Greek word *komeo*, "to take care of," and the early Greek philosophers used it first in the sense of "order," and later in the broader sense of "the world or universe, from its perfect order and arrangement, as opposed to Chaos." Its use as "the World-Soul" came later, and included the earlier conceptions. Its antithesis the word

"Chaos"—has two meanings, viz.: (1) "A yawning empty space"; and (2) "Confusion; or, a mass of matter in confusion without order or laws; a confused mixed, mass, without order or regularity." In both of these usages, Chaos is absolutely opposite in meaning to Cosmos. When we postulate a Cosmos without Law and Order, we are simply applying the term to what is really Chaos—either a Nothing, or else an Orderless Universe. Order always implies the existence of Law—the two are inseparable. There can be no such thing as an universe half Cosmos and half

Chaos. Order and Chaos are antithetical. Law and Chance are antithetical. One annuls the other—they cannot exist at the same time. The three Primary Axioms of Logic show us this fact.

Let us consider them for a moment:

I. *The Axiom of Identity*: "The same quality or thing is always the same quality or thing, no matter how different the conditions in which it occurs."

II. *The Axiom of Contradiction*: "No thing can at the same time and place both be and not be."

III. *The Axiom of Excluded Middle*: "Everything must either be or not be; there is no other alternative or middle course."

These are established axioms of Logic. A leading authority, Prof. Jevons, says of them: "Students are seldom able to see at first their full meaning and importance. All arguments may be explained when these self-evident laws are granted; and it is not too much to say that the whole of Logic will be plain to those who will constantly use these laws as the key."

Therefore we must either hold that the Cosmos is under Law and Order, or else that it is not. And if it is not, then Chance or Arbitrary Decree rule the universe—and the Cosmos is but Chaos. There is no alternative—there can be no half-and-half about the matter. Which is it? We need scarcely to assure the student that the highest modern scientific thought agrees perfectly with the teachings of the ancient occultists, to the effect that the Cosmos is governed by Law in every detail, and as a whole; and that there is universal order, balance, and harmony manifested through it. Not only is this so, but the ordinary human mind is able to discover the existence of Law in the universe, in its every phase of manifestation. The rising of the sun; the flow of the tides; the law of gravitation; the mechanical laws; and Natural Law in all of its phases; show the existence of Law in the Cosmos. Science shows us that the entire universe is held together by the operation of Law—that if the tiniest atom were released from the operation of Law, the entire universe would be resolved into Chaos, so interdependent are its parts, and so incompatible with Universal Law would be the slightest exception thereto. The Laws of the Universe can never be "broken"—if we come in contact with them and refuse to govern ourselves accordingly, we suffer—but the Law remains intact. We do not "break" the Law of Gravitation when we step over a precipice—we only prove its existence. If we could "break" the tiniest Law of the Cosmos, the Cosmos would be Chaos.

And these Cosmic Laws are not the result of the arbitrary fiat or *dictum* of some Being. They are inherent in the very nature of the Cosmos. There never has been a moment in the existence of the Cosmos in which twice two did not make four; never a moment in which a straight line was not the shortest distance between two given points; never a moment in which the laws of mathematics, geometry, and logic were not as true as they are today. Cosmic Laws were not *made*—they are inherent in the Cosmos, and inseparable from it. These Cosmic Laws arise from the *reflected power* of The Law itself—they are superimposed upon the Cosmos in the very nature of the Cosmos.

The Aphorism continues: "Each and every thing, and all things, proceed in Orderly Trend." This is a statement of the Law of Orderly Trend, one of the Seven Cosmic Laws. "Orderly" means: "In order; arranged or disposed in order; observant of order or method; not disorderly; keeping order; well regulated; free from disorder or confusion; characterized by good order; according to established order or method; according to due order or method; duly; regularly; etc." "Trend" is a word derived from an old root meaning "a circle; a ring; round; etc." and its present accepted meaning is: "to move around or about; to extend or lie in a particular direction; to run; to stretch; inclination in a particular direction," or strictly: "to proceed in a particular direction." Its use in the Arcane Teaching implies a "proceeding or moving forward," and also (in the esoteric sense) cyclic progression. Thus the Cosmos is held to "trend" in an "orderly, regular, established" manner, according to Cosmic Laws, and under The Law. Evolution is a manifestation of Orderly Trend and Sequence.

The Aphorism continues: "In the Cosmos there is no Chance; no Disorder; no Inharmony." We have seen that where Law and Order govern and rule there can be no Disorder nor Inharmony. Harmony and Balance maintain where Law and Order govern and control. We wish to add a few words regarding the subject of Chance, owing to the popular misconception of the nature and meaning of this much used word. "Chance" is generally held to be: "an accident; something happening without a cause; a supposed agent or mode of activity other than a force, law, or purpose." The word was derived from the Latin word *cadentia*, meaning "the falling of the dice." An "accident" is "something that happens suddenly or unexpectedly," but the word is generally used in the sense of "something happening without due cause, and out of the established order." The strict meaning of "Chance" is "without cause," and it is generally so used. But with the advancing knowledge of the universal prevalence of causality,

Chance in the original sense of the term is no longer regarded as existent, possible, or reasonable. The word is now employed in the scientific sense of: "The unknown, or unforeseen cause or causes of an event." As Benley says: "Chance is but a mere name, and really nothing in itself; a conception of our minds, and only a compendious way of speaking, whereby we would express, that such effects as are commonly attributed to chance, were verily produced by their true and proper causes." The highest modern philosophical thought agrees with the Arcane Teaching that: "In the Cosmos there is no Chance." Where Law and Order reign, *there can be no Chance*; no "accidents" no "happenings," in the sense of "without cause." Even the cast of the dice is now seen to be as much the result of Law and Order and Sequence as is the motion of the sun, planets and tides. Casualty has been superseded by Causality in philosophical thought.

Aphorism xviii. Know ye that each and every event, and all events, proceed in Orderly and Logical Sequence. There is always a Something Before and a Something After, which men mistakenly call Cause and Effect, but which, in truth, are but relative stages of the Cosmic Sequence.

Aphorism xviii informs us regarding the Law of Sequence, another one of Seven Cosmic Laws. It informs us that "each and every event, and all events proceed in orderly and logical sequence." This Aphorism declares the principle of what modern philosophical thought has called the Law of Continuity, by which is meant that universal principle or law, by virtue of which there is ever maintained a relationship of precedent and subsequent—cause and effect—between all events; the idea being diametrically opposed to that which holds that events are independent and not related to other events. In the Aphorism the word "orderly" is used in the sense defined a little further back. The word "logical" is used in its general sense of "agreeing with the natural reason"; and therefore, is employed in the Aphorism, in the sense of "in a manner which accepted by the human reason as natural, orderly, according to law, and reasonable—and which therefore might be reasonably expected were the preceding events known." The word "Sequence" is used in the sense of: "A succession, or following after, in orderly arrangement and uniformity; a series of things following in a certain order of succession." The word itself springs from the Latin word, *sequens*, meaning "to follow," and the idea of *following in regular order or procession* constitutes the essential meaning of the term.

The Law of Sequence causes all things to proceed in a *continuous stream or procession of events*. "Continuous" means "unbroken; uninterrupted; connected; with no intervening space." An "Event" is a "happening; something that occurs; the consequent or result of any action." Therefore the Law of Sequence causes all happenings, occurrences, or events to flow, proceed, and evolve from previous events, happenings or occurrences; and likewise to result in subsequent events, happenings or occurrences, which flow, proceed, and evolve from them. There is always a "something before" and a "something after" every event, happening, or occurrence. Every event has *reasons*, and is in itself one of the *reasons* for that which must follow after. Just as no link in a continuous chain can escape having a preceding and succeeding link, so no event can fail to have precedent and subsequent events connected with and related to it. No event can be *isolated* from the Cosmic Chain of Sequence, or the Cosmic Stream of Events. No event, and no thing, can *stand alone* in the Cosmos. Everything and every event is interdependent, from the very nature of the Cosmos itself. Thus we see that there can be no such thing as "Chance" or "accidents" in the Cosmos. Nothing ever "merely happens," in the usual sense of the phrase. Everything, every event, every happening, has its preceding causes, and from it will emerge the succeeding effects—all being links in the continuous chain of Sequence.

We recognize these things, dimly, in everyday life, and call them the workings of Cause and Effect. But the Aphorism makes a distinction here and informs us that that which men mistakenly call Cause and Effect, "in truth, are but relative stages of the Cosmic Sequence. Let us proceed to a consideration of this truth.

The statement of this Aphorism apparently conflicts with the accepted philosophical and scientific conception of the Law of Causation, but the difference is largely a matter of expression, and the Arcane Teaching is in full harmony with the advanced conceptions of Causation, as interpreted by the highest authorities. The Law of Causation, as advanced by modern scientific thought, may be stated generally as the conception that everything is an effect of precedent Causes and, at the same time, the Cause of the effects which arise from it—thus each thing is a link in an endless chain of Cause and Effect. Another way of stating this conception is that every event in time, or thing in space, has Causes; and at the same time is the Cause of succeeding effects in the shape of events in time, or things in space. This conception of the Beginningless and Endless Chain of Cause and Effect is seen to be very similar to the Chain of Sequence of the Arcane Teaching. *But here is the difference.* The Arcane Teaching *does not* hold that the Chain of Sequence is Beginningless and Endless. On the contrary, it holds that the

Cosmos emerged from the Infinity of Nothingness at the Dawn of the Cosmic Day—therefore, this particular Cosmos had an actual beginning in time; and likewise, it will have an ending in time, when it again is resolved into the Infinity of Nothingness.

The Law is held to be the only Eternal, using the term in its absolute sense.

The Cosmic Activities proceed according to Law, Order and Sequence. What you are today—what happens this moment— is the logical result of all *that has gone before* in the Chain of Sequence. What is, is not because of Chance—but in accordance with Law, Order and Sequence. What will be tomorrow—a year hence—a million years hence—will be the logical result of all the things and events that are manifesting this moment. There is no break in the Chain. Everything, and every event, proceeds from what has gone before. And from everything, and every event, develop the seeds of future events and things. Everything, and every event, is a blossom— and contains within itself the seeds of future blossoms. Every event is but a stage in the Whole Event of the Cosmos. Everything is but a part of the Whole Thing of the Cosmos. The Cosmos is the Whole Thing, striving, moving, thinking, and doing, in myriads of forms and shapes and manifestations—acting in the countless series of events which together constitute the Whole Event.

At any particular moment in the Cosmic Day—at this very moment that you read these lines—certain things are at certain places, under certain conditions, acting in a certain manner— certain events are occurring under certain conditions. All this is the result of Cosmic Causes operating since the first glimmer of the Cosmic Dawn. And, likewise, at any imagined moment of the future—a year hence—a century hence—a million years hence—at any given moment there will be certain things in certain places, under certain conditions, acting in a certain manner—certain events will be occurring under certain conditions. And this too will be the result of the Cosmic Causes, operating from the beginning—operating and in existence in some stage of Sequence, today—this moment. All that *is* proceeds from all that has gone before. And from all that *is* will flow, proceed and evolve all that shall be even unto the very ending.

And these things and events are "certain," not because of Fate, Destiny or Arbitrary Decree, but because of the operation of fixed and certain natural laws, constant, invariable and immutable. There is no Fate, no Chance, no Accidents. Cause produces Effect. Everything has its precedent, and will have its subsequent. The seeds of the future exist in the present. The seeds of the present existed in the past. No thing or event is arbitrary, separate, disconnected, independent. We are all parts of a Cosmic Whole, taking part in one Cosmic Event. Can you imagine a single thing or event without precedent causes? Can you imagine a Cosmic Law being broken? The parts are conditioned by the Whole. This is not Fate, but Law, Order, and Sequence.

Lesson XII. Dominant Desire; Sovereign Will.

Aphorism xvii informs us that "The Three Principles—Substance, Motion and Consciousness—are equally under Law." The leading scientific minds of the day hold that the Reign of Law is operative not only over matter and motion, but also over mind. There are but few psychologists who hold otherwise, although a few are reluctant to admit that the operations of human volition are caused, and such therefore hold on to the old dogma of "causelessness" although candidly admitting that the only other alternative is the theory of Chance. This reluctance may be explained by the influence of the old theology which held that the admission of cause in volition would annul the doctrine of "free will" (in the sense of free *choice*), and would destroy man's moral responsibility. The theologians, however, do not accept the alternative of

Chance, but murmur something about "special provisions of Providence," without explaining what they mean by this. But all denials of the operation of universal law on the mental plane are in direct defiance of the modern scientific knowledge of the laws of psychology, and the common experience of the race which informs us that people act and choose because of *motives and reasons*. And all human education is based upon this understanding and principle.

The trouble with the theologians is that they confuse Law, Order, and Sequence, with the old fetish of Fate, Destiny, and Predestination. They recognize the logical absurdity of holding one morally responsible for doing what for all eternity it has been predestined, predetermined, or fated one should do. When Determination is divorced from *Pre*-determination, a new light is seen. Notwithstanding the theological reluctance, its advocates nevertheless *act* as if psychological laws were true, in advocating the "training" of the mind, and in offering the "motives" of rewards and punishments for actions. If the volition is free, how could these "motives" influence or affect it. All education and training of the mind implies the existence of mental laws of choice and action. The "Law of Association" is but the Law of Sequence. Without Law in the mental realm, there is but the alternative of Chance—theology to the contrary, notwithstanding.

Aphorism xix. Man on the personal plane always acts and chooses strictly in accordance with the nature of his personal character. His personal character is determined by the nature of his psychical organism resulting from heredity, environment, and experience, and consists of a collection of mental states the motive principle in which is Desire (including Fear, which is but a form of Desire). The personal man, like the lower forms of life, always acts and chooses: according to the sum or average of his desires and fears, the strongest motives always dominating and determining the choice and action.

Each man has a personal character—just as each actor in a play assumes a "character." Each character, as the Aphorism states, is "a collection of mental states." These mental states are manifest as traits, tendencies, temperament, nature, disposition, personality—what we know as "the nature of the person," in fact. Different persons are attracted by different things, in different degrees, and respond in different ways and in different degrees. No two persons are exactly alike. Each person has his own nature, disposition and character. The dictionaries say that Character is: "The personal qualities or attributes of a person." Each character has its personal collection of feelings, desires, wants, inclinations, likes and dislikes, habits of thought, capacity for thought, degree and character of will, etc. Each has its sub-conscious collection of stored up impressions, memories, inherited traits, etc., as well as its conscious mental faculties—in fact, nine-tenths of the mental activities arise from this subconscious region. Each character has its collection of seed-thoughts which constitute its share of the race experience—the experiences of its ancestors. And each has its store of impressions and experiences which have modified it accordingly. The result of heredity, environment and experience creates a personality and character according to which one acts and chooses. This character, at any particular moment, is just what a man is at that particular moment. And as he is, so will he act and choose. He always acts and chooses *by reason of* what he *is*. On the personal plane, he cannot act differently. And what he *is*—his character at the moment—always has as its motive power the sum or average of his desires and fears.

This is the point at which we must consider the objections of the "free will" theologians who will not admit that man acts and chooses according to the sum and average of his desires and fears. These people put forward the three leading "proofs" that man does not so act and choose. Let us consider them, briefly, in detail. They are as follows:

I. *That one may refuse to act on a desire or fear, however strong. He may oppose his will to the desire or fear and defeat its power.*

This statement is unquestionably true, but the explanation is that in so *willing* not to act upon the desire, he is really acting upon other and *stronger* desires or fears which urge him *not to do* the thing in question. Each desire is a motive—and the strongest motive dominates and decides. Before he may will *not to act*, he must first desire or "want to" refrain from the act, or else fear to act. In short he must *want not to* more than he *wants to*. Instead of disproving the action of Desire, it affords a very good proof. He chooses to do that which he "wants to" most strongly.

II. *That one may choose to act upon a higher desire rather than upon a lower one—to act from a higher motive than from a lower one.* This also is unquestionably true—but what is the higher desire" and the "higher motive" but *another form of Desire*. If the "higher" is stronger, it conquers—if the "lower" is stronger, *it* conquers. Whichever is felt by the man to be the *most desirable* according to his reason, experience and feelings is the strongest motive. Sometimes the scales are very evenly balanced, and it requires but a mental speck of dust to tip it one way or the other. But this does not disprove the rule—it only emphasizes it.

III. *That one has the evidence of his consciousness that he is free to act as he pleases—or to choose between two or more different courses of action. One feels most strongly that he has the freedom of choice and action.* This is the "proof" considered unanswerable by the theologians. It is undoubtedly true, so far as it goes, but a moment's consideration will show one that it adds but another proof to the truth of the power of Desire, and the Law of Cause and Effect. Waiving entirely the obvious rejoinder that the feeling or consciousness of freedom has no causal relation to the act, we see that the man merely feels and is conscious of the fact that *he may act and choose as he pleases*. Certainly he may, no one disputes that—*but why does he "please"? Why* does he *want to* do one thing in preference to another? And *why* does he finally *choose* to do one thing instead of the other? Is it merely Chance? Is there no *reason* or cause? Is it not true that he finds it *more desirable*, or *more satisfactory*, to do the one thing? Does he not weigh the motives, reasons, feelings, and desires, by the light of his own reason, experience, nature and character, and then decide in favor of the most desirable course? His *will* is free, of course— but his desires, feelings, "please to," and "choose to" depend upon elements of his character—and the strongest motive, conscious or subconscious, wins the day. Between two things or objects, one chooses that which appeals to him as the "most desirable"—that which he "wants" most, or fears least.

Many will object that if this be true, it is unjust to punish one for doing what he must do according to his character. This objection arises from the old conception of Fate and

Predestination, which held that a man *must* do a certain thing, *in spite of all that might tend to prevent*. This of course would make all "punishment" a rank injustice, and an absurd proceeding. But the doctrine of Cause and Effect does not so hold. On the contrary it holds that one's character may be, and is, changed, modified and altered by the restraints placed upon certain actions. These afford new motives for action or non-action. The theory of *human* Law, at least, is not that one shall be "punished" for wrongdoing *in the spirit of wrath or vengeance*, but that the "punishment" shall act as a deterrent, warning, and *restraining motive* to prevent the recurrence of the act on the part of the criminal, and to prevent others from making the same mistake. It is society's method of protecting itself—not a system of revenge. The very fact that the penalties of the law serve to deter some from wrongdoing is but a proof that the strongest motive dominates. The birch prevents the schoolboy from misbehaving, though he so desires very much. He fears to incur punishment, more than he desires to misbehave. We may *blame* people for acting wrongly, because we regret that their characters were not better developed, or that their judgment was not more perfect. We often make the mistake of blaming *effects*, instead of *causes*. Would it be just to "blame" or "punish" if our acts resulted from Chance? In the same way, remorse and regret mean that we realize that what we did or chose was not wise or desirable, as seen in the light of subsequent events—we regret that the higher, nobler, or wiser motives were not dominant; or feel sorrow at the results of our actions. These latter feelings are often cited by those who deny Cause and Effect on the mental plane. But what, indeed, would be the reason for regret and remorse if our actions had been decided by Chance instead of by causes? If we remove Causes, we are in the hands of Chance—would that be a desirable exchange? If we deny Law, we must attribute all actions to Chance!

Summing up the fact of Dominant Desire, it may be said that people act in accordance with *the line of the Greatest Satisfaction*. This Greatest Satisfaction depends entirely upon the nature of the person—his character—which is regulated by his tendencies, disposition, inherited qualities, results of his experience, environment, education, training, history, etc., all of which, of course, have other causes behind them. Whatever gives to the person the Greatest Satisfaction evident at the moment of action or choice, that will he do or choose. This is the rule—test it most rigidly by applying it to your own acts and decisions, and those of others. But in so testing, do not overlook the effect of Habit as crystallized Desire; nor the effect of Fear as negative Desire. When two desires are otherwise equal, the one most habitual will win the day. The element of Fear, or Aversion, is but a Desire "not to," or "to avoid, or get away from." Compulsion by others may result in action through Fear. And one often refrains from manifesting a desire because he fears to "*pay the price.*"

Did you ever make a choice, or perform an act which gave you the Least Satisfaction, or which you knew to be the *most undesirable* under all the circumstances of the case? If you did so—*Why did you do it?* If you yield to the suggestions, desires, reason or will of another person, against your own inclination and judgment—what is this but the "line of the least resistance," which gave you the least trouble or dissatisfaction at the moment, and in which the negative Desire of Fear had its effect?

In the case of hypnotic influence, or the domination of one's will by another by any means, the rule is not broken, for the stronger person's will influences and arouses the Desire of the weaker person. Even in this case, desire or fear is the motive of action or choice.

In considering this subject, remember that the Aphorism says "the sum and average of his desires—the strongest motives always dominating and deciding the choice and action." We often are forced to "strike an average" between our conflicting desires. And then again, wisdom, experience and intelligence enable us to discriminate between the *desirability* of objects and acts, and thus play an important part in the choice. And imagination gives us a wider range of choice, by presenting a greater number of objects before us for choice. But wisdom, experience, intelligence and imagination result from Causes.

A Dominant Desire always has for its motive the attainment of something which will bring the Greatest Satisfaction, immediate or remote, or the prevention of something which will bring dissatisfaction, immediate or remote—either to the person himself, or to others in whom he is interested. Aversion, fear, or the tendency away from persons or things, are merely the negative phases of Desire, and come under the same rule.

The "most desirable" thing, according to the judgment of the moment, is always chosen—the "most undesirable" thing of the moment is always avoided. Sometimes this necessitates "striking an average." So in the end we do that which we "*like to*"—we do what we "*want to*" do most. The "want to" and "like to" arise from Cause, and are under the Law of Sequence—links in the Cosmic Chain of Eventuality.

And so, the nature of one's character determines his acts. This explains many actions in a strange way. For instance, one man is kind because it gives his nature the greatest satisfaction; just as another gains the greatest satisfaction by being otherwise. One finds satisfaction in doing his "duty"; while another finds satisfaction in escaping it. One finds satisfaction in virtue; another in vice. One finds it in selfishness; another in doing for and giving to others. One finds more satisfaction in giving his life for his country; another finds it in running away and hiding. One finds the greatest satisfaction in giving; another, in getting. One finds the greatest satisfaction in being moral; another in the reverse. One takes the greatest pleasure in being a good citizen; another finds his satisfaction in the opposite. Each acts according to his nature and character—just as a cat and dog acts according to its nature. But man can change his nature, *if he so desires*. And he often so desires, while the lower animal does not—that is the main point of difference.

We have laid much stress upon this subject of Dominant Desire, because we wish to awaken you to a realization, perhaps for the first time, of what an important part Desire plays in the choice and actions of the man on the personal plane of life— how much in thrall to it is the race. When one realizes his bonds, he is in a position to work to rid himself of them. It is only when the slave realizes that he is a slave, that thoughts of freedom come to him. There is a plane above that of Personality—a plane in which Positive Will takes the place of Desire. Sovereign Will is above Dominant Desire. Listen to the Aphorism:

Aphorism xx. When man attains Individuality—Egohood— he enters upon the plane of Will, and rises above the plane of Desire. Desire and Will are the opposite poles of the same Principle—the Centre of Balance being Reason. On the plane of Will, though one still remains under Law, yet he may learn to use Law instead of remaining passive to it. He may learn to oppose Law to laws. He may learn to create Desire by Will, as well as to restrain and master Desire by Will. Furthermore—and this the greatest of all—he may learn to Will to Will. He may learn to complete the Circle of Will. He may learn the Secret of the Excluded Middle. When this last Secret is learned, man is well on the road to Mastery.

By rising to the plane of Will, over and above the plane of Desire, we rise above the lower laws, and acknowledge supremacy only to the higher laws. We may then oppose Law to laws, and counteract and use them. Desire and Will are but the opposing poles of the same principle—Reason being the Centre of Balance, as the Aphorism states. The majority of the race remain centred in the negative pole—few reach the centre—and still fewer learn the secret of swinging the centre over to the positive side. He on the negative plane can do no more than to Desire to Will. He of the positive plane may learn to Will to Will. He who has learned the secret may transmute his desires, and transform his inclinations, tendencies, and tastes. Such a one is the Master of Desire, instead of its slave.

The art of Willing to Will is one of the great feats of occultism—one of the great attainments of the Arcane Teachings. In it lies also the secret of Will Power in its outward manifestations, for he who can change, and create *desires* in himself, can produce similar results in the desire-mind of others. In attaining the plane of Positive Will, one enters into the field of all Occult Power and Attainment—the rest is all a matter of progress, practice, exercise and mastery. When one grasps the Secret of Will, he has laid hands upon the Sword of Power.

Running back from cause to prior cause, and to still more remote precedent causes of his desires, the Individual finds himself at last confronting the Cosmic Will. Retracing his path back to the present, he finds himself confronting his Personal Will, which is moved by Desire. In other words, he finds a Chain of Desire extending from the Cosmic Will to the Personal Will—a chain of countless links, but having a beginning in Will, and an ending in Will—an Endless Chain, because it is a Circle. Thereupon he learns the first lessons of the Arcane Secret of the

Excluded Middle, and thenceforth strives to realize *the union of the two ends of Will*. From the realization of this Union arises the Individual Will—the Positive Will of the Ego. In this process the law of Cause and Effect is not violated, but Will is made the Cause of Will—the Cause and Effect merge. When this is attained—then does Man indeed become the Master!

PART V. THE ASTRAL PLANE.

Lesson XIII. Lower Astral Planes.

There are three great planes of manifestation in the Cosmos—the Material Plane; the Astral Plane; and the Spiritual Plane. There is much confusion in the use of the term "plane" in the occult writings, for it is employed in various ways, from necessity and in the absence of other words with which to express the unfamiliar facts of the case. For instance, many occultists very properly speak of "the physical plane; the mental plane; and the spiritual plane, of Thought," meaning respectively thereby: (1) the plane of thought connected with the sensations of the body, the physical desires, etc.; (2) the plane of intellect, reason, etc.; and finally, (3) the plane of the higher mental activities and manifestations, familiarly known as the Spiritual Plane of Thought. The beginner in the study of occultism is apt to confuse the above usage of the term with that employed in speaking or writing of the Three Great Planes of the Cosmos, the Material Plane; the Astral Plane; and the Spiritual Plane; the second of which, the Astral Plane, will form the subject of consideration in the present lesson, and the two immediately following it in sequence.

The word "plane" has been appropriated by occult writers, from necessity, and given a meaning apparently at variance with the accepted usages. In ordinary language a "plane" is a "perfectly level, flat, and smooth surface." In geometry and astronomy it is sometimes used in an abstract or ideal sense, to indicate "an ideal surface supposed to cut or pass through a solid body or in various directions; as the *plane* of an ecliptic, the *plane* of a planet's orbit, etc." It is also used in a figurative sense, implying "a level, or field" as "on the plane of reason; on the plane of common sense, etc." Generally speaking, its figurative use implies a layer, strata, or *level*, and it is used in occult phraseology in the figurative sense of a level, or strata of Cosmic activity or manifestation.

But the student is cautioned against confusing the term "plane" with any conception of "place." A plane is not a place. A particular place may include several planes, and sub-planes; for the planes interpenetrate each other. A plane has no dimensions in space, and rather more resembles a *state or condition*. It cannot be measured in the three dimensions, and yet it is capable of measurement by degrees in the Scale of Vibrations. These states or degrees of vibration interpenetrate each other, without interference, in which peculiarity they have correspondences or analogies in physical phenomena. For instance, a dozen or more currents of electricity may pass along the same wire, at the same time without interfering with each other, and may then register each on its special instrument, providing that the rate of tension or vibration be different in each case. Or, again, light vibrations, heat vibrations, vibrations of electricity and magnetism of several degrees, vibrations of the X-Rays, sound vibrations, etc., may manifest and remain present in the space of a room, at the same time.

The various planes of manifestation blend into each other, and each of the three planes has seven sub-planes, which in turn are sub-divided into seven minor planes, and so on, until seven times seven acts of sub-division have been made.

On the Physical Plane of the Cosmos occurs the various manifestations of the physical world—the world of matter and energy. It is the plane best known to us, for all of our physical activities are performed on some of its sub-planes. On these planes there are manifestations of matter of degrees unrecognized by the senses of man, as well as the familiar forms and degrees. Likewise there are forces and energies of which man of to-day is totally ignorant, with the exception of a few advanced souls who have risen above the ordinary race limitations. It is not our purpose to enter into a consideration of the Physical Plane in this lesson. Neither is it our purpose to enter into a consideration of the Spiritual Plane, the conception of which is beyond the comprehension of the ordinary human, and which the words of the ordinary plane of life would be utterly inadequate to express. Our subject for consideration here is simply the second plane of the Cosmos—the Astral Plane.

The term "astral" (from the Greek word meaning "a star") is of ancient usage in the occult teachings. Astral "regions" and Astral "beings," were held to be places and beings of a more ethereal and finer order and degree than our material world and beings—so far as the bodies of the latter were concerned, at least. In the Astral regions the disembodied entities and the supernatural beings were held to abide. The term was often used loosely and in a manner tending to confuse the student. In fact, even to-day the term is used with various shades of meanings, by the different schools of occultism, and confusion results by reason thereof. Some schools use the term "Astral Plane" to designate only the *lower* sub-planes of the Astral, using other terms to designate the *higher* planes, which latter they often confuse with those of the Spiritual Plane. Others include the entire series of above-the-Material planes, lower and higher Astral and Spiritual alike, under the general term of Astral Plane.

The Arcane Teaching follows the most approved ancient usage, and applies the term "Astral Plane" to the intermediate plane of the Cosmos—the plane lying between the Material and the Spiritual—including, however, the higher as well as the lower Astral sub-planes. Such has always been the custom of the Arcane Teachers, and it is, moreover, in accordance with the most ancient and authoritative practice.

There are many sub-planes on the Astral Plane, many of which bear close analogies to corresponding planes known to us on the Material Plane. There are also sub-planes containing life activities, which are different from the more familiar ones, and which bear the same relationship to the latter *that the black keys On the piano-board bear to the white keys*. On these "black-key" sub-planes dwell entities strange to human sight and thought, but which, nevertheless, form a part of the universal manifestation of life. These entities are non-human—never were human, and never will be human. Their evolution has been, and will continue, along totally different lines. Occultists group these entities under the general term of "elementaries," or "elementals," although their degrees and characteristics vary greatly, one from another. We shall consider these entities in the following lesson.

Beginning our consideration of the Astral Plane, we must not fail to take notice of one of the sub-planes nearest the material—the sub-plane in which the Thought Currents operate, and also in which the Astral Bodies of the embodied, and the Auric Colors are visible.

On this sub-plane the phenomena of Mentalism manifest. This sub-plane is the one nearest to the ordinary Material Plane, and is often penetrated, unwittingly, by persons whose psychic faculties have become sharpened and who have developed the qualities of Clairvoyance, Astral Sensing, etc.

It is scarcely necessary to explain in detail the facts relating to the Astral Body of human beings, for the student is supposed to have had some preliminary acquaintance with the general subject of occultism. We shall merely note the general facts in passing. The Astral Body of the person is the finer body, or inner envelope, of the entity or soul. This Astral Body has long been known in the traditions of the race, and has been called by various names, such as "the ethereal body"; the "fluidic body"; the "double"; the "wraith"; the "doppelganger," etc. It is composed of Astral substance, which is much finer than the matter with which we are familiar. It bears the same relation to ordinary matter that steam does to ice. The Astral Body leaves the material covering, or ordinary body of the person, at the death of the latter. It also often wanders far from the physical body when the latter is sleeping. Under certain conditions it may leave the physical body during waking hours, and project itself to distant points in space. The familiar "apparitions of the living" are instances of this travel in the Astral, and the phenomena of Clairvoyance is largely due to this form of Astral manifestation. The Astral Body is invisible to the ordinary physical senses, although those possessing Clairvoyant power, or well developed Astral Senses may see it plainly. It may also lower its vibrations and "materialize," as above noted, at which times it becomes visible as a shadowy form apparent to the ordinary physical senses. During the life of the physical body, however, the Astral Body is always connected with the latter by a thin, slender filament, which if broken results in the death of the physical body. Contrary to the ordinary teaching, the Astral Body is composed of seven "sheaths" or "layers" of substance, the grosser of which disintegrate or "sloughs off" when the entity rises to higher Astral sub-planes, and which must be again "materialized" when it revisits the lower planes.

The Aura and Auric Colors of the Astral Body are in the nature of emanations or radiations from the Astral Body, which are manifested in some degree by every person, and which recent scientific investigation has proven conclusively, by means of photographs, etc. The Physical Body, even, has its aura of vitality vibrations, or "Vril," which flow freely from it, particularly when the vitality of the person is strong. This "Vril" is the "human magnetism" of the magnetic healers, and others, and which serves to arouse strength and vigor to those to whom it is applied. The Astral aura, on the contrary, is rather an emanation of the mental states, feelings and emotions of the person's mind. It is egg-shaped, and extends on all sides of the person to a distance of about three feet. It manifests various colors, particularly around the head, the colors corresponding to the character of the mental states being manifested, or those habitual to the person. For instance: Red indicates the animal passions, lust, anger, etc. Blue represents religious emotion, etc.—light blue denoting what is generally called "spirituality," but which in reality is but an ethereal, refined form of religious feeling. Spirituality is more a matter of knowledge and life development, rather than feeling or emotion. Green denotes jealousy, and, in one of its shades, that which is generally called "tact," "agreeableness," "diplomacy," or in its lower forms, "deceit." Gray denotes selfishness. Yellow, intellectuality in its various degrees and forms. Black is the astral color of hate, malice and vengeful emotion. Persons in whom the faculty of Astral Sensing is well developed may see these auric colors plainly, and are thereby informed as to the mental characteristics of the person under observation.

On this lower sub-plane of the Astral are also manifested the thought waves, thought currents, thought-forms, etc., which are manifested in the phenomena of Mentalism.

Thoughts and mental states manifest in objective form. The person manifesting active thought or feeling, emanates waves and currents of thought-force which spread around him in constantly widening circles in every direction. In this way great thought-clouds are formed which hover over and around places to which they are attracted. Thought-clouds of the same general character have a tendency to coalesce and mingle and blend with each other, and to move toward persons, places and localities in which similar thoughts or feelings are being manifested. The Law of Attraction operates in this direction of drawing thought influences toward those who are manifesting similar thought vibrations. Cities, towns and smaller places— even places of business, office-buildings, houses, and rooms have their own particular thought atmosphere, which may be felt by those sensitive to such influences, and *seen* by those possessing the faculty of Astral Sensing.

Akin to these thought-clouds are what are known as thought-forms, which are thought-clouds of great density and power of cohesion, which are also charged with the strong Will or ardent Desire of the persons emanating them—and which are often practically *vitalized* by the "Vril," or vitality of the person, which has been infused into them. Such thought-forms often exert nearly as great a psychic power over those with whom they come in contact as would the sender himself, in person. They are akin to the desire-elementals mentioned in the following lesson.

These thought-clouds and thought-forms abide on the lower sub-planes of the Astral until they finally disintegrate.

They tend to coalesce and gather around places in which the vibrations are harmonious to their own. Some places have their mental atmospheres of vice, others of greed, others of industry, others of the reverse. In short thought atmospheres exist everywhere on this lower Astral sub-plane, just as does the material atmosphere exist everywhere on the material plane. One is just as real as is the other. They have all the correspondences which one might expect. Those who are able to travel in the Astral Body find this thought atmospheric phenomena a source of never failing interest, although at times one is glad to will himself away from some of the scenes, so gross and base are the emotions and feelings manifesting in the dark, heavy suffocating clouds of thought force—so horrible some of the thought-forms. But even these may be driven away by an exercise of the Will, and thought-vibrations of a contrary nature tend to repel them and scatter them away from one's vicinity.

On a sub-plane of a different class from that just mentioned, are found the manifestations of what has been called the "scrap pile of the Astral," and, indeed, that term of the workshop very aptly expresses it. On this sub-plane are to be found the discarded Astral materials of the Astral Bodies which have been "sloughed off" by entities which have discarded them as they have moved up higher. Also, the disintegrating Astral bodies of entities which have failed to survive and whose souls have been resolved into their original elements and become merged into the general principle of Consciousness, as described in a previous lesson. Remember, please, that these remnants of the Astral bodies so discarded and disintegrating, are not in any way related to the souls which formerly inhabited them.

They are mere shells, *without soul or mind*, and yet preserving a slight degree of vitality, or "Vril." They are astral *corpses*, just as much a corpse as is the discarded physical body. But, just as the physical corpse may be aroused into apparent life activity by a strong galvanic current, and will roll its eyes, move its limbs, and even utter groans—so may these astral corpses be "galvanized" by the "Vril" of a medium (unconsciously by the latter), if the conditions be favorable, and may be materialized so as to appear as a shadowy form, acting, moving and even speaking, the only *mind* in it, however, being supplied by that of the medium or the persons present at the seance. These astral corpses also become visible under certain conditions, often around graveyards, battle-fields, etc., and are thought to be ghosts, or "spirits" of those who formerly inhabited them.

They are, however, generally but the grossest astral covering of the Astral body—its "shell" so to speak, and are no more to be regarded as the deceased person himself than is the physical body lying in the grave—both are discarded coverings, or "corpses."

A psychic who, by means of untrained or misdirected psychic development, happens to wander on to this plane of the Astral, experiences a most unpleasant sight. It is not pleasant to roam in this charnel house of the Astral—this tomb of the Earth. An old Egyptian sage thus recorded his impressions of it: "What manner of place is this I see. It hath no water. It hath no air. It hath no light. It hath no foundation. It is unfathomably deep. It is as black as the blackest night." A modern investigator has said of this region—this Golgotha of the Astral: "Most students find the investigation of this section an extremely unpleasant task, for there appears to be a sense of density and gross materiality about it which is indescribably loathsome to the liberated Astral Body, causing the sense of pushing its way through some black viscous fluid, while the inhabitants and influences encountered there are unusually undesirable."

"And are there inhabitants of such a place?" one naturally asks. Alas, yes! There *are* denizens of this loathsome place— inhabitants of this horrible abode. Entities, however, not placed there for *punishment*, for no Being would entail such a fate upon the meanest and most depraved—or invent such a Hell. They are there because of their own abnormal desires and tendencies, which unfit them for the planes of even the lowest of disembodied human entities, and which also render them unfit for association with the disembodied astral forms of the beasts, which latter persist for a short time after physical death.

"Then, what manner of creatures must these be?" you ask. "Fit for neither man nor beasts. Were they *human?*" And, one is forced to answer, "Yes!" Subject to the laws of humankind they are not allowed the privilege of rapid annihilation bestowed upon the beasts—they must live out their peculiar life to the end. They are the pariahs, the ghoul-like scum of the human race, who have removed themselves from the race fate and have entailed upon themselves a fate of their own. Their fate is a Living Death—a conscious life in a corpse-like body, among corpses of the Astral. These creatures are the disembodied entities of those who degenerated along abnormal sex lines—who attempted to reverse the Cosmic Law of Sex Polarity, and thus brought upon themselves the Recoil of the Life Forces. They were the lowest of the human Satyrs. Nature finally casts over them the spell of a deep sleep, from which they never awaken, and from which they pass into disintegration and annihilation.

They polluted the Sacred Altar. They stole the Divine Fire for devilish rites. They committed the Unpardonable Sin. They removed themselves from the trend of Cosmic Evolution. Their own Desire was their Fate. We wish it were possible to speak plainer—but the time has not yet come.

Lesson XIV. Astral "Black-Keys."

Before passing on to the sub-planes higher in degree and scale, let us call your attention to some of the minor sub-planes—the "black-keys" of the Astral scale. On these sub-planes dwell the non-human, or semi-human creatures which are grouped together in the occult classification under the general name of "elementaries" or "elementals." It is impossible for us to enter into a detailed consideration of this class of entities in a work of this general nature intended for popular reading. The reasons therefor would involve explanations which would crowd out of the space intended for them certain other details of the Astral Planes, and would even then be most incomplete and unsatisfying. Enough to say that occultists know that this planet, the earth, is the field and theatre for *three* distinct processes of evolution—that of the world that we know, human, animal, and vegetable; and two others of a different order. These two other fields of evolution have their own planes which are totally unrelated to ours. But these other evolutionary processes, although distinct from ours, nevertheless blend slightly with certain sub-planes of our Astral Planes—that is, the "edges overlap," if such a clumsy term may be used. Consequently, on certain of the "black-key" planes of our Astral, there may be found elementaries of a scale of life different from our own. This is but a general statement, the faults of which will be obvious to every advanced occultist who reads it—and yet such advanced student will see the necessity for the purposely imperfect statement in this place.

Those who have read Bulwer's occult stories—notably "Zanoni," will recognize the nature of the entities of which we speak.

While the Arcane Teaching includes within its store of knowledge and information full details regarding these particular sub-planes which we have designated as the "black-keys" on the scale of the Astral Plane, and its Initiates who have attained certain degrees are fully informed regarding the same, still we are unable to make public at this time, place, and through this particular channel, the inner Arcane Teaching regarding the same. Personally, we think the time is ripe for such information to be plainly stated, accompanied by the necessary warnings; but those higher in authority among the Custodians have said to us: "Nay! Wait in patience! When the propitious hour is indicated by the planetary symbols—then may you open the sealed volume to those who would free its riddles! For the present, the vow of silence maintains!" So there is naught left for us but to bow to the superior authority in the matter.

However, while we are not permitted to state the inner Arcane Teaching in this particular detail, the prohibition does not extend to our using quotations from other authorities who have already reported concerning these sub-planes of the Astral. And, believing that the said reports would be interesting to those of our students who take a scientific interest in this phase of occultism, we have decided to give you, in this lesson, very liberal quotations from a leading authority of another school of occultism, who has paid much attention to the phenomena of certain phases and planes of the Astral Plane, both in the direction of studying older and more advanced authorities, and also in the direction of personal investigation and exploration of these sub-planes, of the Astral. The latter is a task surrounded with dangers and risks which but few even advanced occultists care to undertake, and although we doubt the wisdom of the task, nevertheless we must admire the scientific ardor of the investigator.

The remainder of this lesson, indicated by quotation marks, consists of quotations from the said authority, investigator and explorer of these dark regions of the "black-keys" of the Astral.

The elementaries may be grouped into several general classes, although the classification is more or less unsatisfactory and imperfect, at the best. One of these classes comprise the entities which some writers have called "Nature Spirits," which term, however, is less accurate than poetical. These entities have been known in the legends by various names, prominent among which are the following: Earth-spirits, or gnomes; water-spirits, or undines; air-spirits, or sylphs; fire-spirits, or salamanders; fairies; pixies; elves; brownies; peris; djinns; trolls; fauns; kobolds; imps; goblins; little people; good people, etc., etc., of which the aforesaid authority says:

"Their forms are many and various, but most frequently human in shape, and somewhat diminutive in size. Like almost all inhabitants of the astral plane, they are able to assume any appearance at will, but they undoubtedly have definite forms of their own, or perhaps we should rather say favorite forms, which they wear when they have no special object in taking any other. Under ordinary conditions they are not visible to physical sight at all, but they have the power of making themselves so by materialization when they wish to be seen. There are an immense number of subdivisions or races among them, and individuals of these subdivisions differ in intelligence and disposition precisely as human beings do. The great majority of them apparently prefer to avoid man altogether; his habits and emanations are distasteful to them, and the constant rush of astral currents set up by his restless, ill-regulated desires, disturbs and annoys them. On the other hand, instances are not wanting in which nature-spirits have as it were made friends with human beings, and offered them such assistance as lay in their power, as in the well-known stories of the Scotch brownies or of the fire-lighting fairies. This helpful attitude, however, is comparatively rare, and in most cases when they come in contact with man they either show indifference or dislike, or else take an impish delight in deceiving him and playing childish tricks upon him. Many a story illustrative of this curious characteristic may be found among the village gossip of the peasantry in almost any lonely mountainous district; and anyone who has been in the habit of attending *séances* for physical phenomena will recollect instances of practical joking and silly though usually good natured horse play, which almost always indicates the presence of some of these lower orders of astral spirits.

"The life periods of the different subdivisions vary greatly, some being quite short, others much longer than our human lifetime. We stand so completely outside such a life as theirs that it is impossible for us to understand much about its conditions; but it appears on the whole to be a simple, joyous, irresponsible kind of existence, much such as a party of happy children might lead among exceptionally physical surroundings. Though tricky and mischievous, they are rarely malicious unless provoked by some unwarrantable intrusion or annoyance; but as a body they also partake to some extent of the universal feeling of distrust for man, and they generally seem inclined to resent somewhat the first appearance of a neophyte on the astral plane, so that he usually makes their acquaintance under some unpleasant or terrifying form. If, however, he declines to be frightened by any of their freaks, they soon accept him as a necessary evil and take no further notice of him, while some among them may even after a time become friendly and manifest pleasure on meeting him.

"The Adept knows how to make use of the services of the nature spirits when he requires them, but the ordinary magician can obtain their assistance only by processes either of invocation or evocation; that is, either by attracting their attention as a suppliant and making some kind of bargain with them, or by endeavoring to set into motion influences which would compel their obedience. Both methods are extremely undesirable, and the latter is also excessively dangerous, as the operator would arouse a determined hostility which might prove fatal to him. Needless to say, no one studying occultism under a qualified Master would ever be permitted to attempt anything of the kind at all."

On other low planes of the Astral there is another class of elementaries, which have been called "artificial or man-created entities," of which the aforesaid authority says:

"This, the largest class of Astral entities, is also much the most important to man. Being entirely his own creation, it is inter-related with him by the closest bonds, and its action upon him is direct and incessant. It is an enormous inchoate mass of semi-intelligent entities, differing among themselves as human thoughts differ, and practically incapable of anything like classification and arrangement. The only division which can be usefully made is that which distinguishes between the artificial elementals made by the majority of mankind unconsciously, and those made by magicians with definite intent; while we may relegate to a third class the very small number of artificially arranged entities which are not elementals at all.

"The elemental essence which surrounds us on every side is in all its numberless varieties singularly susceptible to the influence of human thought. The action of the mere casual wandering thought upon it, causing it to burst into a cloud of rapidly-moving evanescent forms, has already been described; we have now to note how it is affected when the human mind formulates a definite, purposeful thought or wish. The effect produced is of the most striking nature. The thought seizes upon the plastic essence, and molds it instantly into a living being of an appropriate form—a being which when once thus created is in no way under the control of its creator, but lives out a life of its own, the length of which is proportionate to the intensity of the thoughts or wish which called it into existence. It lasts in fact just as long as the thought-force holds it together. Most persons' thoughts are so fleeting that the elementals created by them last only a few minutes or a few hours, but an often-repeated thought or an earnest wish will form an elemental whose existence may extend to many days. Since the ordinary man's thoughts refer very largely to himself, the elementals which they form remain hovering about, and constantly tend to provoke a repetition of the idea which they represent, since such repetitions, instead of forming new elementals, would strengthen the old one, and give it a fresh lease of life. A man, therefore, who frequently dwells upon one wish often forms for himself an astral attendant which, constantly fed by fresh thought, may haunt him for years, ever gaining more and more strength and influence over Him; and it will easily be seen that if the desire be an evil one the effect upon his moral nature may be of the most disastrous character.

"Still more pregnant for good or evil are a man's thoughts about other people, for in that case they hover not about the thinker, but about the object of the thought. A kindly thought about any person, or an earnest wish for his good, will form and project towards him a friendly artificial elemental. If the wish be a definite one, as, for example, that he may recover from some sickness, then the elemental will be a force ever hovering over him to promote his recovery, or to ward off any influence that might tend to hinder it. In doing this it will display what appears like a very considerable amount of intelligence and adaptability, though really it is simply a force acting along the line of least resistance—pressing steadily in one direction all the time, and taking advantage of any channel that it can find, just as the water in a cistern would in a moment find the one open pipe among a dozen closed ones, and proceed to empty itself through that. If the wish be merely an indefinite one for his general good, the elemental essence in its wonderful plasticity will respond exactly to that less distinct idea also, and the creature formed will expend its force In the direction of whatever action for the man's advantage comes most readily to hand. In all cases, the amount of such force which it has to expend, and the length of time that it will live to expend it, depend entirely upon the strength of the original wish or thought which gave it birth; though it must be remembered that it can be, as it were, fed and strengthened, and its life-period protracted by other good wishes or friendly thoughts projected in the same direction. Furthermore, it appears to be actuated, like most other beings, by an instinctive desire to prolong its life, and thus reacts on its creator as a force constantly tending to provoke the renewal of the feelings which called it into existence. It also influences in a similar manner others with whom it comes into contact, though its *rapport* with them is naturally not so perfect.

"All that has been said as to the effect of good wishes and friendly thoughts is also true in the opposite direction of evil wishes and angry thoughts; and considering the amount of envy, hatred, malice and uncharitableness that exists in the world, it will be readily understood that among the artificial elementals many terrible creatures are to be seen. A man whose thoughts or desires are spiteful, brutal, sensual, avaricious, moves through the world carrying with him everywhere a pestiferous atmosphere of his own, peopled with the loathsome beings which he has created to be his companions. Thus he is not only in sadly evil case himself, but is a dangerous nuisance to his fellow-men, subjecting all who have the misfortune to come in contact with him to the risk of moral contagion from the influence of the abominations with which he chooses to surround himself.

"It occasionally happens, however, that an artificial elemental of this description is for various reasons unable to expend its force either upon its object or its creator, and in such cases it becomes a kind of wandering demon, readily attracted by any person who indulges feelings similar to that which gave it birth, and equally prepared either to stimulate such feelings in him for the sake of the strength it may gain from them, or to pour out its store of evil influences upon him through any opening which he may offer it. If it is sufficiently powerful to seize upon some passing shell (discarded astral body) it frequently does so, as the possession of such a temporary home enables it to husband its dreadful resources more carefully. In this form it may manifest through a medium, and by masquerading as some well-known friend may sometimes obtain an influence over people upon whom it would otherwise have little hold. ... Many a well-meaning man, who is scrupulously careful to do his duty toward his neighbor in word and deed, is apt to consider that his thoughts at least are nobody's business but his own, and so lets them run riot in various directions, utterly unconscious of the swarms of baleful creatures which he is launching upon the world. To such a man an accurate comprehension of the effect of thought and desire in producing artificial elementals would come as a horrifying revelation.

"Since such results as have been described above have been achieved by the thought-force of men who were entirely in the dark as to what they were doing, it will readily be imagined that a magician who understands the subject, and can see exactly what effect he is producing, may wield immense power along these lines. As a matter of fact, occultists of both the white and dark schools frequently use artificial elementals in their work, and few tasks are beyond the powers of such creatures when scientifically prepared and directed with knowledge and skill; for one who knows how to do so can maintain a connection with his elemental and guide it, no matter at what distance it may be working, so that it will practically act as though endowed with the full intelligence of its master.

"By some of the more advanced processes of Black Magic, also, artificial elementals of great power may be called into existence, and much evil has been worked in various ways by such entities. But it is true of them, as of the previous class, that if they are aimed at a person whom by reason of his purity of character they are unable to influence, they react with terrible force upon their creator; so that the medieval story of the magician being torn to pieces by the fiends he himself had raised, is no mere fable, but may well have had an awful foundation in fact. Such creatures occasionally, for various reasons, escape from the control of those who are trying to make use of them, and become wandering and aimless demons, as do some of those mentioned under the previous heading under similar circumstances; but those that we are considering, having much more intelligence and power, and a much longer existence, are proportionately more dangerous. They invariably seek for means of prolonging their life, either by feeding like vampires upon the vitality of human beings, or by influencing them to make offerings to them; and among simple half savage tribes they have frequently succeeded in getting themselves recognized as village or family gods. By the vitality they draw from their devotees, they may continue to prolong their existence for many years, or even centuries, retaining sufficient strength to perform occasional phenomena of a mild type in order to stimulate the faith and zeal of their followers."

While the above quoted authority has placed what we consider to be undue emphasis upon the power of the elementals—for the human Will is sufficient to overcome their power, and they are prevented from coming to the mental atmosphere of all who do not attract them by virtue of the character of their own mental vibrations—nevertheless, we have thought it advisable to give you the benefit of this investigator's reports, for the purpose of warning you against dabbling in Evocations, and certain so-called "magical" methods and practices. Black Magic in all of its forms result only in pain and evil to those indulging in them. He who invades planes of life foreign to his own, takes upon himself the risks inherent on such planes.

Lesson XV. Higher Astral Planes.

We have now reached the point where we are called upon to consider the phases of the Astral Plane concerned with the state or condition of the disembodied entities of human beings. We call these the *higher* Astral Planes, only by way of contrast with the lower planes mentioned in the preceding two lessons, for some of these "higher" planes are quite low indeed as compared with the highest Astral Planes. Let us begin with the consideration of the lowest of these higher planes of the Astral, and then proceed to consider the planes higher in the scale.

In the first place, we must remember that the disembodied human soul leaves the physical in a state or condition akin to sleep. It is carried by the attraction of its nature and character to the highest plane consistent with its nature—that is, to a plane corresponding with the highest qualities existent within itself. And upon that plane it gradually awakens into the Astral life of that particular plane. The conditions of the Astral Life are so different from that of the Material Plane that it is difficult to intelligently describe it in terms of the latter. For instance, the souls on the higher planes are able to enter into conscious relationship with those on the lower planes, but those on the lower planes cannot enter into conscious relationship with those on the higher planes except through the act of those dwelling on the higher. Each plane has planes higher and lower than itself, the above law being operative in all cases. The higher plane souls have access to the lower, but the lower may not invade the higher. And this *access* is not in the nature of a *physical visit* from the higher to the lower, but is in the nature of a psychic consciousness, akin to Clairvoyance, in which the soul, while remaining on its own plane, still seems to have traveled to the others, there to converse with other souls on these planes.

The soul itself, unless very advanced, does not realize the nature of the connection but thinks that it actually *travels* to the scene of the lower planes. The analogy of Clairvoyance on the Material Plane will give you the idea of the process.

When a soul awakens on its own plane of the Astral, it finds it difficult to realize that it is not alive in the flesh, and often much time is required before it realizes its true condition. Then it begins to manifest an interest in its surroundings, and pays many visits on its own and other planes (in the manner before mentioned) renewing old acquaintances and relationships, and manifesting the activities quite natural for a human being under such circumstances. But sooner or later this life begins to pall upon it, and it passes into the Idealistic State, which we shall describe a little further on. Enough for the moment to say that in the Idealistic State the soul begins to manifest its ideals—the things it has hoped for, dreamed of, and longed for in its earth-life. The greater the idealistic quality of the soul, the greater the extent and range of its Idealistic State. But before considering this interesting phase of Astral Life, let us see what happens on the lower planes, to those who have but few ideals, and those of a most material nature.

On the very lowest of these planes of the Astral we find the "earth bound" entities, or souls, of many degrees. These are the souls of those who are so material in their tastes, habits and trend of thought and desire that they can never rise to the higher states and conditions of the Astral. They stay close to the earth, mingling unseen in the scenes which they so loved during their life in the body, and yet being unable to actually participate in the carnal manifestations, unless, indeed, some particularly attractive dweller in the flesh opens his physical organism to the obsession of some affinitive and congenial companion of the lower Astral Planes and allows the entity to manifest through his physical body. These entities are found in great numbers in the astral atmosphere of low resorts, and similar places, where they poison the psychic atmosphere to such an extent that their presence may be *felt*, and often *seen* by sensitive persons who happen to visit such places. We may add as a caution to those who are fond of dabbling in the psychic process of Evocation, that it is largely from this class of entities that many of the "spirits" appearing at *séances* are drawn. It is this class of entities who so often impersonate your disembodied friends and relatives, and whose sneers and ribaldry are scarcely concealed behind the loving messages and "spirit wisdom" which they pass on to the wondering mortal in the flesh who would not dream of associating with their kind in earth life.

The life of these entities on the Astral Plane is not long. They find but little pleasure, and much torment, in life apart from the physical, for their desires are altogether along physical lines. They are filled with dissatisfaction, *ennui,* and weariness. As a writer has said: "The disembodied learn that the Hades of Immortality is the lack of a physical body." Their dissatisfaction soon sets into operation the *desire to be relieved of the burden*, and the "Will-not-to Live" manifests itself. They drop into a dream-state, or somnambulistic condition, in which they *dream out* their desires and tastes to the end—until they have exhausted every mental longing within their nature. There being nothing left of them, when these mental states have been lived out, they weaken and pass into unconsciousness, which is followed by death on the Astral with consequent disintegration and annihilation as entities. Their dream state is, in a way, their Idealistic State—all the Idealistic State they are capable of, at any rate. This is not in any way a *punishment*—merely a natural consequent of their nature. As the old saying goes: "One cannot make a silk-purse out of a sow's ear." Nor can one get more than a pint out of a pint measure. *Desire* is the cause of their life, and of their death. Balance is manifested and preserved. Water cannot rise above the level of its own source. These entities receive "their own," as much as do those on the higher planes.

There is no injustice manifested here.

Rising in the scale we find souls who while attached to material things nevertheless have had *ideals* during their life— things for which they had hoped, and dreamt, prayed and longed. As the scale advances we find that the nature of the ideals advance from lower to higher—but the principle is the same. And for the lowest to the highest of these ideal degrees, the Astral Life contains that peculiar and wonderful condition or state known as the "Idealistic State." And this Idealistic State is the real Astral Life of the soul, into which it enters after it has tired of the conditions it finds at first on the Astral Plane. It is composed of a condition or state, or series of such conditions or states, in which *it lives out in vivid imagination, or realistic dream-like states all of its unrealized personal ideals, hopes, expectations, desires, ambitions, aspirations, longings, and inclinations of its nature.*

It may be objected to that this is but a state of illusion or delusion, and not a reality. But it must be remembered that even on the Material Plane: *"Dreams are true while they last."* On the Astral Plane, in the Idealistic State, these dreams exceed in vividness and reality anything that the embodied mortal ever experiences. So far as the soul is concerned the experiences through which it lives in the Idealistic State are just as *real* as anything that it ever experienced in physical life. Every element of reality is there. And there *is* a reality about it that all advanced occultists recognize. At the last, one's experiences in physical life may be resolved to a "series of mental states"— and what less than this does the Astral dreamer experience? And what more than a Dream, after all is the experience of the earth-life of three-score-and-ten of the average person? "Like dreams they come, like dreams they go." In its way, and on its plane, the Idealistic State is just as *real* as the physical life.

In this Idealistic State, the dreaming soul lives out countless lives, of infinite variety. Just as in an ordinary dream, Time is annihilated and one may live out a lifetime in the space of a second, so in the Idealistic State the soul lives out centuries of experiences in a moment. To all intents and purposes, the soul—every soul in fact— lives an Eternity in the Idealistic State, although the entire experience may occur in a few years (as *we* know time). Time is measured only by "happenings," and the happenings of an Eternity may be crowded into a very short space of ordinary time, in the

Idealistic State. Every possibility within its personality is lived out, outlived, and exhausted in interest, in the Idealistic State. Just as in the moment of physical death, the soul sees as in a flash its entire earth-life in one great panorama—past and present being at once—so in the Idealistic State the soul lives out every personal desire, aim, aspiration, hope, ambition, longing, and wish, in an infinite series of states or lives. *It realizes every personal ideal* inherent within it, to the utmost. Its fullest personal Heart's Desire is attained. There is no unsatisfied personal longing, or unrealized ideal, left at the end of the Idealistic State of the soul on the Astral Plane. Think what this means, please. Think what it must mean to live out to the full "The Might Have Been," which is in the life of every human being. Think what it must mean to manifest one's love to the utmost—to have every wish granted—every ambition satisfied. Think what it must be to live out one's life *as one wishes it had been lived*—with all the mistakes corrected, all the errors remedied, all the problems solved, all the atonements made, all the injustices rectified. The Idealistic State is the living over of your life As You Wish It Could Have Been. Nay, more, living it over countless times, each variation bringing out some new point and feature of unrealized ideals, desires, and wishes! It is a state in which the verse of Kipling comes true:

> *"And only the Master shall praise us, And only the Master shall blame;*
>
> *And no one shall work for money, And no one shall work for fame;*
>
> *But each for the joy of the working, And each in his separate star,*
>
> *Shall draw the Thing as he sees it*
>
> *For the God of Things as They are!"*

But it is only a *dream*, you say. Nay, more than a dream as you understand the term. A dream it is, but a dream so *real* that naught but Omniscience could distinguish the difference. A dream so *real* that it equals the thing that we call Life, in every element of reality. In the end, one is as Real as the other—Earth Life and the Astral Idealistic State. And, also, in the end, one is as Unreal as the other.

But not only are the high personal desires, aspirations and ideals so lived out in the Idealistic State. The low personal desires, aspirations and ideals are also passed through this threshing-mill of the Idealistic State. One lives out to the utmost, in some of the series of these dream-lives, *all* the possibilities of his nature or character—good and bad alike. In fact, the lowest desires and ideals are the first to manifest, and the first to die out and be lived out. To those who have no others, the end then comes. But to those who have higher ideals and desires mingled with the lower, there then comes a stage of living out the higher part of their nature. And as time passes, the soul rises far above all the dross and grossness of its nature, and lives in the higher regions of itself—enjoying to the fullest the satisfaction which comes only from those higher states. But, the soul must *possess* the higher in order to manifest it. Unless the higher be involved within the soul, it cannot be evolved.

What does not exist cannot be manifested.

While in this Idealistic State, the soul may be attracted by those on earth who are related to it by the old ties or affection or interest, and in such case it may manifest by communications. But these communications can contain *only that which the soul knows and experiences at the time*. It merely reports what it is experiencing—merely its own personal experiences of the Idealistic State. And even this it reports in a dazed, dreamy fashion. Thus the devout Christian soul will report that it is dwelling in a Heaven of orthodox surroundings—the golden streets, harps, and milk and honey being described in detail. A good Catholic soul will report a Catholic Heaven, with all the saints present; while a good Baptist soul will report a Heaven along strictly Baptist lines—close communion, and only immersed souls being in evidence. A Moslem will describe himself as enjoying all the delights of the Heaven promised by Mohammed. And the soul of the Unbeliever will inform you that "there is nothing in this Heaven business at all"; and that the "after life" is merely a life among congenial companions, thinking along the same lines as himself; and that he is of the opinion that the church people have perished, instead of having gained immortality. And so on, each "painting the Thing as he sees it" as the world of "Things as They Are." And each is telling the Truth, as he sees it, from his own viewpoint. Strange, but true!

Those who complain of the absence of the qualities of Heaven and Hell in this Idealistic State have not thought deeply enough regarding it. In the attainment of the highest ideals and aspirations, there is contained all that men have pictured as the joys of Heaven—*and infinitely more*. And in the living out of the consequences of evil desire and low ideals, and all that goes with this state, there is all that the most fervent Calvinist could wish for in a Hell—*and infinitely more*.

But, remember always, that the Heaven and Hell of the Idealistic State is not a punishment or reward bestowed for good or evil deeds—it is but the working out of Cause and Effect— the fullest manifestation of Desire and one's Character. And, in the adjustment acts restrained by Fear equal Acts performed. "As a man thinketh in his heart, so is he" in the Idealistic State. In the working out of Cause and Effect in the Idealistic State of the Astral, it is indeed true that: "He who hates is an assassin; he who covets is a thief; he who lusts is an adulterer; that the gist of a crime is the desire behind it." This Idealistic State of the Astral Plane is not Fate, not Providence, not Destiny, not Reward and Punishment—it is but the operation of natural laws of Cause and Effect, Orderly Trend, and Logical Sequence, on the Astral Plane. "From one, know All."

And, in the working out of the Idealistic State of the Astral, the most unpleasant experiences are lived through first, and then the higher ideals begin to manifest themselves—the soul rising to higher and still higher flights, until at last it reaches the highest degree possible to it by reason of its constitution, nature and character. And in that Life, if it be prepared to receive it, it may receive instruction from Beings higher in the scale, as well as from the more evolved souls of our own race who are attracted to it by reason of its desires and ideals. Many a soul has received the help which led it to Individuality, in this Idealistic State. Many an Individual soul has so received instruction which led to better conditions for growth in the next incarnation. "When the pupil is ready, the Master appears" on the Astral Plane as on the Material Plane. If you possess the seed of the ideal, the blossom and the fruit will surely be yours.

When the impulses arising from the personal desires, aspirations, and ideals of the soul have expended themselves fully, and the "personality" of the soul has been "lived out and outlived" in the process—when there remain no further impulses of personality to exert themselves in the Idealistic State—then the soul finds that it "has nothing more to live for" along the lines of personality. It feels aged, tired and weary, and the desire for *rest* creeps over it, and it gradually sinks into a dreamless sleep, which ends in the Death of the Personality. If Egohood has *not* been attained by the soul, then it never awakens into a new life, for Personality being all that it possesses, and all personality being expended and exhausted, then there is nothing left to persist in new birth. But if Egohood has been attained, and the soul realizes that it is more than the "Me" of itself, then when the "Me" dies away, the "I" finds itself still existent and filled with the impulse of the Will-to-Live of the Cosmic Will, which urges it forward to re-birth in new bodies, to seek further and more advanced experience. Even in this case the soul falls into the deep Astral sleep, but awakens therefrom when it is reborn into a new body, under circumstances and environments in accordance with the Law of Attraction resulting from the *essence of the past life*, the latter inhering to it. The Ego then will be free from its lived-out desires and will no longer be hampered by them. It will be attracted toward new scenes and fields of activity. In its new body it will have to combat the inherited impulses and desires of its new "Me," but it will always feel its superiority to the latter, and will feel the ability to *stand aside and look at its personality.*

The advanced Ego, in time, reaches the stage of *conscious* re-birth, in which the Ideal Life is *consciously continuous* with the old life, and which is *consciously* followed by the new birth. We have spoken of these things in our lesson on "Survival of the Fittest," which you should now re-read in the light of the present lesson.

There are many planes of the Astral much higher than even these which we have described, but a description of them would be impossible except to highly advanced occultists. Some of these higher Astral Planes transcend the imagination of the average person leading the personal life today, on earth. And yet, over and above the entire Astral Plane, there is the great Spiritual Plane, which we would lack words to even faintly designate. And yet, even these exalted Planes await your coming, O Neophyte, whose feet are now well set upon The Path!

PART VI. OCCULT FORCES.

Lesson XVI. Psychic Phenomena.

For the sake of convenience in considering the various phases of the phenomena of the Occult Forces operative in the Cosmos, we have divided the same into three general classes, as follows: (1) Psychic Phenomena, consisting of the manifestation of the phases generally known as Clairvoyance, Clairaudience, Psychometry, Telepathy, etc., the distinguishing feature of which is the "knowing" of events other than through the ordinary senses; (2) Mentalism, consisting of the manifestations of Mental Influence, Mind-Power,

Thought-Force, Mental Magic, etc., the distinguishing feature of which is the exerting of the influence of one mind over other minds; (3) Invocation and Evocation, consisting of the "calling upon" supernatural beings, or the "calling forth" of disembodied entities; elementals; vitalized thought-entities, etc., from the Astral Plane.

These manifestations, and the force which produces them have been called "Occult" because of the fact that they belong to the less understood phases of natural forces and phenomena. The word "Occult" means: "secret or hidden from the eye or understanding; not seen or understood; mysterious, invisible, unknown, undetected, etc." To many persons, Occultism is considered to be concerned with supernatural forces, things, and manifestations. This is erroneous, for there is nothing *super*-natural—nothing outside of or over nature, of which we can ever have any knowledge. Everything in the Cosmos is *natural*, and under natural laws. The Law is the only *super*-natural that there is or can be—and we can know It only as being in actual existence; we can know nothing of its inner nature, for it is not a "thing" with attributes, qualities or limitations, as we understand those terms. Everything in the Cosmos is *natural*—the unknown as well as the commonly known. Therefore, when we say "occult" we mean merely some natural thing, force, or manifestation, not commonly known or recognized by men. When a thing, force, or manifestation becomes commonly known, it ceases to be regarded as "occult." Electricity was once regarded as an "occult" force—but today it is commonly known and employed, although its real nature is still a mystery. To the trained and advanced Occultist the so-called Occult Forces are just as familiar and *natural* as are the manifestations of force common to the knowledge of the race.

The Occult Forces are simply finer forces of nature, which are not recognized, known or understood by the average person of the race, today. We wish this to be thoroughly understood. There are no supernatural forces, things, or manifestations—all are natural, and under natural laws. Let us now proceed to a consideration of the class of occult phenomena which we have grouped under the sub-title, "Psychic Phenomena," and which are known severally as Clairvoyance, Clairaudience, Psychometry, Telepathy, etc., the distinguishing feature of which is the "knowing" of events through other channels than the ordinary senses. These several phases are but modifications of one general phenomenon— Astral Sensing.

The majority of modern writers upon the subject of Psychic Phenomena lay great stress upon the "vibrations, waves, currents, etc.," by which psychic impressions are transmitted from one mind to another, or by which one "senses" occurrences in points of space far removed from him. We have no objection to these terms, for they represent the best available words to describe the actual details of the manifestation—but these words must be used understandingly. The idea, so commonly advanced, that these "vibrations" or "waves" or "currents" are but forms of *etheric* vibrations similar in nature to the waves of light, heat, electricity, material magnetism, etc., is erroneous, and gives a materialistic tinge to phenomena which are of a much higher plane than that of material forces and substance. While there is a general resemblance between all planes of the Manifest Cosmos, owing to the Law of Analogy which causes "correspondences" on all planes—"as above, so below"—and "from one know all"—still the vibrations, waves and currents concerned in Psychic Phenomena and Mentalism belong to an entirely different plane from that of those concerned in the manifestation of light, heat, electricity, etc., which belong to lower planes.

In the preceding lessons, we have shown you that there are three Principles manifesting and active in Cosmos, viz., Substance, Motion, and Consciousness. In each of these three Principles, there are manifested correspondences which we may call "vibrations," "waves," "currents," etc. On the plane of Substance, we have vibrations and waves of matter, which result in the various forms, shapes, and action of material objects. This is caused by the Principle of Motion acting upon the Principle of Substance. Much that we call energy or force is but the appearance of fine degrees of Substance energized by Motion. Electricity, for instance, is but a fine form of Substance, so energized. The Ether, itself, is but a fine form of Substance, almost approaching Pure Energy, but not passing over the line which divides Energy from Substance. There are also vibrations and waves of Pure Motion, which may be considered, mentally, as independent of Substance, although we can never know them as such. There is a plane of Pure Motion, which is unthinkable except to minds which have been trained to grasp the subject. And, likewise, there are vibrations, waves, and currents in the *Principle of Consciousness*, produced by the action of Motion upon that Principle. And it is to this plane that the "vibrations, waves, and currents" concerned with Psychic Phenomena properly belong. They are *not* "waves in the Ether," for the Ether is on the material plane. They are "waves in the Mind Principle" itself, which is quite another thing.

Without attempting to lead you into an extended discussion of the scientific details of the matter, we would call your attention to this one fact which should serve to give you a plain mental picture of the phenomenon—a general outline of a picture, into which you can fill the details as you proceed in the study and experimental work along these lines. This general statement is as follows: The Cosmos is known to be practically a great World-Brain, in which Thoughts become Things, taking on Substantial Form. With a Cosmos *mental in nature*—consisting in fact of but One Universal Mind in which all particular things are but *Centres of Consciousness*—can you not see that there must be a Circulation of Consciousness, or Currents of Thought, just as there is a circulation of water in and by the currents of the ocean; or as there is a circulation of air by reason of the currents therein; or as there is a circulation of electricity, light, and all other forms of what we call Energy. *Consciousness is a Principle*, just as is Substance or Motion, and *what is true of one Principle is true of the other two*, according to the Law of Analogy. Therefore, there are Vibrations, Waves, and Currents of Consciousness, just as truly as there are corresponding manifestations on the material plane. And you may use these terms, very properly—always avoiding the mistake of confusing them with the material correspondences.

In Clairvoyance, Clairaudience, Psychometry, and Telepathy, we have several forms of manifestation of the existence of these Mental Waves and Currents, for so we shall call them to avoid the necessity of longer terms. But how does the mind of the person receive and register the impressions received through these Mental Currents? It is known to be a fact that no mind can receive impressions without the agency and medium of *some form of material organ,* though that material organ may be extremely subtle and fine. And this rule holds true in the case of the phenomena which we are now considering. And such organs *do* exist, and are called the Organs of Astral Sense. In the lessons treating of the Astral Plane, you have been informed of the existence of the Astral Body, the subtle counterpart of the Physical Body. This Astral Body is endowed with counterparts of the physical senses, which it may use in sensing the objects and impressions of the Astral Plane. In this way Astral Sensing becomes possible. The average person has not used these Astral Senses sufficiently well to develop them for active use, but this development is possible to those who have sufficient interest and patience to undertake the task. But here and there are found persons whose Astral Senses manifest their existence in a degree not known to the average person. These persons become very sensitive to the impressions of the Astral Plane, and although, as a rule, they are untrained and do not comprehend the nature of the phenomena, still they afford conclusive proof of the existence of the faculties in question. We shall not attempt to "prove" the existence of Psychic Phenomena in these lessons. We have not the space at our disposal, nor is it within the scope of this particular work. Evidence of such nature as to convince any unprejudiced persons may be found in many books on the subject, notably the reports of the English Society for Psychical Research. Moreover many persons have experienced these facts in their own lives.

Let us first consider the phenomenon generally called "Clairvoyance," which is defined as: "A faculty or power by which the clairvoyant is able to see mentally things concealed from sight; to see and describe things happening at a distance." With the exception of cases in which the person actually travels in his Astral Body to distant scenes, and there witnesses with his Astral Senses the events actually occurring there, all Clairvoyance results from one general cause, and in the same general way. Let us suppose an event occurring at a distant place. In the manifestation of that event there occurs a constant, regular and continuous series of conscious states on the part of all things concerned therein. Not only on the part of all living things is there consciousness manifested, but there is a consciousness manifested by all inanimate things present upon the scene,—things inorganic as well as organic, in the usual use of these terms. As we have said on page 60 (Lesson IV): "Those who have studied along occult lines have become aware of the existence of mind and consciousness in so-called inanimate objects—the minerals, metals, etc., and even in the atoms—and finally in the Ether. Everything in the Manifest Cosmos has *some degree* of Consciousness." This being so, it follows that such Consciousness must follow the natural law, and transmit waves or currents—waves and currents of Consciousness—which travel and *circulate* on the Astral Plane where they may be sensed by those astral organs attuned to receive them. Just as the Marconigrams may be received only by instruments keyed to the proper degree of receptivity, so may these currents be received only by those who are in tune with them.

One whose Astral Senses are sufficiently sensitive, and attuned, may receive and register these currents, just as the physical eye registers the light waves of the ether, or the ear the sound waves of the air. There is not necessarily a projection of the Astral Body to the scene of the happening—the Astral Senses may register the impressions received from the currents of Consciousness. To those who may doubt the reasonableness of *sensing* things and events over thousands of miles, we would say that it is simply an Astral correspondence of the Physical phenomenon of Sight, whereby impressions are received from the distant stars, over billions of miles—over distances so vast that it requires centuries for the light waves to travel. And, remember this—the physical eye never actually sees the outer objects themselves, but merely sees the effects produced upon the nerves by the waves of light. Nor does a person fail to see the outside object, but he also fails to see even the light-waves themselves—he merely *sees* certain vibrations of nerve-substance set up in the brain by the action of the light vibrations. And this is in every sense no less wonderful than the phenomena of Astral Sensing which we have just described— merely a little more common and familiar, that is all. If we had as full and common a development of the Astral Senses as we have of the physical, we would consider it no more remarkable to *see* events occurring in India, than to witness the changes on the planet Mars. One is as natural as the other. Clairaudience is but another phase of Astral Sensing, by which the Astral Senses receive the impression of sounds, instead of sights. The principle involved is the same.

So far we have spoken only of Clairvoyance in its phase of sensing distant objects. There are other phases, to the consideration of which we shall now pass. But before leaving this phase, we wish to put ourselves squarely on record regarding the nature of the majority of cases of genuine Clairvoyance. In spite of the opinions of many able authorities, we believe that the manifestation of the above form of Distant Clairvoyance is very rare and uncommon. We believe that but few persons ever experience it, even spontaneously. We believe that the majority of recorded cases of Distant Clairvoyance are instances either of Telepathy of a high order, or else of actual Astral Projection, which we believe to be far more common than is usually believed. We believe that a great number of cases of Clairvoyance are due to the unconscious projection of the Astral Body to the distant scene, if even but for a moment— for time is practically annihilated in Astral Projection.

Clairvoyance of Past Events, is explained by the Arcane Teachings as resulting from the fact that in the Cosmic Brain events leave their records and impression, just as the events of the experience of a man leave records and impressions in *his* brain. These recorded impressions constitute subconscious Memory, in the case of both the man's brain and the Cosmic Brain—"from one know all"—"as below, so above." On the Astral Plane there are preserved the records of the Cosmos— the Cosmic Subconscious Memory, in fact. Everything, action, thought, deed, or activity of any kind, degree or description, that has been manifested since the Dawn of the Cosmic Day, is there recorded in the great unforgetting Subconscious Memory of the Cosmos. All occultists know this, and have called this Subconscious Memory Record by different names. Some minds, peculiarly attuned, occasionally enter into conscious relationship with this Cosmic Subconscious Memory, and are able to record, generally more or less imperfectly, what they sense there. This may be done, either through psychic sensing of mental currents arising from these states of Subconscious Memory, or else by actual contact with them in the Astral Body. But, the phenomena is far less common than is generally supposed, and many cases are explainable upon the hypothesis of Telepathy—that is the impressions are thought impressions, either emanating from the mind of some person now living in the physical, or else some persistent thought-currents which have maintained their coherent properties over long periods of time.

Clairvoyance of the Future, is a misnomer. It implies actual existence somewhere of a foreknowledge or Foresight of the Future—which does not exist. If such existed, then Fate or Predestination would be true. The Cosmic Mind does not *know* before the manifestation—for the knowing causes the manifestation. But the phenomena which is known by the name of Clairvoyance of the future, *does* exist, although the theories concerning it are erroneous. It is true that occasionally individuals seem able to foretell with more or less accuracy, the events which afterward come true at least partially. The secret consists in the fact that the Laws of Orderly Trend and Sequence being operative, there must always be in existence the "shadows cast by the approaching events"—that is active causes operating in the direction of bringing about certain effects. Among these active causes, Desire and Mental Pictures in the minds of living human beings play an important part.

The Clairvoyant perceiving the evidences of these active causes in the Astral is often able to make very good guesses or intuitive conjectures of the events which will follow. Just as one may predict something that will happen tomorrow, from something that is happening to-day. But there is no *certainty* about the prediction, in either case. For there may be, and generally are, other causes which will play their part at the time of action, and thus defeat the entire prediction. Clairvoyance of the Future perceives *probable effects of existent causes*—but no more. The Future is not in existence in the mind of any being—not even in the Mind of the Cosmos. Make no mistake about this. Even Astrology can indicate only "probabilities" of the future. Psychometry, or the receiving of impressions from inanimate objects, by which one enters into *rapport* (or psychic connection) with the previous environment of the object—thus learning its previous history, particulars of its environment, etc., is explained by the fact that in the object's consciousness (for all objects possess a degree of consciousness) there is preserved a memory of its past environment, history, etc., which may be read by the mind attuned to the impressions. Not only this, but the object is still astrally connected by psychic filaments with its previous environment, and the Clairvoyant may thus enter into *rapport* with the latter and its stored-up memories. The object gives the Clairvoyant "the loose end" of the psychic ball of memory and association, which he then unwinds.

Lesson XVII. Mentalism.

Under the head of "Mentalism" we shall group that general class of occult phenomena which consists of the manifestations of what has been called Mental Influence, Mind Power, Thought Force, Mental Magic, Mental Suggestion, etc., the distinguishing feature of which is the exerting of the influence of one mind over other minds. This phase of occult phenomena is well known to the general public of to-day, by reason of the great interest which has been manifested in late years regarding the influence of the mind over physical states, and the investigations and literature which have resulted by reason thereof. But this power, and the knowledge thereof, is no new thing, by any means. We find traces of it in the history of every one of the ancient peoples, as well as in the records of the nations of comparatively modern times. The hierophants of ancient Egypt, Chaldea and Greece were adepts in all of the various branches of mentalism and understood the true underlying principles far better than do the majority of the teachers and writers upon the subject to-day. The traditions and legends coming to us from old Atlantis, inform us of the high degree of knowledge of these things were possessed by that wonderful people who inhabited what is now the "Lost Continent."

To understand Mentalism, one must understand the nature of Telepathy, or Transference of Thought. We hear much of Telepathy in these latter days in the many books and magazines devoted to the subject, in plays, and in the teachings of the various metaphysical cults which have sprung into prominence. Many are the theories advanced to account for the phenomena, and manifold is the error that has arisen from imperfect and incorrect statements of the underlying principles. On the one hand, we hear much of theories of "the ether waves" which carry the "thought vibrations," both being likened to, and held as, but higher forms, of the other vibrations of the ether. On the other hand, we hear many theories which seek to account for the phenomena on supernatural grounds—the desirable forms being considered the evidences of divine power, and the undesirable being regarded as arising from diabolical sources. But there is nothing supernatural about the matter, nor are the waves and vibrations "etheric." We have explained the matter in the preceding lesson, and have shown how the Circulation of Mind is sufficient to account for the phenomena.

That the Thought of man is an actual, moving force, is a fact well known to all occultists, ancient and modern. That thought waves travel in currents and waves is a fact not only believed because of the ancient teachings, but also because those who are able to sense on the Astral Plane are able to *see* the passage of these thought waves, and currents, as they pass from one mind to others. Not only is thought-force exerted consciously, and with direct intent, but also unconsciously and with direct intent and purpose on the part of the person who exerts it.

Thought is as real a force as is electricity, although it operates on an entirely different plane. It may be compared to magnetism and electricity, because it is the correspondence of the physical fine forces, on the mental plane. But one must not make the mistake of supposing that these thought waves or currents, or other forms of influence, travel through the ether as do light, electricity and material magnetism. On the contrary, they have nothing to do with the ether as a medium. They travel through the Universal Principle of Mind.

We have seen, in preceding lessons, that the Three Cosmic Principles pervade all space—the Cosmos—and one of those Principles is Consciousness—Mind. Do you realize just what this means? That all the space there is, or can be—Infinite Space—is occupied by the Mind Principle of the Cosmos? That pervading all space there is a great Cosmic Ocean of Mind, living throbbing, pulsating with life and energy, in the depths of which there is the quietude of eternal calm and peace—on the surface of which are ripples, eddies, waves, currents and whirlpools— upon and in which there is manifested the phases of the fiercest tempest and of absolute calm, rest and peace. And in this great Ocean of Mind—in the Cosmic Mind Principle—occur all the multitude of manifestations of Consciousness that are known on the lower planes of life—on the human plane—and on the planes far beyond any possible conceptions of beings on the lowly scale of mankind of today?

The would-be authorities and instructors on the subject of Mentalism speak learnedly of the "etheric waves" by which Thought is carried from mind to mind. They do not dream, these founders of latter-day schools and cults, that for thousands of years the Arcane Teachers have known and taught that even this much vaunted Universal Ether in which is supposed to abide the foundation principles of all things—this Something which Science says is a No-Thing containing the infinite possibilities of Everything—is but the lowest of the scale of the *seven Ethers* known to the occultists, and which highest and lowest Ethers are but manifestations in the Cosmic Brain, *a result of Mind!* And to suppose that Mind needs this lowest Ether to convey its currents of mental energy is as much a folly and inversion of Truth as that conveyed in the materialistic dogmas that "mind is a secretion and by-product of Matter!" These pseudo-mentalists do not know the first principle of Mentalism, when they assert that Mental Currents are but higher forms of "etheric waves" and energy.

In time, they will learn that the Ether is the byproduct of Mind, and rests in the Ocean of Mind just as the dissolved salt rests in the Ocean of Water. We do not say this in the spirit of captious criticism—that would be a waste of words and time— but because we realize that unless the fundamental Truth is comprehended and realized the study of Mentalism will be but a phase of the study of *physical* science, which it infinitely transcends in importance.

Mind requires Substance in order to manifest itself, *but it travels in its own medium*. Its waves are waves of Mind—its currents are currents of Mind—its vibrations are vibrations of Mind. Activities in a Centre of Consciousness are not confined to that particular centre of manifestation, but extend in all directions in rapidly widening circles, unless the sender deliberately concentrates his thought force in a special and particular direction, either by conscious intent, or else by reason of intense Desire. This Thought-force flows out in currents and waves, exerting more or less influence upon all minds with which it comes in contact, the degree depending upon the degree of harmony to the particular vibrations which are manifested in the receptive minds.

But all this is an old story to the majority of our readers. There is scarcely need for us to write regarding these fundamental facts of Mentalism. They have been told, and often very well told, by the many writers on the subject, who have discovered the facts of the operation of these mental forces, although often in ignorance of the fundamental principles involved in the phenomena. Every student of these lessons has read much regarding the operations of thought influence, and to repeat these familiar facts would be akin to repeating the instructions in kindergarten work, and the alphabet, to advanced students.

We shall, therefore, take it for granted that the student is informed regarding these elementary facts in Mentalism, and shall now merely show how they are explained by the underlying principles of the Arcane Teaching. In our supplementary work,

"The Arcane Formulas; or, Mental Alchemy," we shall give the formulas for the actual demonstration and manifestation of these principles. These lessons are not for beginners, but for those who have acquainted themselves with the reality of Mental Influence and Thought-Force, and who have passed the kindergarten stage of occult attainment and knowledge.

The existence of Mental Influence in its various phases has been fully established to the satisfaction of thousands of investigators. The facts of hypnotism are now common property. The existence of "absent treatments" and other phases of telepathic influence is now accepted as fact by the majority of students of the subject. What is known as "personal magnetism" is now understood to result from purely mental causes. The Attractive power of Thought—the Drawing Power of Mind—the operation of the great Law of Mental Attraction— these things are recognized by students of the subject, and hundreds of books have been written explaining (?) them under one hypothesis or another, and giving more or less valuable instructions in their use. We shall not dwell upon these details at this place—our little book "The Arcane Formulas; or, Mental Alchemy" will furnish the "how" side of this subject, in a condensed, plain, practical and "usable" form. What we wish to do now is to acquaint you with the real underlying principle of Mental Influence—the one fact which illumines the entire subject—which has been known to and taught by the Arcane Teachers for thousands of years, but which does not seem to be known to the latter-day teachers along these lines. We ask you to pay close attention to what we have to say on this point, for when you grasp this underlying principle you have the key to the whole range of phenomena.

The secret of Mental Influence—the effect of one mind over the other minds—lies in the fact that *there is sex in mind*. Under the Law of Opposites, in its phase of Sex Polarity, we find the interesting fact that there is to be found evidences of Sex Polarity on all planes of activity and in all forms of activity, inorganic as well as organic. Sex Polarity is manifested even by the atoms, in the attractions and repulsions. In electricity and magnetism the polarity manifested is all along the lines of Sex Polarity. (We explain this in our supplementary work entitled, "The Mystery of Sex; or, Sex Polarity.") And on the mental plane this principle is found in full operation. The manifestation of Will is the action of the Masculine Principle. Desire and Imagination are phases of the Feminine Principle. Thought, Reason and Intellectual activities result from the union of the two principles. Desire, the female principle of Mind, arouses and attracts the Will, the Masculine element, and draws it into action. Imagination, another phase of the feminine principle, acts in the same way. But, yet, the action of Will is the inciting cause of the activities of Desire and Imagination. The Will can *create* only by its action upon the feminine principles of Desire and Imagination—it cannot create by itself. On the other hand, the feminine principles of Desire and Imagination cannot produce and create without the union with the Will. This is merely the general outline of the activities.

But, and here is where the explanation of Mental Influence is seen, both the feminine Desire and, the masculine Will of a person may be incited into activity by the Will or Desire, as the case may be, of another person. The Will of another person may incite and arouse the activities of one's Desire and Imagination, and render it so active that it will drag into action its own mate, the Will of the person affected. And, in the same way, a strong Desire in the mind of a person, may act to arouse into activity the Will of another, taking the latter away from its lawful mate—the Desire of the person affected. In the same way, two Wills (that of the person affected and that of the person affecting) may struggle for the control, mastery and possession of the Desire and Imagination of the first mentioned person. And, likewise, there is often found the struggle between the feminine principle of Desire in two persons, each wishing to maintain and exert influence over the Will of one of the persons. In this statement is contained the actual secret of the Mental Influence of one person over another in direct personal relations and contact. It is the secret underlying hypnotism, mental influence, personal magnetism, psychic influence, and all the other forms of direct mental influence.

The same principle is operative in the case of mental influence at a distance. In it is found the explanation of the Law of Attraction; the Drawing Power of the Mind; Absent Treatments; etc., as well as in the various forms of phenomena generally grouped together under the head of Mental Magic.

There is found the effect of the masculine Will principle in the thought-waves and mental currents upon the feminine principle of Desire in the minds of those affected. And likewise there is found the attractive force of the strong feminine Desire thought-waves or mental currents, which tend to attract and arouse into activity the masculine principle or Will of those affected. *It should be unnecessary to state that every person, male or female, has this dual-principle of mind within him or her—the masculine and the feminine mental phases of mind.*

The feminine principle of mind acts always in the direction of exerting an attracting, drawing influence upon the will; and also in the direction of creating and conceiving ideas, mental images and other forms of mental creative activity. The masculine principle of mind always acts in the direction of inciting activity within the feminine principles of mind. The feminine principles of mind may be said to be dominated and ruled by the masculine principle, so far as the apparent workings of the mind is concerned; but as a matter of fact, a closer examination will disclose the interesting fact that the masculine principle is always attracted and *"managed"* by the feminine principle, either its own lawful mate, or else the feminine principle of some other mind. We have seen in a preceding lesson, that the Will is "free" and theoretically at least may act without restraint from within, but that in reality it never *does* act unless aroused by Desire. It can "act as it *pleases*," but the "pleases" depends upon Desire, the feminine principle. So that in mental phenomena, as in human life, while the masculine is apparently, and theoretically, the master, as a matter of fact, the feminine causes her mate to do as *she* "pleases," at the same time allowing him to think that it is *he* who "pleases."

The men and women of strong Will Power, who dominate all around them, and often those far removed from them in space, really emanate strong currents charged with Will Power, which coming in contact with the feminine principles in the minds of others arouse the latter and cause the desires of those persons to be in accord with the Will of the strong individual. Great masters of men possess this power to a great degree, and then "work their Will" upon others in this way. Their influence is felt far and near, and they make people do as they like by making them "want to" do that way, or else by causing them to "fear," which is but a negative form of Desire, as we have said in another lesson. In the same way, men of strong Desire and Imagination—feminine principles of the mind—may and do exert powerful influence over the minds and Wills of others, and lead them their way. The "magnetic" persons manifest these feminine principles—they attract, allure, draw on, and often actually seduce the Wills of other people. They are emotional, and capture the Will of others, and at the same time produce a consequent reaction on the emotional natures of the others, by sympathetic vibration. The "electric" persons manifest the masculine principle and cause others to "want to" do as the person wishes. They are "motional" and not only arouse the Desire in others, but also overawe and terrorize the Will of the others. The men and women of the greatest power are those who manifest both the masculine and the feminine principles and consequently affect others on the lines of both poles of their mentality. One moment they exert the power of Will; the next the attracting, drawing, charming power of Desire. If you will test all instances and classes of the phenomena of Mentalism by this principle of Mental Sex Polarity, you will see that it affords an explanation and a reason for them all. We shall have more to say on this subject in our supplementary book,

"The Mystery of Sex; or, Sex Polarity," of which general subject it forms a phase and part. The principle of Sex is strongly in evidence on the mental plane—as it is on the physical—and as it also is on the spiritual. He who leaves Sex Polarity out of the consideration loses the Master Key to the Creative Activities of the Cosmos. It lies indeed at the very heart of the cosmos itself.

So much for the influence of mind over mind. What of the influence of Mind over Things? The answer to this question is very simple. There *is mind in everything*, to respond to the more positive mind. Moreover, *everything is in mind*—in the Cosmic Brain. As we have said elsewhere: If Thoughts become Things in the Cosmic Brain, then following the Law of Analogy, it is possible for Thoughts to materialize as Things on other planes of activity. The same principle is involved—the principle of mental creative activity....With a Cosmos, *mental in its nature*, with energy and substance; matter and motion; all receptive, responsive, and plastic, and obedient to Mind— what cannot be accomplished by those who understand the Laws of Mentalism? With Will as the great creative Power in the Cosmos—what is not possible to him who understands the Art of Willing? With Desire as the great creative energy, can we not see why Desire should be harnessed, controlled, directed, mastered and employed in our lives, careers and destinies?

Lesson XVIII. Invocation and Evocation.

Under the head of "Invocation and Evocation" we shall group that general class of occult phenomena which consists of the "calling upon" supernatural beings; or the "calling forth" of disembodied entities; elementals; vitalized thought entities; etc., from the Astral Plane of Existence. The word "invoke" means "To call for solemnly, or with earnestness; to call upon or address in prayer; to solicit in prayer for assistance or protection." The word "evoke" means: "To call out or summon forth; often used in the sense of calling forth of the disembodied souls, and similar entities."

Invocation of the power of superior, or supernatural beings, by means of prayer, offerings, sacrifices, and other ceremonial forms is seemingly as old as the race. All the ancient peoples invoked their greater and lesser deities, and other supernatural beings, and down to the present time we find prayer actively employed in all forms of religious worship. Even outside of the field of religion, we find many instances of invocation of the power of genii and other supernatural beings, by means of ceremonial magic and similar practices. The old works upon the Magic Art are filled with directions for ceremonials of this kind. The modern mind, however, regards these latter things as merely the effects of silly credulity on the part of ignorant people, the prejudice generally extending to the religious practice of invoking the power of the angels, saints, and other superior disembodied entities.

But, even the most ardent objector to the invocation of lesser beings, if he remain in the bosom of the churches, is apt to adhere to the old and well established custom of calling upon Deity for assistance in the affairs of his life, often going so far as to offer to Deity supposedly valuable hints and bits of advice regarding the conduct, operation and management of the Universe at large. To a mind which has grasped the realization of the transcendent ideal of the Absolute and the Infinite, it is startling to hear many devout "class-leaders," deacons and clergymen, particularly among certain non-ritualistic denominations, addressing their Deity in terms of easy familiarity and good-fellowship, giving Him their opinion on things in general; finding fault; administering patronizing commendation and flattery; and in general informing Him how they, the invokers, wish the world to be managed and run. Burns's poem, "Holy Willie's Prayer" gives us an excellent example of this form. This, however, is a statement of an extreme abuse of the principle, and our natural revolt at the same must not blind us to the fact that prayer in other forms constitutes a source of great spiritual comfort and consolation to many a soul in hours of trouble and pain.

The modern rationalist, seeing no intellectual "reason" for believing in the efficacy of prayer, is apt to dismiss the entire subject as but a part of the outgrown superstition of the race. But this will not do, for an unprejudiced observer will find before him many striking and undoubted instances of "answer to prayer"—of results occurring in almost exact accordance with the nature of earnest and sincere invocation. These instances are too numerous and common to be dismissed as mere coincidence—they must be admitted, and the cause looked for further. And in the examination and search, we must not lose sight of the too often overlooked fact, that these "answers to prayer" come to people of all shades of heterodox religious belief—heathen, pagan, idolaters, in all parts of the globe, and in all times—as well as to "true believers" in the particular faith which happens to be "orthodox" in our particular land at this particular time. The worshippers of the ancient gods of Rome and Greece had their prayers answered; the Egyptian worshippers had the same favors granted them; the Hindus, ancient and modern, received great benefits from prayer; the Mohammedans are a people of great prayers, and many are the answers received by the faithful Moslem. And so, the investigator must either accept the polytheistic idea of the existence of many gods of many people, all of whom hear and answer the prayers of their worshippers, or else the alternative idea that all of these various worshippers, while worshipping at their respective shrines and altars, in reality bring themselves in psychic communication with higher spiritual powers, and thus set in operation natural psychic forces which tend to bring to them their "heart's desire." Which of the two ideas seem the most rational and in accordance with the known facts of the universe?

The Arcane Teachers have always held and taught that every true and earnest prayer coming from the heart of a sincere and devout worshipper, tends to bring that person into a closer relation to the great Cosmic Spirit—the Essence of the One Life of the Cosmos. This, not by a reaching out of the person's mind toward some far away Something, but by means of an Inward Unfoldment, by which the Spirit within each soul unfolds itself and is recognized as present and existent. This experience of the Indwelling Presence of Deity, or the Union with Deity, is common to the religiously inclined soul of all lands, times, and phases of belief—it is common to the race. Instances are found in the records of the transcendental of all times.

This experience, when it occurs to one, leaves him with a sense of renewed power and strength, which often operates in the direction of the person being able to accomplish that for which he prayed.

Not only does it act as a Comforter, but also as a Source of Power. And this is not to be wondered at, when we realize that it means that the individual is thus brought much closer to the very Essence of Being—the One Life. An understanding of this fact will enable us to understand many instances of renewed strength resulting from prayer, meditation, and self-communion, which cannot be dismissed lightly as "mere imagination." All advanced occultists realize the benefits which result from "Meditation," in which the same principle is invoked. When one comes into close relationship with the Cosmic Will, is it any wonder that Power results?

But there is more to the subject than even this. The person who prays earnestly and with *faith in the result*, assumes the mental attitude of Confident Expectation, which is one of the first stages in Attainment by occult methods. Earnest Demand; Confident Expectation; Positive Will—these are the three Co-ordinates of the exercise of Occult Power. And the first two elements are present in all earnest, faithful prayer. And the final stage is very often awakened by the exercise of the two former. Moreover, in demanding earnestly, and expecting faithfully, the person creates the mental image in the Imagination which is an important part in all manifestation of occult power. By exerting these mental forces, all of them important and effective, is it any wonder that the person sets into operation the mental forces which tend to draw to him the things that he needs—and to materialize the ideals that he is holding in his mind? It would be a source of wonder to all occultists if the said results failed to manifest in some degree. The laws of Mentalism are set into full operation by earnest, heartfelt, faithful prayer—it is one of the most potent forms of invoking the operation of well-established laws of Mentalism. This is apparent to all advanced occultists—and will be to the student, if he will but analyze the processes and methods employed unconsciously by the devout worshipper.

And, moreover, none of us can afford to sneer at the tales of the interposition of "the saints" and "angels," and other "holy beings" of the several religions. These are no mere fantasies, and vain imaginings. While many of the beneficent results attributed to them are really due to the causes above mentioned, still all occultists know that there are many advanced beings on the higher planes of the

Cosmos, who are undoubtedly attracted by persons on the lower planes who bring themselves in *rapport* with them by manifesting the proper mental and spiritual states. "There are many more things in heaven and on earth" than are dreamt of in the philosophies of the day. But, of course, any and all results of prayer are in full accord with natural law, and result through the operations thereof. These things are not supernatural—they are but a part of Nature's hidden workings.

Let us now consider the subject of "Evocation."

One of the most common of all forms of Evocation is the familiar "materialization" of disembodied human beings by means of a "medium," or person in the flesh, whose vital power is used by the disembodied entity in manifesting itself once more on the material plane. In some of the instances of this form of manifestation the disembodied entity voluntarily and consciously makes use of the vitality of the medium in order to manifest itself to persons in the flesh for the purpose of communicating with them, or else merely to gratify a desire to assume earthly form and garb once more, and to mingle with persons in the flesh. But all true occultists are aware that a large percentage of these manifestations are not the entities which they purport to represent, but are imposters from the Astral Plane, who assume the image of friends and relatives of those present, copying with more or less perfect detail the mental image of the departed one which exists in the mind of the person in the flesh, and which is called forth by memory by the associations and suggestions of the *seance*.

Another form of Evocation, also quite common in *séances*, is that where the disembodied entity is actually "called forth" by the strong desire and affection of some of the visitors attending the seance, in which case the materialization is effected through the vital powers of the medium, inspired into activity by the strong desire of those who wish to communicate with and see once more the form of those who have passed out of the flesh. In these cases the disembodied entity is scarcely conscious of the manifestation, and is like a person in a dream, or rather like one who walks in his sleep. This fact accounts for the dazed, startled condition of mind often manifested by these materialized entities when they are summoned forth at a *seance*.

They are dwelling in the life of the Astral Plane, wrap in their owns dreams and meditations, and it is cruel to disturb them. In fact, it is quite as unnatural to place a disembodied entity in this condition as it is to plunge a person in the flesh into some abnormal psychic state. Advanced occultists, unanimously, condemn the prevalent practice of evoking these entities, and disturbing their Astral life.

There is a class of earth-bound entities on the lowest sub-planes of the Astral Plane, who hover around their old scenes on earth so long as they are allowed to do so by the laws of the Astral World. These entities swarm around materialization séances, and other similar psychic performances, taking great delight in manifesting their presence as forcibly as may be, and playing as many pranks as possible. These entities often act the part of some celebrated character of history, or some friend or relative of those present, and make "exhibitions" of themselves by making Shakespeare write doggerel verse; or Napoleon tell someone what to take to get rid of a cold; or Plato to warn a maiden to "beware of the 'light-completed' woman." This fact has brought genuine spiritualistic phenomena into disrepute in many quarters where the state of affairs is not known, and caused much pain and heart-burnings among the sincere early followers of spiritualism who were not acquainted with these psychic facts, but who accepted as "gospel truth" every communication reaching them from the "spirit world."

The average spiritualist of to-day, however, is much better informed, and is disposed to be quite as particular in forming "spirit" acquaintances and friendships, as he is in forming earthly ones. Much of the testimony given at *séances* by even reputable and truthful entities is more or less incorrect for reasons that will be apparent to those who have read what we said in our lesson on the "Astral Plane." That is to say, these entities, as a rule, are familiar only with the particular environment familiar to them by reason of their affiliations and their particular character. The best proof of this is the totally contradictory evidence offered by such entities. Their reports range all the way from the "happy hunting grounds" of the savage, to the state of transcendental bliss of the idealistic soul. And each of these reports are equally true, for each reports "the Thing as he sees it," for the world "of Things as they are" on the Astral Plane.

When these facts are understood, one may begin to reconcile the apparent discrepancies of the reports of the *seance.*

In some cases disembodied entities may fall in with the desires of those in the flesh, and will endeavor to aid them in their purposes in the earth-life. But they can accomplish no more than if they were in the flesh—they can employ the thought-force in the same manner—that is all. They cannot affect a person whose thoughts are of a higher degree of vibration, any more than can be done by one still in the flesh.

The influence of these entities has been grossly exaggerated by some writers on the subject. They are governed by the Law of Attraction, and can go only where they are attracted. Moreover, they are apt to end in tormenting those who have invoked them for unworthy purposes. We caution all against attempting to make use of such aid, even if offered.

There is also the Evocation of what are called in a general way, "the elementaries" or "elemental forces." We do not consider it wise to enter into a detailed consideration of this subject, for reasons which will be apparent to all advanced students of occultism. We have spoken of it in a previous lesson. Enough to say that in nature there are semi-intelligent living forces, which under certain conditions may be evoked and guided by the intelligence of human beings, in certain forms of Black Magic. Such practices are extremely unworthy, and invariably result in disastrous results to those dabbling in the forbidden practices. We assure the student, however, that these influences can work no harm to those who stand on the higher plane of thought and life, although those on the lower planes of thought and life may suffer annoyance from them. The Law of Attraction governs and regulates these things—"like attracts like"; "entities, like water seek always their own level."

Another form of Evocation, very common and yet scarcely recognized by many thinkers along these lines, is the evocation of Thought Forms, Desire Nebula, etc. These peculiar Things are the result of strong and vital currents of Will and Desire thrown off from the minds of persons who have lived, and who may still be living. They have a tendency to coalesce and combine, and following the Law of Attraction they gather in the vicinity where similar mental influences are being exerted. They are like gathering clouds on the horizon, non-active in themselves, but capable of manifesting lightning and thunder under certain conditions. These lacking conditions are often supplied by persons of strong Desire or Will, who attract them to them and vitalize them by the energy of their own emotions or motive mentality. These thought-clouds then act as if they had been sent out by the mind of the person animating and energizing them, and manifest all the phenomena of the thought currents.

They may either be directed toward the accomplishment of certain ends of the person, if he be capable of such direction; or, on the contrary, they may involve him in a psychic whirlwind or tempest until he is almost torn asunder. The consequence is that one often "sows the wind, and reaps the whirlwind" is literal truth. Beginning with manifesting these mental states, one is finally carried off his mental feet by them, and caused great pain and misfortune. The lives of many prominent men show examples of this phenomena, although the public does not understand it.

Akin to the above, is the evocation of the Desire Elementals, and "artificial entities" mentioned in our lesson "The Astral Plane." In this case the effect is even more startling that that arising from the evocation of Thought Forms, etc., to which the Desire Elementals are closely related. The difference between the Desire Elementals and active Thought Forms is only a matter of degree, and many writers confuse the two forms of manifestation.

It should be unnecessary for us to add that the Arcane Teachers most positively condemn the practice of evoking the elementals, and forbid it among their students. In fact, they withhold the inner teachings on the subject of certain sub-planes of the Astral, as we have seen, in order to prevent unworthy persons taking advantage of certain of the teachings.

The practice of Evocation often leads directly to Black Magic, which involves the practitioner in whirlwinds and whirlpools of psychic energy and occult forces, and often causes his destruction. There are many to-day practicing Evocation, under high sounding names, and clothed with the garments of high pretensions. But such will feel the Law of Cause and Effect. The Law is never mocked. It moves with the pitiless and unerring certainty of a machine. Each draws his own to him. None can escape their own good—or evil.

Beware of Evocations! Do not play with fire. Do not toy with Edged Tools!

PART VII. ARCANE SECRETS.

Lesson XIX. The Secret of the Opposites.

Let us now consider The Law of Opposites, or Polarity, the mastering of which constitute one of the Arcane Secrets. Listen to the Aphorism:

Aphorism xxi. Everything in the Cosmos has its opposite. Every quality, attribute or condition has its opposite. Everything and every quality, attribute or condition is one of a Pair of Opposites—and yet contains within itself a Pair of Opposites. Polarity is inherent in everything. Everything has its Two Poles; and also is, itself, one pole of something else. The Pairs of Opposites—the two Opposing Poles—are but phases of the same thing. In the union of the Two Poles, or Pair of Opposites, there is to be found the "thing-in-itself" of a thing. There is always a Reconciliation and Agreement possible between Opposites— always a possible Synthesis of Opposing Thesis and Antithesis. Everything "is" and "is not" at the same time, in its qualities, attributes and conditions—and the Reconciliation, Agreement and Synthesis reveals a new "Is." And yet the Reconciliation, Agreement, or Synthesis—the new "Is"—is but one Pole, or one of a Pair of Opposites, of a new and higher Polarity or Pair. And, so on, to infinity. In this Aphorism is contained the Secret of the Understanding of all things in the Cosmos.

This Aphorism states a fundamental truth of the Arcane Teaching—the truth that everything is but one pole of a Pair of Opposites. And that while everything has its Opposite, still the two Opposites, together, form the Real Thing. Every truth is but a half truth. Everything is a paradox. There is "the other side" to everything. There are the "two extremes" to everything. In this great Cosmic Law is found the fact that diametrically opposed things, physical, mental and spiritual, are in reality but the different poles of the same thing. In this Law is found the explanation of all physical phenomena—the mental activities and states—and the Secret of Sex-Generation and Regeneration—and many other important facts and laws—of Cosmic Activity.

When one has had his attention directed to the existence of The Law of Opposites, he will see evidences of its presence and operation on all sides, and in all phenomena of the Cosmos. He will soon see that no matter what may be the quality of a thing, another quality diametrically opposed to the first one will always be found. Sometimes it is difficult to discover the opposing quality—but the Law is invariable and constant, and a careful search will always reveal the Opposite. The principle may be called to your mind by reference to a few familiar instances. Thus: You will always find an Up and a Down; a High and a Low; a Right and a Left; a Hard and a Soft; a Heavy and a Light; an Abstract and a Concrete; a Long and a Short; a Broad and a Narrow; a Hot and a Cold; a Sharp and a Dull; an Easy and a Difficult; a North and a South; an East and a West; a Positive and a Negative; a Male and a Female; a Large and a Small; a Good and a Bad; a Light and a Dark; a Day and a Night; a Love and a Hate; a Courage and a Fear; a Truth and an Untruth; and so on until you will find that, the moment you notice a quality of a thing, that same moment you will recognize an opposite quality.

Your first impression after noticing these Pairs of Opposites is that they are composed of things entirely different from each other—entirely apart—and far from being "the same thing." But examine a little closer, and what do you see? Where do you draw the line between Up and Down? You may say that one thing is "up" and another "down," in comparison with each other, or in relation to some other thing. But, in the abstract, apart from comparison and relativity—where is your dividing line which causes one direction in Space to be "up" and another to be "down." You will find that there is no such absolute division, and that your "up" and "down" are but relative and comparative terms, depending upon some imaginary or temporary dividing line. Astronomers recognize this fact, and one of the first things they teach their students is: "There is no 'up' nor 'down' in Space!" The same is of course true with High and Low; Right and Left; etc. Also with the cardinal points, which consist of Pairs of Opposites. Travel North as far as you can go, and reaching the North Pole you find yourself in a position in which whatever direction you travel your next step will lead you South. Travel East as far as you can and you will find yourself returning to your starting point *from the West*—for there is no "East or West Pole." What is West to us, is East to others. China and India are in the "Great East," but they are West to America. We can reach them by traveling either East or West.

You think that Hard and Soft are two entirely different things, do you not? Then tell us where you draw the line between Hard and Soft. What constitutes a thing Hard or Soft—except relativity and comparison? Where is your Absolute Hard, or Absolute Soft. Hard and Soft are but names for *degrees* of a Something the two Opposites or Poles of which we call "Hard" and "Soft," respectively. The same is true of Heavy and Light. Where is your dividing line? The terms are but *relative degrees* of weight, are they not?—poles of the same thing. What is the difference between Long and Short—Broad and Narrow— Sharp and Dull? These contrasting qualities are but *degrees* in the same thing. What is the difference between Large and Small? What particular size makes one thing Large and another Small? Where is your standard? What is the difference between an Easy thing and a Difficult one? Is there a positive standard— are they not merely *degrees* of the same thing, and relative to the strength of power employed?

Perhaps this point can be brought out more clearly by a consideration of "Hot and Cold." At first thought no two things seem further removed from one another than these two—they seem to have nothing in common. But let us see. We find that science assumes the existence of a certain Something called "Temperature." The word is derived from a Latin Word Meaning "measure; proportion; degree." Science uses it to indicate the "intensity of radiant heat." And Heat is held to be simply a "state or condition of matter, resulting from vibration." Temperature then is merely a term used to indicate *varying degrees of vibration* of a certain kind. Therefore we see that "Hot and Cold" have no real existence as things-in-themselves, but are merely *degrees* in the scale of Heat, the latter being but a term indicating certain kinds of vibrations. Therefore "Hot and Cold" are but degrees of the same thing, in the end—and that "same thing" is but a quality of Something Else—a quality of Motion, having its own Opposite in a higher scale.

Moreover, even on the lower plane "Hot and Cold" are seen to be but relative and comparative. At what point on the thermometer would you draw a line dividing "Hot" from "Cold"? Everything is a little "hotter" than something else, and a little "colder" than a third thing. So far as the sensation of "Hot" and "Cold" is concerned, it is quite relative and comparative. Come from a cold hallway, into a warmer room, and you feel quite warm, even though those in the room be shivering. Dip one hand into ice-water, and the other into boiling water, at the same time—and then plunge both hands into a basin of luke-warm water, at the same moment. What is the result? To one hand the water seems quite warm, while to the other it seems quite cool—and yet the temperature of the water is fixed. Where is your "Hot and Cold," then? You say that to-day is "warm" meaning that it is warmer than it has been. A month from now, you may call the same temperature "cool." In the end you will find that "Hot and Cold" are but names designating *degrees* of Heat vibration. You know very well what you mean by each term—you recognize them as Opposites—and yet you are unable to fix a dividing line between them or to separate things into two distinct classes of "Hot" and "Cold" respectively. You find that they blend into each other, and that the shades of differences between close degrees are almost indistinguishable in sensation. You see that they are but a Pair of Opposites, and together form Two Poles of the same thing—Heat. The very "Cold" thing is as much *a degree of Heat* as is the very "Hot" thing—the distinction is merely one of *degree*.

The same Law is operative in the field of Good and Bad. (We do not refer to "Right and Wrong" in the moral or religious sense, although even that comes under the Law, and is a matter of *degrees* upon a standard erected by some particular school, religion, or custom—the standard varying greatly among the schools, sects, or localities. It is often very difficult to determine between "Right and Wrong" in any particular standard or scale, so closely do the degrees shade into each other.) We refer to "Good" in the sense of: "desirable; conducive to satisfaction and happiness"; and to "Bad" in the sense of: "undesirable; conducive to dissatisfaction and unhappiness." We find, upon analysis and examination, that these two terms are but another Pair of Opposites, which represent degrees of a Something which we may call "Satisfaction" or "Happiness." A "Good" thing is one which causes Happiness and Satisfaction; a "Bad" thing, one which produces Unhappiness and Dissatisfaction. We readily distinguish between these two results, in general. But when it comes to drawing a fixed line between them on the scale, we find it impossible. Some things are "better" than others; some things are "worse" than others; but these degrees are comparative, and relative. A dirty crust of dry bread tastes very "good" to a starving man; while the same thing would be very "bad" to the taste of a well fed person. And so it is with everything "Good and Bad"—all relative.

Moreover, the same thing may be both "Good and Bad," at the same time—that is, "Good" for some purposes and "Bad" for others. So we must always inquire "Good" for *what*? "Bad" for *what*? And, likewise, the same thing may be both "Good and Bad," at the same time, for the same purpose, *for two different people*. "It's an ill wind that blows Nobody any Good," says the proverb. "One man's Good is another man's Bad," says another. "One man's Loss is another man's Gain," says a third. "One man's Meat is another man's Poison," says a fourth. And so on, each illustrating the truth of the general statement. A "Good day's fishing" may be a "Bad day's work" for the fish. "Good!" says one man when wheat advances on the Board of Trade—and yet that advance may mean the greatest "Bad" for another. A writer on Natural History once pointed to the long legs and long beak of the Crane, so well adapted to catching fish, as a "mark of the Goodness of Providence." The fish probably thought it an exceedingly "Bad" provision.

Let us begin with the Positive Pole of Love-Hate, which we call "Love." We find here a high degree of the emotional quality which consists of the states of "affection; regard; attraction; affinity; etc." Then, on the extreme Opposite of the scale— the Negative Pole-we find the quality which we call "Hate," which consists of "aversion; dislike; repulsion; etc." These two emotional states seem as different as any two things can be, do they not? It seems almost impossible to conceive that they are but the Opposite Poles of what we may call "Regard," or

"Attraction," or "Affinity"—and yet such is their real relation. Returning once more to the pole of "Love," let us descend the scale. Moving down a little on the scale we find states of "less regard," or "less attraction." Then still further down, we find states in which the regard or attraction is very greatly reduced. Finally we come to a point at which there appears to be *no* regard or attraction, and still *no* repulsion or dislike. This is the neutral point of balance which is always to be found somewhere in the consideration of every Pair of Opposites, and yet which is not a fixed or absolute point, but which varies according to circumstances, persons and various influences. Then passing down the scale we find manifested a slight repulsion or dislike; this increases as we move down the scale. Finally we notice degrees of intense dislike and repulsion, until finally we find the Negative Pole of "Hate." You will understand this readily— you have noticed the different degrees of Love and Hate, and have also noticed how these degrees rise and fall according to circumstances and conditions. But have you ever noticed that extreme Love often is suddenly transmuted into extreme Hate, and *vice versa*, under extreme emotion or exciting cause. Who has not seen instances where a woman's intense Love has been transformed into burning Hate, by the influence of some new cause. In some cases the emotion moves rapidly backward and forward, to-and-fro, between these two poles, until the person does not know whether he or she Loves or Hates. As in one of Kipling's poems a woman says: "I 'ate you, grinnin' there….Ah, Gawd, I love you so!"

It will be seen that all these transmutations of emotional states from one pole to the other—from Love to Hate—from Fear to Courage—are but changes of Polarity, or a shifting of position on the emotional scale. But these changes are *always* along the scale of the emotion which has the two poles—and not from one emotion to another. Emotions of different scales cannot be transmuted one to another—they must belong to the same scale. Water may be transformed into Steam, and Wood into Smoke; but Water cannot be transformed into Smoke, nor Wood into Steam. And so it is with the emotional states—*the transmutation must be along the degrees of, or between the poles of, the same scale.*

And, so, now we arrive at the point of the Arcane Teaching in which is made plain the processes of Mental Transmutation in its phase of Change of Polarity. This forms an important part of the Arcane Processes of Mental Transmutation. By the application of the trained Will, it is possible for the student to transmute one emotional state to its opposite, by changing the polarity. Thus, one may change his Love into Hate, or his Hate into Love, simply by concentrating the Attention and Will upon the Opposite Pole of the state or quality. In the Arcane processes, the student is never told to "fight" or "kill out" an undesirable emotional quality by opposing sheer Will to it— this is a waste of energy, and is moreover quite unscientific. The proper method is to concentrate on the Opposite Pole, and thus change the vibrations and shift the emotional center of Balance.

In the same way, and under the same Law, the emotional states of others may be influenced by polarizing their minds on the opposite pole of the scale of the emotion in question. Hate is not to be combatted...by Hate—this only adds fuel to the fire. The proper way is to form the mental image of Like and Attraction, in your mind, and then concentrate its effects upon the other person. Just as you may change you own emotional states, so may you change his, under the proper conditions and by the proper methods. And, remember this, this process does not consist in the sentimental, negative, rabbit-like attitude of mind that many teachers preach to the students—it does not consist in "turning the other cheek" to be smitten. Far from it, this process is purely volitional and not emotional. It is the bringing into play of the scientific principles of Mentalism— not wishy-washy emotional sentimentalism, or the practice of "kissing the rod that smites you." The Arcanes are not sentimentalists, nor emotional weaklings. On the contrary, they live in their heads with their Balance in the Will. But, nevertheless, they tell you that the way to combat Hate is by its opposite Pole. This is a Paradox which requires thought to solve. It is the principle taught in the old fable, in which the Sun and the North Wind dispute their power to tear away a man's cloak from him. The harder the North Wind blew, the closer the man hugged the cloak around him. But when the Sun tried the effect of its heated rays, the man soon dropped the cloak because he found it uncomfortable. Polarizing in an Opposite, negates the first condition.

If you are strong enough to hear the full truth, listen to these words: The advanced occultist regards *both* Love and Hate as emotions of the "Me" side of oneself. Therefore he rises above both, and neither Loves nor Hates, in the ordinary meaning of the terms. He maintains a balance in his "I," like the man on the tight rope with his balancing pole, first shifting the balance to one side, and then to the other, as occasion renders advisable. He thinks that the slave to Love is as miserable as the slave to Hate—and he avoids both extremes. He finds that the synthesized Love-Hate is in itself but one pole of a Something Else—and he moves up higher to that Something. Instead of being compelled to sail according to the wind of Emotion, he ploughs his way through the Sea of Life by the power of the Steam of Will. He knows the Opposites—the Two Poles—of everything, to be but phases of a Synthesis of opposite qualities. He changes them to suit himself and his purposes. He solves the problem of the "two ends" *by tying them together*. He is Balanced between the Two Poles. He neutralizes unnecessary qualities, and undesirable ones, by changing their polarity. He grasps both horns of the Dilemma. He embraces the Paradox as a Whole. He claims all—but allows naught to claim him. He uses all—but allows naught to use him. Along this road lies Mastery!

Lesson XX. The Secret of Rhythm.

Let us now consider the Law of Rhythm, the mastery of which constitutes one of the Arcane Secrets. Listen to the Aphorism:

Aphorism xxii. In the Cosmos every thing moves. Every thing is in constant motion. Every thing is undergoing constant change. Every thing "beats time." Vibration is universal, and, manifesting according to the Law of Rhythm, constitutes the difference of degree existing between things on all planes. Every thing moves to-and-fro in Rhythm, between its two poles. Every thing rises and falls, in Rhythm, within the limits of its nature. Every thing advances and retreats, in Rhythm, within the limits of its power.

The Aphorism informs us of the truth that in the Cosmos everything moves; is in constant motion; is undergoing constant change. This is one of the fundamental principles of the ancient instruction of the Arcane Teachers, which has been steadfastly adhered to throughout the centuries, until now the most advanced modern science has moved to the same position. Heraclitus, the famous Greek philosopher, who lived nearly twenty-five hundred years ago, and who was affiliated with the Arcane School, made this principle the basis of his philosophy.

His basic principle was: "Everything moves; everything changes; everything is in flux; everything is constantly 'becoming.'" Clodd, the English scientific writer, says: "Nothing escapes the law of change. The shrewd speculations of Heraclitus, the Ionian, who lived two thousand five hundred years ago, that everything is in a state of flux, and, therefore, that the universe is always "becoming," have added confirmation in every discovery of modern physics." Buddha (b. c. 600) said: "Everything changes but Change."

Huxley said: "The more we learn of the nature of things, the more evident is it that what we call rest is only unperceived activity; that seeming peace is silent but strenuous battle. In every part, at every moment, the state of the cosmos is the expression of a transitory adjustment of contending forces; a scene of strife in which all the combatants fall in turn. What is true of each part is true of the whole. Natural knowledge tends more and more to the conclusion that 'all the choir of heaven and furniture of the earth' are transitory forms or parcels of cosmic substances wending along the road of evolution, from nebulous potentiality, through endless growths of sun and planet and satellite; through all varieties of matter; through infinite diversities of life and thought; possibly, through modes of being of which we have neither a conception, nor are competent to form any, back to the indefinable latency from which they arose. Thus the most obvious attribute of the cosmos is its impermanence."

The universal and ceaseless motion of all things is caused, of course, by the operation of the Principle of Motion—one of the Three Cosmic Principles, which acts upon Substance in the many manifestations arising principally from the action and reaction of the dual principles of, or rather the opposite poles of, Attraction-Repulsion. Its forms and varieties are as manifold as are those of Substance, or Consciousness—that is to say, they are practically infinite. The basic activity of Motion, however, is that which we call Vibration, of which the Aphorism says; "Vibration is universal, and manifesting according to the Law of Rhythm, constitutes the difference of degrees between things on all planes." Modern Science now stands "on all fours" with the Arcane Teaching in this respect, and not only holds that all things are in constant vibration, but also, that the rates of vibration determine the difference in the elemental nature of all things. Everything, from the tiny corpuscle, or electron, of which the atoms are composed, to the greatest masses of matter known to us, manifest the law of Rhythmic Vibration. Moreover, Science has demonstrated that the sole difference between the "elements" which make up the different forms of matter, arises from the rate and degree of vibration manifested by the electrons composing them—that is to say, they are *but varying degrees of vibration*. The difference between Gold and Lead consists but of differences in Vibration. The difference between Light and Beeswax is but a difference in Vibration.

In previous lessons you have seen that the Cosmos, when resolved into the Infinity of Nothingness, is practically Motionless—the Principle of Motion is in a condition of Absolute Rest. And yet, that Absolute Rest is analogous to Motion of such a high degree of Vibration as to be practically Motionless and at Rest. In this condition, or state, the two poles of Motion have been resolved into one—the extremes have merged—Absolute Motion and Absolute Rest are seen to be identical. But from the first Dawn of the new Cosmic Day, there is manifested Vibration on a constantly descending scale, until the lowest point is reached—then the upward trend begins. And in these varying degrees of Vibration is manifested every thing that is in the Cosmos, not only the physical things, but also the mental states. Every mental state, of any and all kinds, has its own degree of Vibration, which makes it what it is, and constitutes its difference from other mental states. And these mental Vibrations may be transmitted from one brain to another, in the phenomena of Mentalism.

It should not be necessary here to inform the student that that which we call sound, light, heat, magnetism, electricity, the X-Rays, and other forms of energy, are but varying forms of Vibration. And that even the most solid piece of material substance—a diamond or piece of steel, for instance, is composed of a countless number of tiny atoms, which in turn are composed of minute electrons or particles—all in constant vibratory motion, manifesting intense energy, dashing about and circling around each other, bounding and rebounding from each other, each atom resembling a solar system with its circling planets in constant motion. The elementary text-books on physical science inform their readers that every thing, and all things, of which we have any knowledge through our senses, are but appearances arising from differing rates of Vibration. And that, moreover, our only consciousness of them is the result of Vibration.

But, what of the "Law of Rhythm" which causes everything to "beat time," as the Aphorism states? Let us consider this Law, for it has a very important bearing upon Mental States and phenomena.

"Rhythm," according to the accepted usage, is "movement in measured time," the most familiar instance of which is the "time" in music, which is measured by the "beats" of the metronome or the baton. And scientific investigation, as well as the ancient occult teachings, show us that *everything in the Cosmos "beats time,"* and moves in accordance with Rhythm. We see this in the swing of the planets; the beating of the human heart; the in-breathing and out-breathing of the lungs; the rise and fall of the tides; and in the operation of Vibration on every plane, in every thing. As Vibration is universal—so Rhythm is universal.

A moment's thought will show you that all the phenomena in Nature manifest this law of Rhythmic movement between two extremes. There is always the ebb-and-flow of things. Always the rhythmic swing of the pendulum between the two extremes of the thing. Day is succeeded by night; summer by winter; action by reaction; work by rest; activity by inactivity; intermittent symptoms in diseases; "good times" by "bad times" in business; exaltation by depression. On every plane may be observed instances of this universal "pendulum swing" of Rhythm, which carries the thing to-and-from between its two polar extremes. As the Aphorism says: "Everything moves to-and-fro, in Rhythm, *between its two poles.* Everything rises and falls, in Rhythm, *within the limits of its nature.* Everything advances and retreats, in Rhythm, *within the limits of its power.*" Modern science holds that the Evolution of worlds must have had its precedent Involution, and the Evolution must be followed by Devolution—and so on, to Infinity. It holds that just as the suns and planets were evolved by stages from the nebula, so must they return to the nebula, in time; again to begin a new series of evolutionary world-building. Notice the quotation from Huxley, in the first part of this lesson. Herbert Spencer makes this law of Rhythm one of the principles of his philosophy.

The Arcane Teaching also shows the Law of Rhythm to be operative in the form of the Days and Nights of the Cosmos— the swing of Rhythm between the Manifest Cosmos and the Unmanifest Cosmos. The Law of Polarity, and the Law of Rhythm are twin-laws— they are bound to each other for Eternity. You will notice the resulting effect, that the rise and fall, or rhythmic pendulum swing, is determined, governed and restrained by the length of the scale of

Polarity. Nothing can swing beyond the limits of its poles—nothing can exceed the limits of its nature or power. Consequently, if a thing swings far in one direction, it swings back equally far in the other. If its swing is great, its extremes are widely apart—if the swing is small, then the extremes are close together. The pendulum illustration may be applied to the phenomena on all planes. A short beat of the metronome allows the rod to move only a short distance each way—the long beat admits of a wide swing.

And so, those who enjoy keenly also suffer keenly; while those whose natures allow of but limited suffering, are also capable of only a limited degree of capacity for enjoyment. A pig suffers but little, and enjoys but little; while a highly organized, sensitive, "high strung" human being, suffers the joys of heaven at times, and also the pain of hell at others. The pendulum swings as far in one direction as in the other. *Only by a Mastery of Mental Rhythm can man hope to escape the pain that his high development would otherwise bring him.*

The Arcane Teachers instruct their pupils in the Art of Mental Transmutation, by an understanding of which they may apply the energy and power of Mental Vibrations intelligently, and under the control of the Reason and the Will. When it is understood that the difference between Mental States is like the difference between the Physical Elements—merely a rate of Vibration— then Mental Transmutation or Mental Alchemy, becomes as real as the Physical Transmutation, or Physical Alchemy, of the ancients, which science is now on the eve of rediscovering. An understanding of this give one the Mastery of Self, and also the Secret of Mentalism. Moreover, an understanding of the Law of Rhythm enables one to take advantage of the flood-tide of Mental Rhythm, and a neutralizing or rising above the ebb-tide. With an understanding of the Law of Balance, one may so balance and counter-balance himself that he is not disturbed by the backward swing of the pendulum of Rhythm, but instead may take advantage of its energy and transmute it into desirable things. In this understanding comes the Poise of Power.

Let us now consider the Law of Cyclicity, which is akin to the Law of Rhythm. Listen to the Aphorism:

Aphorism xxiii. Cyclicity is akin to Rhythm, and arises by reason of it. All events tend to move in Cyclic Trend—in constant circular movement of continuous recurrence. The only escape from Cyclicity is found in the process of transmutation into Spirality. This is accomplished by Advancing the Central Point of Motion. The conversion of the Circle into the Spiral is one of the highest forms of Mental Alchemy.

The Law of Cyclicity manifests in the universal tendency of things to swing in circles. Cyclicity is an outgrowth, or more complex form, of Rhythm. The primal manifestation of Rhythm is action to-and-fro in a straight line or path—a movement backward and forward between the limits of the poles. This would be the invariable movement if the particular force manifested were the only manifestation of force or energy in that particular field of the Cosmos. But when the swinging pendulum (free to move in *any* direction) is subjected to the conflicting attractions and repulsions of other manifestations of force and energy, then is manifested the universal tendency toward the *circular* trend—the tendency to convert the straight path of the swing into a circular path or cycle. The action and reaction, the attraction and repulsion, arising from the conflict between the force of the Rhythmic swing in a straight line on the one hand, and the attractive and repellant forces from without, on the other hand, tend to swing the moving thing in a perfect circle around a Central Point of pivotal centre. And these conflicting forces are in operation through the Cosmos, and the manifestation of Cyclicity may be noticed on all planes.

There is ever the evidence of the cyclic trend of things and events—the tendency to move in circles. The electrons in the atoms move in circles, just as do the planets around the sun; and just as does the sun move around some other center in space.

The highest occult teachings, as well as the highest speculations of science, inform us that there is always a movement in circles around some given point; and the movement of *this* center of motion around some other center; and so on to Infinity.

The Aphorism states that: "All events tend to move in cyclic trend—in constant circular movement of continuous recurrence." And the experience of man, aided by the reports of history, bear out this statement. The student of human history is struck by the continuous cyclic trend manifested throughout the ages of history. The student of philosophy is attracted by the same evidence in his own field. And so it is with every field of human thought—Cyclic Trend is noticeable everywhere. Races and nations rise, flourish, decline and fall; only to be succeeded by others traveling over the same lines. "Westward, the star of Empire takes its flight," the center of political power constantly changing. The civilizations of Atlantis, Egypt, Chaldea, Rome and Greece arose and passed away. Our civilization is but traveling over the same general lines. All forms of political government, monarchic, autocratic, democratic, in all their variations, were known in the past as in the present. The same law is observable in the history of philosophical thought. Theories popular in Greece over two thousand years ago afterward fell into disrepute, but are now again forcing their way to the front. The scientific theories of Causation, Continuity, Determinism, and Evolution were popular in Ancient Greece over two thousand years ago. And they were likewise popular in Ancient Egypt and in India centuries before that time. Fashions in literature, dress, and manner constantly recur—traveling 'round and 'round their little circles. Laugh as we may at the absurdity of fashion in dress, nevertheless it proceeds according to Cyclic Law. Religious ideas are as old as the world—pantheism, polytheism, monotheism, and atheism—all have played their parts of fashion in religious thought, over and over again—and will play them again. The present-day revival in interest in occult thought arises from the same law.

And the life of individuals manifests the same trend and tendency. A little thought will convince you that the majority of people travel in circles in life. The same old thing over and over again, recurring at intervals of greater or lesser duration, according to the "nature" of the person. The majority of persons are like the squirrel in the cage who travels all day on his whirling wheel—but ends where he began.

"But," you may say, "if the Cosmos travels around in a continuous circle it would never progress or advance into increased consciousness." Very true! And if the individual continued in the "constant circular movement of continuous recurrence" he would never advance on The Path. The Aphorism gives us the Secret when it says: "The only escape from Cyclicity is found in the process of transmutation into Spirality. *This is accomplished by advancing the*

Central Point of Motion." If the Central Point of Motion of a Circle is moved forward, then the

Circle is converted into a Spiral. The Central Point is advanced in the Cosmos by the Cosmic Will urging forward the entire Cosmic Process, and thus converting the Cyclic Trend into a Spiral Trend—onward and upward, in advancing and rising circles toward Progress. And by a similar process, the Individual may convert the Circle of his Life Motion into an Advancing and Rising Spiral, which while carrying him around the Life Circle will at the same time raise him a stage higher at each turn. While apparently traveling around a circle, like the average person, he will be *a stage higher at each turn.* The Mountain of Attainment, around which winds the Spiral Path, is traveled only in this way. 'Round and 'round the Pilgrims travel, seemingly retracing the same steps—but in reality reaching a stage higher each circle they make. They often complain (until they learn better) saying, "I have gone 'round and 'round, and still reach nowhere." But when they compare their present stage with that of a year ago, they see that they have *advanced*. Is this not the case with you, friend? Have you not used these very words? Heed the lesson!

By advancing the Central Point, by the Will, the wise and strong convert the Cycles into Spirals, and thus attain and advance. As the Aphorism says, this "is one of the highest forms of Mental Alchemy."

Lesson XXI. The Secret of Balance.

Let us now consider the Law of Balance, the mastery of which constitutes one of the Arcane Secrets. This Law may be considered in its three phases of Counterbalance, Compensation, and Poise, respectively. Let us now consider the first phase, viz., Counterbalance. Listen to the Aphorism:

Aphorism xxiv. Know ye, that in the Cosmos every thing is Counterbalanced. Everything is set-off and offset by other things. There is always Check and Countercheck in every manifestation, on every plane, of the Cosmos.

This first phase of Balance, which is known as "Counterbalance," is a law, the operation of which is evident to every investigator of physical science. "Balance" in the Arcane usage may be defined as: "Equipoise; equilibrium; and equality of weight or force."

"Counterbalance" is defined as: "Compensating balance; weight or force opposing equal weight or force." This phase of the Law of Balance, like its other phases, arises from the existence and operation of the Law of Opposites, or Polarity. Everything in the Cosmos is dual. There is always something opposed to, counterbalancing and checking something else. The Manifest Cosmos could not exist and remain operative without this law.

Just as the watch or clock requires a nicely adjusted system of counterweights, countersprings, and counterbalances, in order that their opposing action may render the movement of the timepiece uniform and regular, so does the Cosmos require, and possess, an equally nicely balanced and counterbalanced system, in order that its activities may be uniform and regular.

The regular and uniform movement of the planets around the sun is made possible only through the operation of the counterbalancing forces of centrifugal and centripetal gravity, the former manifesting in the tendency of the planet to fly from the central point, the sun; and the latter manifesting in the tendency of the planet to move toward the central point, the sun. The counterbalance of these two opposing tendencies produces regular and constant movement in the elliptic orbit.

In the same way the two phases of Force or Energy oppose and counterbalance each other—one tending to build up, and the other tending to tear down. Some authorities have adopted the use of the term "Force" to designate that form of Motion which tends "to bind together two or more particles of ponderable matter, and which retards or resists motions tending to separate such particles"; for instance, Gravitation, Cohesion, Chemical Affinity, etc. The same authorities use the term "Energy" to designate that form of Motion which tends "to separate two or more particles of ponderable matter, or of the ethereal medium, or which resists or retards the Force tending to bind them together." Clodd says: "If Force had unresisted play, all the atoms in the universe would gravitate to a common center, and ultimately form a perfect sphere in which no life would exist, and in which no work could be done. If Energy had unresisted play, the atoms in the universe would be driven asunder and remain forever separated, with the like result of changeless powerlessness.

But with these two powers in conflict...the universe is the theatre of ceaseless redistributions of its contents."

All through living Nature is this same law of Counterbalance in force. The plant-life nourishes the animal-life, and the latter by means of its waste matter and its disintegrating forms nourishes the former. Moreover, the very *breathing* of the two great forms of life, tend to support life in each other. Animals breathe in oxygen in order to support life, and breathe out carbonic-acid gas, the latter being poisonous to animal-life. At the same time the plants, under the action of the sun's rays, break up the carbonic-acid gas, absorbing the carbon which nourishes plant-life, and releasing the oxygen needed by animal life. Thus the refuse element of the plant is the life-giving element of the animal; and the refuse element of the animal is the life-giving element of the plant. As Emerson says: "Whilst the world is thus dual, so is every one of its parts. The entire system of things gets represented in every particle. There is somewhat that resembles the ebb and flow of the sea, day and night, man and woman, in a single needle of the pine, in a kernel of corn, in every individual of every animal tribe. There action, so grand in the elements, is repeated within these small boundaries. For example, in the animal kingdom the physiologist has observed that no creatures are favorites, but a certain compensation balances every gift and every defect."

In Nature there is always the operation of the "Check and Countercheck" mentioned in the Aphorism. Each life-form is kept in check by some other life-form. If this were not so, particular life-forms would overrun the earth. Darwin says; "There is no exception to the rule that every organic being naturally increases at so high a rate, that, if not destroyed, the earth would soon be covered by the progeny of a single pair." Clodd adds; "If all the offspring of the elephant, the slowest breeder known, survived, there would be in seven hundred and fifty years nearly nineteen million elephants alive, descended from the first pair. If the eight or nine million eggs, which the roe of a cod is said to contain, developed into adult cod-fishes, the sea would quickly become a solid mass of them. So prolific is its progeny after progeny that the common housefly is computed to produce twenty-one millions in a season; while so enormous is the laying power of the aphis, or plant-louse, that the tenth brood of one parent, without adding the products of all the generations which precede the tenth, would contain more ponderable matter than all the population of China, estimating this at five hundred millions."

It is the same in plant life. If any single species were to remain unchecked, the entire globe would be covered with it inside of less than twenty years. The fungi, and other lower organisms, multiply so rapidly (some a billion-fold in an hour) that they would cover the earth in a year, if not counterchecked by nature. But the countercheck is always there. Each animal, plant or fungus has its natural enemy which preys upon it for food. *Every living thing lives upon other living things*—each according to its kind. This is one of the forms of Nature's counterchecks.

This law is brought forcibly to mind when certain plants or animals are transported to other regions, without their natural enemies accompanying them, the result being that they speedily become a danger to the land, and their natural enemies have to be brought to the new region to keep them in check. Students of Evolution see in Natural Selection, and other laws of Evolution, many phases of Counterbalance and Countercheck in the Cosmos—the working out of the law that "Everything is set-off and offset by other things," as the Aphorism says.

And now let us consider the second phase of the Law of Balance—the phase of Compensation—the Debit and Credit phase of the Cosmic Activities. Listen to the Aphorism:

Aphorism xxv. Know ye that there is always a Cosmic Debit and Credit. In the Cosmos there is Absolute Compensation. The Cosmic Accounts are always evenly balanced. There is nothing furnished Free—No thing given for Nothing—in the Cosmos.

The Equivalent is always demanded and rendered. The Price for Every Thing is always fixed—and Paid.

The truth embodied in the above Aphorism is recognized by the world's greatest thinkers, although the average person endeavors to deny it, and refuses to look the Truth in the face. That wonderful essay upon "Compensation," by Emerson, carries the truth to every open mind. All true philosophers have recognized the principle as in existence. Any one may see the fact, if he will stand apart and view the world-picture in the proper perspective. The idea of

Compensation is based upon the phases of Counterbalance and Countercheck—upon Set-off and Offset. In short, it is always a matter of "Paying the Price." We cannot have the cake, and keep our penny, at the same time. We must always give up one thing to obtain another—we must always relinquish to attain—we must always die to live. Life is a continuous "Pay, pay, pay!" As the Aphorism informs us: "There is nothing furnished Free—No Thing given for Nothing—in the Cosmos"; "The price for Every Thing is always fixed—and Paid." For every advantage gained, another must be surrendered. This is the Law of the Cosmos, as all wise men know it. It does one no good to deny or ignore it—it is Law, fixed, constant, immutable.

Emerson, in his essay on "Compensation," says: "The theory of the mechanic forces is another example. What we gain in power is lost in time, and the converse. The periodic or compensating errors of the planets is another instance. The influences of climate and soil in political history are another.

The cold climate invigorates. The barren soil does not breed fevers, crocodiles, tigers, or scorpions. The same dualism underlies the nature and condition of man. Every excess causes a defect; every defect an excess. Every sweet has its sour; every evil its good. Every faculty which is a receiver of pleasure has an equal penalty put on its abuse. It is to answer for its moderation with its life. For every grain of wit, there is a grain of folly. For everything you have missed, you have gained something else; and for everything you gain, you lose something. If riches are increased, they are increased that use them. If the gatherer gathers too much, nature takes out of the man what she puts into his chest; swells the estate, but kills the owner. Nature hates monopolies and exceptions. The waves of the sea do not more speedily seek a lever from their loftiest tossing than the varieties of condition tend to equalize themselves. There is some leveling circumstance that puts down the overbearing, the strong, the rich, the fortunate, substantially on the same ground with all others. Is a man too strong and fierce for society, and by temper and position a bad citizen—a morose ruffian, with a dash of the pirate in him?—nature sends him a troop of pretty sons and daughters who are getting along in the dame's classes at the village school, and love and fear for them smooths his grim scowl to courtesy. Thus she contrives to intenerate the granite and feldspar, takes the boar out and puts the lamb in, and keeps the balance true. The farmer imagines power and place are fine things. But the President has paid dear for his White House. It has commonly cost him all his peace, and the best of his manly attributes. To preserve for so short a time so conspicuous an appearance before the world, he is content to eat dust before the real masters who stand erect behind the throne. Or do men desire the more substantial and permanent grandeur of genius? Neither has this an immunity. He who by force of will or of thought is great and overlooks thousands, has the responsibility of overlooking. With every influx of light comes new danger. Has he light? he must bear witness to the light, and always outrun that sympathy which gives him such keen satisfaction, by his fidelity to new revelations of the incessant soul. He must hate father and mother, wife and child. Has he all that the world loves and admires and covets?—he must cast behind him their admiration and afflict them by faithfulness to his truth, and become a byword and a hissing."

As we have said in a previous lesson: *The greater the capacity for joy, the greater the capacity for pain.* The swing of the pendulum of Rhythm between the two poles of the Opposites measures our relative happiness and unhappiness— comparative satisfaction or dissatisfaction. The capacity for pain is the symbol of advanced Evolution. The tramp *has* nothing and *desires* nothing beyond his immediate wants. His arc is small. Another will have much, but desires still more. His arc is large. Each, and both, fall a little short of what would constitute happiness for them. Query: which of the two is the happiest, or the most miserable? The answer of Compensation is: "They are equal in their degree of happiness and unhappiness—in satisfaction and misery. They are twin-brothers of equal heritage."

A financial panic which makes the millionaire writhe in fear and terror, passes entirely over the tramp. The more one has, the more afraid of losing it is he; and the harder the blow if the loss occurs. Many ancient philosophical writers insisted that the measure of pain and pleasure is equally distributed between persons—although the degrees of each vary greatly. The man who makes two dollars a day and is able to save a half-dollar out of it, is possibly happier and better satisfied than he who makes a hundred and spends half as much more. What would bring happiness to a savage would bring misery to a college professor. Happiness is comparative, and so is unhappiness. We find happiness where we least expect it—and unhappiness where it surprises us. Just as "to know all, is to forgive all"; so, to know all, is to understand the relativity of satisfaction and happiness. It is said that the "back is always made strong enough to bear the burden"—we do not assert this, as a fact, but we feel *that the back gets used to the burden*, and feels it not more than other backs feel lesser burdens. And while the proverb that "God tempers the wind to the shorn lamb" may not be scientifically correct, still it is true that *the shorn lamb becomes tempered to the wind*, and "gets used to it."

Clodd says: "The simplicity of the simplest forms has been their salvation. A high organization brings with it many disadvantages, for the more complex the structure the more liable is it to get out of gear. We cannot have highly convoluted brains and at the same time digestive organs simple and renewable like those of the sea-cucumber. Death is the price paid for complexity." And pain is the natural consequence and counterbalance of complexity in life, knowledge, and possessions.

Each one has his troubles and his joys. Each his pains and his pleasures. If we knew all the inside facts concerned with others' lives we would not be willing to exchange with them, *providing we had to live exactly their same lives*. Who would wish to exchange his personal life with that of another—taking all that goes with the other's, and giving up, completely, *all* that composes his own? Each man's "cross" is fitted exactly to his particular shoulders—and each man's "crown" is adjusted nicely upon his particular brow. It takes a philosophical mind to realize this—the tendency is to consider one's own lot the very worst of all—and the other man's lot much the better. The other man is probably thinking the same about your's. *Neither would exchange, if he knew the full facts of the case*— all the counterbalances and counterchecks. Each has his own "character," *and all that goes with it*. Each has his own arc of happiness and satisfaction—with their opposite poles. As the old Egyptian proverb ran: "'What will you have?' said the gods to man. '*Take it, and pay for it!*'"

And now, let us consider the third phase of the Law of Balance—the phase of Poise. Listen to the Aphorism:

Aphorism xxvi. Poise is Power. Poise results from Balance. Balance is secured by adjusting and maintaining the Centre between the Poles of the Pairs of Opposites. By Balanced Poise the Master neutralizes Polarity and Rhythm, by resolving them into Unity. In the Heart of the Storm is Peace. In the Centre of Life there is Poise and Power. Seek it ever, O Neophyte—for in it thou shalt find thy Self.

In this Aphorism is contained the seed-thought generated in the centuries of thought and experience of the Arcane Teachers. Do not pass it by because of its simplicity. Poised Balance is the aim and goal of the Arcane Initiates. It is the Secret of Mastery. There is always a Center of Everything. But the Center exists only because of the existence of the Circumference. There is always a Point or Poise between the Poles of every Pair of Opposites. But that Point exists only because the Extremes exist. And in the Central Point is always found the Power of the Whole Event or Thing. In the Center of Gravity of the Earth, one would be able to remain in a position of Perfect Poise, unsupported except by the Concentrated Gravity of the Whole Earth. So nicely Poised that a mere effort of the Will would exert sufficient energy to propel him in any desired direction. The Power of the Opposites are concentrated at the Central Point. There is all Power to be found—and *there* only. The axiom: "Action and Reaction are Equal" indicates a Central Point in which exists the True Lever which will move the Whole. At the Center one is enabled to *use* Action and Reaction without being subject to either. The Arcane Initiate strives to attain this state of Equilibrium and Absolute Poise. He yearns to master the art of traversing the Razor-edge Wire of Life, balancing himself perfectly, like the trained mental athlete that he is, by the Balancing Pole of the Opposites which he has firmly grasped. Pitting the Opposites against each other—neutralizing Pole by Pole—balancing Law by Law—the Master traverses the slender thread which separates the World of Desire from the World of Will.

Oh, Neophyte, in the Center of Life shalt thou indeed find Poise and Power. In the Heart of the Storm shalt thou find Peace. In the Center of the Cosmos shalt thou find thyself. He who finds the Center of Himself, finds the Center of the Cosmos. For, at the last, they are one.

BOOK TWO
THE ARCANE II.

THE ARCANE FORMULAS

Lesson I. Egohood.

In the "Arcane Lessons" you have seen that the individual is but a Centre of Consciousness and Force in the great Life Principle, Cosmic Will or Spirit. As Aphorism XII has informed you: "There is but One Life and not Many Lives. Separateness is but relative and partial—illusory—the creative fiction of the Cosmos... In the Cosmic Will there is but One Life in which, and by which, is manifested the Many."

You have also seen that Egohood is evolved and earned—not given as a universal birthright, or general natural right of the race. As Aphorism XIII has informed you: "The Ego is evolved from the Personal Self. Every living thing possesses a Personal Self, but, even among men, many fail to reach Egohood. Egohood is earned, not bestowed as an universal natural gift. Many personalities are born, but few Egos are evolved."

Egohood is the state of Realization of the Ego—the Perception and Realization of the I am. As an old English writer once said: "Whether we try to avoid it or not, we must face this reality some time—the reality of our own Egohood—that which makes us say 'I,' and in saying 'I' leads to the discovery of a new world."

The average person is surprised, incredulous and even indignant when he is informed that but very few of the race really have this *awareness* or consciousness of the I am within them. He will insist that *he* is fully aware of the existence of the "I," and cannot imagine that anyone can have the audacity to dispute the proposition. But a little self-examination will reveal the fact that he has but the first glimmering of Self-Consciousness, which is far from being the Consciousness of Egohood. We have no desire or intention of entering into an extended metaphysical inquiry in these pages, but we *must* point out to you what Egohood is *not*, as the first step toward showing you what it *is*, and how it may be acquired.

The very elementary life-forms have merely the consciousness of "something outside" evidenced in sensation or feeling. The atoms manifest a faint degree of awareness (consciousness) of other atoms, which is evidenced in attraction and repulsion.

There is in chemical affinity a higher degree of elementary consciousness. The crystals manifest a still higher degree in their activities of building-up form. The cell-forms of the lowest animal and plant life show an awareness of objects of food and of other forms which seek them for food—and consequently they move toward the first, and away from the second. Rising in the evolutionary scale we find constantly increasing degrees of consciousness. Among the higher animals, and the lower forms of men, we find what science has called "simple-consciousness," by which is indicated that *awareness* of outside objects, accompanied by a greater or lesser degree of reasoning regarding them. The dog, horse, and other higher animals give us a typical example of this form of consciousness, which degree is but little surpassed by the less developed of the human race, many of the latter not having advanced further in the scale. Simple-consciousness may be described as a state of *knowing, but not knowing that one knows*. It is a consciousness of outside things received through the senses, and also of the physical sensations arising in one's own body.

But, as man advanced in the scale there came to him the degree of consciousness which is known as "self-consciousness," in which the sense of "I" comes to him—he differentiates between the Self and the Not-Self, as he understands it. He not only *knows*, but he begins to *know that he knows*. He begins to understand that he has a "knowing machine" by means of which he knows, thinks and is consciousness. The mental gaze, in this stage, begins to turn itself *inward* as well as outward. But the majority of the race possess this self-consciousness to but a limited degree. As a leading psychologist has well said: "Many persons never have more than a misty idea of such a mental attitude. They take themselves for granted, and never turn the gaze inward." Self-consciousness, like simple-consciousness, has many degrees on its scale. One has but to study his fellow men in order to perceive these varying degrees. We cannot pause here to consider this stage in detail—our concern is with higher degrees.

In a general way, and in order that you may make the clear distinction between simple-consciousness and self-consciousness, we suggest that you think of the former as *an awareness of the outside world, and one's own physical being*, and of the latter *as an awareness of one's own mind*. Or, the former may be thought of as *physical consciousness*, and the latter as *mental consciousness*.

But, here and there among the multitude of men are evolved a few who have attained a higher stage of consciousness— the Ego-Consciousness, or consciousness of Egohood— which surpassing the physical-consciousness and the mental-consciousness, just alluded to, may be styled *spiritual consciousness*. For the Ego-Consciousness is really the consciousness of Spirit, in an elementary degree—there are many other and higher degrees.

Ego-Consciousness, or Realization of Egohood, is more than an awareness of the outside world, or of one's own body as distinct from the bodies of others and other things. It is more than even the awareness of one's own mind, even when this awareness is carried to a high degree of development. It is difficult to describe this plane of consciousness to those who have not attained it, but it may be stated as *an awareness of Individuality*, rather than *an awareness of Personality*.

Personality is but the *character* in which the One Life is playing a certain part. As we have said in The Arcane Lessons, the very word "person" is derived from the Greek word *persona*, meaning "a mask used by actors."

Your personality is merely the part in life you are playing—"the John Smith part of you." And, consequently, the awareness of Personality is merely an awareness or consciousness of your own personal character, *just as an actor is aware and conscious of the character of the play he is enacting*. If you can imagine the actor forgetting his real Self, and becoming so earnest and wrap in the play that he imagines that he really *is* Hamlet or Richard III, or Mephistopheles, you may gain a clearer idea of the state of consciousness of the man on the plane of Personal Consciousness. When he shakes off the illusion, and realizes that he is something more than the assumed character—when *you* awaken to the fact that you are something more than "John Smith,"—then the personality is seen to be in reality but an assumed character, or "mask used by actors."

The Consciousness of Individuality is an awareness by man that he is above the limits and character of Personality—that he is a Centre of Consciousness and Force in the One Cosmic Life.

This awareness must, however, be more than a mere *intellectual* acquiescence in the teaching to that effect, or an agreement with some teacher. Important as these steps are in approaching the realization, they are but foot-hills above which tower the mountains of the real Cosmic Knowing. The individual must *know* that he is an individual—just as he knows anything that he has experienced. For indeed, he must really *experience* the fact that he is an Ego-Centre in the Cosmic Life or Spirit. He must realize that *he is* more than body and mind—that he is, indeed, Spirit in Spirit. No mere intellectual acquiescence or understanding will supply the real experience of Egohood.

It is not necessary for one to have experienced Cosmic Consciousness—or the awareness of his identity with the Cosmic Spirit as a whole—to gain Egohood. This experience belongs to a higher stage. The Individual must, however, experience the realization that he is an Ego—a spiritual entity, before he attains Egohood. Many grow into this stage naturally and by slow and gradual steps—in fact all development must be along natural lines. One cannot be dragged or pulled up into this stage—one must grow into it naturally, as the plant develops and blooms into flower. But—and here is an important point, and one upon which depends the usefulness of these lessons—there are many who are ready and prepared to throw off the sheath of personality and to enter into the fuller life of Egohood, who are struggling with the confining bonds of Personality which they find hard to throw off. To these, and to these only, the methods and exercises, herein given, will appeal. If they appeal to *you*—if they attract you and you hunger to put them into effect—then know that *you* are ready for them, and ready to throw off the confining sheaths that are binding you and holding you back.

As we proceed, you will see that in this Realization of Egohood lies the Secret of Attainment—the Key of Power. Before you can exercise the Power of Spirit, you must realize that you *are* Spirit. Spirit is the Essence of the Cosmos. The Ego is a focal point or centre in that Essence.

Lesson II. Establishing the Ego I.

To "establish" is "to settle or fix firmly; to make steady, firm, or stable; to place upon a firm foundation; to ordain permanently and with authority;" etc. Therefore is this Formula—one of the oldest known to Occultism—called *establishing* the Ego. Its mastery imparts the sense and power of firm settlement and steady foundation of the consciousness of the Ego—the identification of the self with the Self.

The Arcane Teachers instruct the Neophyte that he must first of all develop this awareness of the Ego, by degrees, until at last the Ego-Consciousness may become the habitual and natural consciousness, at all times and under all conditions. Once firmly fixed, the Ego-Consciousness never leaves one. Once found, it becomes a Tower of Strength in which one may ever take refuge from the trials of the personal life—and from which one may safely defy the things of personality.

The first step of the Formula is that of acquiring a clear, distinct, positive and absolute realization that the Ego is *not* the body or physical organism, but is superior to and master of them. Even those students who have entered the plane of Mental-Consciousness require additional drilling in order to escape completely and fully from the bonds of the physical body. The following exercise is recommended for this purpose:

Exercise.

Let the Neophyte place himself in a quiet place, away from the disturbances and distracting influences of the outside world. Let him assume a position of rest, relaxing the tension from muscles and nerves.

Then, let him fix his attention upon his physical body; first the body as a whole, and then beginning at the feet let him move the attention upward until the whole body has been included in attention, step by step, until the brain is reached.

During this process the Neophyte will become aware, by degrees, that he is a Something inside of the body, viewing and considering the latter in all of its details, *instead of being identical with the body.* There will be found a dawning realization that the body is but the physical envelope or sheath in which the Ego dwells— or a garment which the Ego has assumed for the conveniences of physical life. This realization will not come all at once, but will gradually dawn upon and in the consciousness, increasing by practice. When a degree of proficiency and realization of this stage has been acquired, then may the Neophyte proceed to the next stage, as follows:

Let the Neophyte now concentrate his attention upon his feet, until he is able to regard them as but tools or instruments whereby the Ego may walk in physical form. Then let him, using his imagination, realize that even if his feet were not there, attached to the body, the Ego would still be fully existent and in being—that, although deprived of useful tools, the Ego would *still be the Ego*, unimpaired and undisturbed in its real being.

Then bring the entire lower limbs into attention, and after fixing them firmly in consciousness, let the Neophyte realize that these limbs are but instruments for physical progress—useful and important, but not indispensable to the being and reality of the Ego. Let him see that if these limbs were not there that the Ego would still *be*, complete and fully existent.

Then, let the Neophyte bring into attention the pelvic organs (the reproductive organism, etc.) and, after realizing their uses and purposes—important to physical life—let him realize that the integrity and being of the Ego is in no way dependent upon them. Let him, in imagination, separate himself from them in consciousness, and thus realize that even if that part of the body were removed, and missing, nevertheless the Ego would be fully existent in its entirety of being.

Then let the Neophyte, in a similar manner, consider the abdominal organs—the stomach, liver, etc.—and while realizing their value and utility in physical life, let him also realize that they, too, are but physical *instruments* of the Ego for certain purposes, and that the Ego would dwell unimpaired in being, existence and reality, were they absent.

Then let the Neophyte likewise consider the chest organs, the lungs, etc., and while respecting and realizing their usefulness and wonderful adaptability to purpose, also realize that the Ego would be full existent and real even if these organs or parts of the body were absent.

Then let the Neophyte pass on to the consideration of the head, with its various organs of sense; its brain centres and convolutions—the machinery of thought, and then realize that although it would be impossible to live as a physical being in the body without these organs, still if they were absent the Ego would still be the Ego—complete, existent, in reality, with integrity unimpaired.

Then let the Neophyte again consider the whole body, as one organism—the wonderful instrument of the Ego, adapted for physical life. But let him fully realize that this wonderful machinery is but *a created machine* in and through which the Ego manifests physical life and activity. And, that the Ego is above, independent of and apart from the physical body, in the true sense—for it may dwell apart from, and out of the body.

After performing these mental exercises, throw the mind into and over the entire body and into and through all of its parts— the purpose of this concluding process being to re-energize the physical organism which has, in a measure, become devitalized during the analytical process. You will find that you will be able to re-charge the body with vitality and make it stronger and more virile than it was before the exercise, after you once realized that it is but an instrument, or machine, which is used by and directed by the Ego. The realization of the Mastery of the Body by the Ego brings with it a new power of energizing and vitalizing the body or any part thereof.

Throwing the attention to parts of the body, after this realization has been gained, tends to direct to the particular parts an increased supply of Vril or Vital Energy.

After having mastered the above exercise to a satisfactory degree, let the Neophyte pass on to the following exercise:

Exercise.

Let the Neophyte, in imagination, leave the physical body and gaze upon the latter. A little mental practice will enable one to do this in imagination, thus bringing fully to the mind the realization that it is possible for the Ego to leave the body and dwell apart from it. When the mind has once grasped this possibility, the body will ever after be recognized as merely a physical machine, sheath or covering, of the Ego—and one will never again commit the folly of identifying the "I" with the physical body.

To those who may object that this is merely an exercise of the imagination, proving nothing, for the reason that "one may imagine *anything*," we suggest the trial of the old Occult Test whereby the Neophyte was instructed to try to imagine himself as *dead*. A trial will show that this is impossible—all that can be imagined in this direction is that the *physical* body is dead, while the soul either (1) stands apart, fully alive, viewing the body; or else (2) inhabits the dead body—in either case it being the physical body alone which is dead, the Ego being always alive.

Then let the Neophyte imagine himself as leaving behind his physical body, until, as Holmes says: "...Thou at length are free, leaving thine outgrown shell by life's unresting sea." Let him then imagine himself as occupying other and different bodies, one at a time, in different phases of life and condition, in different ages, etc. This will bring about a realization that the Ego is something higher and independent of the particular physical shell or machine that it is now using, and which it may have at one time considered identical with itself. Then will the particular body occupied seem, in reality, "*my body*," instead of "I," or "Me."

The Neophyte is cautioned against learning to despise his body when he realizes that it is not his "self." The body is to be respected and well cared for, for it is a necessary instrument for expression at this period of the evolution of the Ego. Do not make the mistake of so many who have grasped half-truths, and who *despise* their bodies. This is a great mistake, and we would warn all Neophytes against it. The physical body is the bridge which is carrying you over a wild stream—do not undervalue it—treat it well, with loving regard and care. The physical body is the Temple of the Spirit—make it a worthy one. Keep it clean and in good condition. Let it be a worthy dwelling place of the Most High.

Lesson III. Establishing the Ego II.

The practice of the exercises indicated by the Formulas described in the preceding lesson, if carefully and faithfully practiced, will give to the Neophyte a new sense of existence. He will realize by actual mental experience that he—the Ego—is an entity having its existence on a plane higher than that of the physical body, and superior to the latter. He will also experience a realization of the power of mastery over the physical body, which he may employ in the direction of mentally treating the latter for physical wrong functioning, weakness, or irregularities of any and all kinds. With a little practice he will be able to make his physical body a most responsive instrument of his mind and will, and may build it up and strengthen it as he may desire. This power, once acquired, will also enable him to treat the physical bodies of others to excellent advantage. When the Neophyte actually realizes that he is independent of, and superior to, the physical body, he will realize that he has the power to command his physical functions, and those of others who have not attained the realization.

But let not the Neophyte make the natural mistake at this point, of considering that he has escaped the bonds of Personality—for he has not. The Arcane Teachers first free their Neophytes from the trammels and retarding influences of the physical body, and in thus doing build up a still higher sense of Personality. Later, this higher sheath is, in turn, discarded, and the Ego focalizes upon its spiritual nature—its individuality. But the step of building up the incorporeal higher Personality must be attained before the next higher is possible. There O Neophyte, be not in too much haste to pass on to the next step. Master each step as you proceed—thus do you rise naturally and easily on the Ladder of Attainment.

Following the exercises indicated in the preceding lesson, the Neophyte may now proceed with the work of Establishing the Ego, in its first stages, as follows:

Exercise.

Placing himself in a position and condition of ease and repose, let the Neophyte meditate on the incidents of Incorporeality, or Life independent of the Physical Body. Thinking of oneself as a physical being, one naturally and properly takes into account the incidents of corporeality or life in the body. For instance, he realizes that he may be hurt by fire, water, earth, air or ether. He may be burned by fire, drowned by water, smothered or bruised by earth, swept away by air, or injured by ethereal vibrations such as electricity, etc. And, again, he may be wounded, meet with physical accidents, laid low by sickness, etc. These are the incidents of Corporeal Life.

But, in meditation, by using the imagination intelligently, he is brought to a realization that none of these incidents are in effect upon the plane of the Incorporeal Life. Meditation and intelligent imagination will show the Neophyte that in his Astral Body he might pass through fire unscathed— through water untouched—through earth without hurt or interference—through air without being swept off his feet— through the ether without regard to ethereal vibrations. None of these things of the physical plane have any effect upon the Astral Body, or disembodied Ego. In some of the ancient occult initiatory rites the Neophyte was taken out of his physical body, and in his Astral form was bidden to plunge himself in the flames of the hottest fiery furnace; to throw himself from the highest precipice; to drop into a bottomless lake. Not realizing that these things could not affect him in his Astral form, and being bound up with the memory of the Corporeal Life, the Neophyte would often shrink from the tests. But after being encouraged by example and precept he would submit to the test, joyfully, with a laugh on his lips, as he realized that to him in his Astral form these corporeal things were nonexistent— mere dreams of the physical plane.

Of course the actual experience in the Astral is far more convincing than is the mere realization of the truth in meditation, but the latter must not be despised for it gives one an intuitive realization of the truth, which, once attained, tends to destroy fear and to impart a new sense of courage, invincibility and invulnerability and mastery, which permeates the entire being and causes one to radiate power and strength.

Likewise will come the realization that the Ego, in itself, is incapable of hurt, harm, wounds, or sickness. These things belong to the Corporeal Life, and have naught to do with the Higher Self.

The Neophyte is enjoined to persevere and practice until he gains the *actual experience* and recognition that his Higher Self—his Real Self—is superior to all the incidents and accidents of the Corporeal Life, and that let come what will to his physical covering he, *himself*, is unhurt, whole, untouched, undisturbed.

An old Arcane Teacher, over two thousand years ago, was once told that the world was coming to an end. "Well, what is that to me!" he replied, resuming his study. He realized fully his invincibility. A similar tale is told of Emerson, who was halted in the street by an excited Millerite, who informed him, in strained tones: "Mr. Emerson, the world will be destroyed in ten days!" "Well, *what of it?*" replied Emerson, calmly, "I don't see but what we shall get along just as well without it."

The Nineteenth Century Transcendentalist voiced the truth as clearly as did his predecessor in Ancient Greece. The sense and realization must be experienced before it can be understood. It may be realized by practicing the Formulas, as given herein.

The next step indicated by the Formulas, is that of Focalizing the Consciousness on the Ego. This is still within the realm of Personality, but on a very high plane of that realm—a plane which gradually blends into the higher plane of Individuality. It consists of bringing about an acute realization of one's existence as a Centre of Consciousness and Force. It tends to gather up the dissipated sense of personal existence, and bringing it to a focal point, into vivid and actual conscious realization, preparatory to it being transmuted into the higher sense of individual existence. The following exercise will tend to bring about the desired realization:

Exercise.

Let the Neophyte place himself in a position, and condition, of rest and calm. Let him then meditate upon the great Ocean of Life in which the individual entities are but focal Centres of Consciousness and Force. Let him picture himself, in imagination, as being an actual Centre, with all the universe revolving around him. Let him see himself as the pivot around which the universe moves—the Central Sun around which the infinite world and planets circle in their cosmic flight. Let him feel himself to be the Focal Centre of the Cosmos. And this is indeed, in accordance with the centuries old occult axiom which informs us that "The Cosmos is infinite—its circumference is nowhere—its centre is everywhere." Let the Neophyte lose all thought of the outside world, in this meditation,—let him regard it as totally unmanifest if he likes—but see himself in Actual Existence and in Full Power. Let him realize "I am" to the fullest extent of his power of imagination and conception.

A student of the Arcane Lessons has written us of his experience in this stage of Realization. We quote from his letter, for it affords a typical instance of the phenomenon of the Establishing the Ego-Centre. He says: "On first reading, the Arcane Lessons appeared to 'wipe out' my 'I,' and to cause it to disappear within the One Life when it resolved itself into the Infinity of Nothingness, at the end of the Cosmic Day. Right here, I began to 'sit up and take notice,' with the result that my 'I' in a fierce effort to preserve itself from going to sleep, shone with such fierceness, clearness, and determination, that all was an Infinity of Nothingness right then. *There was nothing remaining but just 'I.'* Then I fully understood how the One Life could go to rest at the end of the Cosmic Day, and how 'I' would be the awful *lone* witness of its rest. I had made the separation of the One Life and the Real Life, or distinguished the Manifested Life from the Unmanifest." We quote this testimony because it brings out several steps in the evolution of the "I am" conception.

This student passed through the several stages at one leap—attaining in rapid succession the realization of the Centre, and then, immediately following, the realization of the impersonal or Individual Ego, or Real Self, this latter stage forming the subject of our next lesson. The now familiar occult statement of "I am!" should be used freely in practicing these exercises, for it tends to bring out the actual realization of Real Egohood which is the aim and goal of the Formulas. The statement has been used by the Arcane Teachers, and other advanced Occultists in all lands, for thousands of years. Its recent use is but a revival of the ancient initiatory exercises and rites. It is a tremendous Statement of Being—and should be used reverently and with awe.

Lesson IV. Establishing the Ego III.

In the preceding lessons we have directed your attention to the process of mentally freeing oneself from the restrictions imposed by the illusory identification of the Self or Ego with the physical body—the Corporeal Self. If the Neophyte has caught the spirit of the Formulas, and has put the same into practice, he will have at least evolved into a partial consciousness or realization of the Incorporeal Self.

But even this is but the first step toward Freedom and Attainment. Even with the highest conception of the Incorporeal Self, when the latter is bound by the illusion of Personality, one fails to realize his true Egohood. Only when the bonds of Personality are loosened, does the Ego begin to realize its true nature.

Just as one is bound by the illusion of the corporeal nature of the "I," so is it further bound—and even more closely bound— by the illusion of the *personal* nature of the Ego. The Ego is not only more, and greater, than the physical body it uses—but it is also more, and greater, than that part of the mind, consisting of a series of inherited or acquired impressions which constitutes the "Me." There is a great difference between the "Me and the I." *The "Me" is the individual as he thinks he is*—a bundle of prejudices, tastes, ties, etc. *The "I" is the Individual as he is in reality*—free from mental ties of all kinds. The "Me" is the character being played by the Ego—the "John Smith" part of him. The "I" is the real player of the part. It is often very difficult for one to disentangle and free himself from the overwhelming force of Personality, so completely is the average person self-hypnotized and race-hypnotized with the "John Smith" idea.

The Arcane Teachers have several Formulas for unloosening the bonds of Personality. Let us consider them.

Let the Neophyte place himself in a position, and condition, of restful, calm repose. Then let him take mental stock of himself. Let him ask himself the question: "What am I?" He will find, upon self-examination, that he considers himself to be a certain person—"John Smith," for instance, "aged 45, grocer, of Cincinnati, Ohio." This "John Smith" has a "character" of his own, which he supposes to be *himself*. Laying aside the illusion of the appearance, shape, form, etc., of the body, he will still find that he has decided personal characteristics. He *likes* certain things—he *hates* certain others. He is tied tight by his likes and dislikes, his loves and hates, his tendencies, his general "nature" and "characteristics" in short. He imagines that these things are *himself*, and that if they were taken away from him, he would cease to exist.

Then let him proceed as he did when divorcing himself from the illusion of the Corporeal Self. Let him set aside first one like, and then another—first one hate, and then another. Let him, in imagination, visualize himself as being divested of first one "characteristic" and then another. As the process continues, the Neophyte will find, much to his surprise, that notwithstanding that his most cherished and firmly rooted "characteristics" are sheared away from him, he himself remains. He finds that when all his mental feelings, as well as the objects thereof, are removed from his mental vision, he, himself, remains. He will find a Something remaining that is back of, underneath, and at the centre of all these "feelings" and "characteristics," and which persists in full vigor when they have been stripped away from him.

Then let him, mentally, in imagination, see himself as *acting out other characters*. He will find that he is able to play out Hamlet, Richard III, Mephistopheles, Micawber, and a host of other characters, as well as he has been playing the old "John Smith" part, which he has been imagining was Himself. He will then see that just as the body was but an instrument and covering, so is this habitual "character" but an instrument and mental covering—useful but not essential to his being—something that can be put on, and taken off—something that could be exchanged without affecting the "I." He will realize that this "character" is but his "Me"—and that he may have other "Me's" at will. But the "I" remains the same in each case.

But, try as he may, he will never be able to shake off or discard the "I." He will find that this "I" is unchangeable, and cannot be gotten rid of—for it is Himself, his Real Self. He will find this same "I" always at the centre of every "character" he assumes— always behind every mask he places before him. He will find that it will always be the same old "I," of which he can always, and *must* always, say "I am." No one can truthfully assert of his Real Self, "I am not." Such a statement is always a lie upon the face of Truth. One may say "I am not *this*, or I am not *that*"—but he can never say of that Central "I," that it is *not*.

This "I" is always the Actor—the Doer—the Seer—the Thinker. It is always the Centre Divest it of every characteristic and there will always remain that Something that is.

This "I" is absolutely subjective, or inner—all else is objective, or outer, to it. It cannot be classified with any mental state— for all mental states are objective to it. It cannot be described in terms of objective consciousness, for these terms denote things subordinate to it. We are conscious of it, not through any channel of sense. or feeling,—it impresses itself upon us directly. We cannot separate ourselves from it—for it is the Self, itself. We cannot stand off and examine it, nor set it off for examination—for where *it* is so must *we* be, for the two are one. It is never objective to anything else in us— but everything else in us is objective to *it*. It may, in our ignorance, be influenced and moved by our feelings, emotions, etc.—but when we know the Truth it turns on these feelings and emotions, and changes, kills, or creates them. It is at the basis of all activities—it is identical with the will.

Divorce this "I" of all its mental "characteristics," feelings and emotions—and instead of seeming weakened, it is increased in strength. It then appears as untrammeled, and unrestricted will. It gives and can give, but two reports of itself: (1) it must always, and does always say of itself: "I am"; (2) it must always say, and does always say, of itself: "I do." This is all. This is what the "I" is— the Something that is, and Something that does. All the rest of the mental furniture belongs to the "Me," and is changeable, inconstant, and shifting. The "I" is always the same—there is nothing else for it to be.

By practicing this "mental stock-taking," and self-examination, the Neophyte will soon be able to at least partially divorce his "I" from his "Me"—at least he will be able to do so in imagination, sufficiently to testify to the different elements of the two. Other Formulas, in this book will aid him in this attainment. For this is the Centre and Heart of all Attainment. It is the one thing, which, when found, gives us the key to all the rest.

The following exercise is also taught by the Arcane Teachers and other advanced Occultists. In connection with the others given in this book, it will serve to loosen the bonds and ties of Personality, and enable the Neophyte to spread the Wings of the Self, and soar in the free ether of Individuality.

Exercise.

Let the Neophyte place himself in a position and condition of calm, restful repose. Then let him meditate upon his own identity, as distinguished from the outside objective world. Let him reach mentally into the very centre of his being—the inner recesses of his soul, until he meets his Real Self face-to-face. Let him, in this meditation, repeat softly to himself *his own name*— that is, the name which he applies to himself at times when he thinks of himself in the third person. Or, else, his favorite "short name" or familiar "nickname," such as "Jim," or "Will," or "Jack," etc.—in short, the name which he most familiarly identifies with himself. Let him repeat this name over and over again, softly, to himself, throwing into it his earnest attention *as if in that name, or word, were contained the Secret of His Existence*. In many cases the Neophyte will find that he is lifted up to a higher plane of being or consciousness, in which he sees more clearly the Light Within, and hears a few strains from the great Song of Life. If the experiment succeeds, he will realize, as never before, the reality of the "I" the Secret of the Ego.

Rudyard Kipling, in his great story of Hindu life, entitled "*Kim,*" speaks of this practice familiar among Oriental people. He describes his hero, "*Kim,*" attempting to gain this state of consciousness. We quote from this book, as follows:

"A very few white people, but many Asiatics, can throw themselves unto a mazement, as it were, by repeating their own names over and over again to themselves, letting the mind go free upon speculation as to what is called personal identity.....

"'Who is Kim-Kim-Kim?'

"He squatted in a corner of the clanging waiting-room, rapt from all other thoughts, hands folded in lap, and pupils contracted to pin-points. In a moment—in another half-second—he felt that he would arrive at the solution of the tremendous puzzle, but here, as always happens, his mind dropped away from those heights with the rush of a wounded bird, and passing his hand before his eyes, he shook his head.

"A long-haired Hindu *bairagi* (holy-man) who had just bought a ticket, halted before him at that moment, and stared intently. 'I also have lost it,' he said sadly. 'It is one of the gates of the Way.'

"'What is thy talk?' said Kim, abashed.

"'Thou wast wondering there in thy spirit what manner of thing thy soul might be. ... I know. Who should know but I?'"

Tennyson, the great English poet, in his letters to and conversations with his intimate friends and relatives, testified to having experiences of this kind, occasioned by repeating his name to himself in a manner resembling the practice of the ancient occultists, and of the Hindus of to-day, as mentioned in "*Kim*." He stated that he was lifted into another world in which he was given a positive assurance of his spiritual nature and immortality—a condition in which the fear of death became laughable. He also stated the same idea in the following verses:

> "And more, my son, for more than once when I Sat all alone, *revolving in myself*
>
> *That word which is the symbol of myself,*
>
> The mortal symbol of the self was loosed,
>
> And passed into the Nameless, as a cloud
>
> Melts into Heaven. I touched my limbs, the limbs

Were strange, not mine—and yet no shadow of doubt, But utter clearness, and through loss of Self

The gain of such large life as matched with ours

Were Sun to spark, unshadowable in words,

Themselves but shadows of a shadow-world."

Lesson V. Will-Focalization

The Neophyte who has advanced to the stage in which, in the ancient Occult parlance, he "has *found himself*," has discovered that his Real Self is something far different from anything that he ever had imagined it to be. Instead of being an entity with distinctly marked characteristics and personal peculiarities, he discovers that it is a something the *nature* of which can be stated only in the sense of Potentiality. We do not mean for a moment that the Ego is existent only in a potential sense—on the contrary, it is actually existent in the most extreme and positive sense. In fact, its existent being is endowed with such a degree of actuality that all else seems to fade into relative non-existence. There is no question of "I Am Not" about the Ego—it is first, last and always a Something of which the positive "I am" can, and must be, asserted. It is only when we come to examine the nature, attributes and qualities of this "I am" Ego, that we are forced to use the terms of Potentiality instead of actuality. Let us consider this a little further, for in its understanding lies the solution of many occult paradoxes.

In the first place, if we are keen analysts, and understand the precise terms of philosophical psychology, we will see that the Formulas for Establishing the Ego, and the practice of the exercises arising therefrom, have divorced from the Ego the usual attributes, characteristics and personal peculiarities which are popularly supposed to belong to, and to be inseparably connected with it. Setting aside as the "Not I" first one feeling and then another; first one emotion and then another; first one characteristic and then another; first one personal peculiarity and then another; and placing them in turn in the "Not I" category—the Neophyte finds that after he has stripped the Ego of all the attributes of Personality, there is still a

Something left—an irreducible element—an insoluble residuum—a *surd*, or something which while actually existent yet is incapable of being described, expressed or designated by rational terms—a final algebraical x, or Unknown Ultimate Element. As to the existence of this Unknown Element, or Ego, there is no doubt in the Occult Teachings, differ as the modern philosophies may about the matter—moreover, it is a matter which may be determined by the conscious experience of anyone who will practice the exercises of the Formulas, in the proper way. The "I am" will always be found at the centre of the self, and will always respond "I *Am!*"

But when we attempt to *describe* this Ultimate "I"—when we attempt to endow it with attributes, qualities, or peculiarities, then do we find ourselves at sea, for these things all belong to the plane of Personality, while the "I" transcends Personality, and cannot be expressed or designated in the terms of the latter. But, nevertheless there is found a way of identifying the "I." Philosophical psychology, both occult and popular—both esoteric and exoteric—gives us a term whereby we may discuss and consider the "I," or Ultimate Element of Self. This "I," which we have stated as the final algebraical x, or unknown ultimate element of the Self, is found to be identical with the highest philosophical and psychological conception of what has been called the *Will*. Thus the x equals The Will. Let us then try to understand the "I" by considering what the highest human thought reports regarding the Will. By studying the *symbol* we may understand the *reality*.

Brushing aside as unworthy the popular conception of the

Will, we find that the highest philosophical and psychological thought uses the term "The Will" to designate the underlying Essence of Being—the fundamental life-mind-spirit principle of the Self. The Ancient Greek Philosophers so used the term; the original Buddhist philosophy so employs it; we find it so used by eminent thinkers all through the history of philosophical thought; Schopenhauer, Nietzsche and Wundt used the term in this sense. The Arcane Teachers identified the Principle of Will with Spirit—the Essence—the "beingness" of Being. The Will is that Essence or Spirit, in the Cosmos and in the individual, which is ever moving, changing its manifestations, flowing, evolving, proceeding, desiring, attaining, seeking, accomplishing. It contains within itself the potentiality of

Everything, but it itself cannot be said to be any of the things it manifests.

Prof. William Sturgis Bigelow, in his lecture on "Buddhism and Immortality," delivered in Harvard University, 1908, (Published by Houghton Mifflin Company, New York), beautifully states the esoteric conception of Will, in describing the Buddhist conception of life and immortality. We take great pleasure in calling your attention to the following quotations from the said lecture. Prof. Bigelow says:

"We are all, as we familiarly say, conscious of our own existence. Under this statement we habitually include, in more or less confusion, several distinct elements. First, the existence of our material bodies as objects of sensory perception. ... Second, of certain sensations, pleasurable or painful, originating not outside but inside the body itself. Third, of certain disturbances... that we classify as passions or emotions. Fourth, of what we call aptitudes and their opposites. Fifth, of desires or inclinations and their opposites. Lastly, of something of a wholly different character, consciously closer to the centre than anything else, and differing from the other forms in being the only form of consciousness to which we are not passive. This we call Will.

We say, I feel sensation, pain or emotion; but we never say, I feel my Will. It is always subjective and active. ... This Will is a part of the normal consciousness of each one of you, yet it is neither a part of sensation nor emotion, but, on the contrary, is capable of dominating both. What is it? Ask your own consciousness. Sensations originate outside and inside the body; emotions, inside. But the Will is deeper than either, and they are both objective to it. We cannot classify it with anything else. We cannot describe it in terms of any other form of consciousness. We are conscious through our bodies and of our bodies, but the consciousness of the Will is direct. We cannot separate ourselves from it. We cannot stand off and examine it. We cannot modify it by anything else. It itself modifies everything within its scope. Other forms of consciousness are objective to it, but it is never objective to them. It may be overpowered by sensations, emotions, or passions, through its own weakness or their strength. It often is. But its attitude towards them, whether resisting or directing them, is always essentially and necessarily active. It exists in no other form than the subjective form. It is inconceivable in any other form.

If it is not active, it is not Will. There is nothing in our consciousness deeper. It underlies and overlies and permeates all other forms, and, moreover,—what is of immeasurably more importance,—it can if need be, *create them*. ... Will is the assertion of a form of consciousness from the centre outward. When this is opposed by another form of consciousness, intruding from the circumference inward, we recognize a hindrance to the free action of the Will, and we talk of 'necessity.' But such intrusive forms ... come from or through ... the material, separate personality. If it were not for these the Will would act freely. The separate personal consciousness with its offshoots is, therefore, the only obstacle to complete freedom of the Will. Complete freedom of the Will is complete freedom of consciousness, and complete freedom of consciousness from the habitual and empirical limitations of personality is complete freedom of the Will. The terms are interchangeable. The only Will that is not free is the *personal* Will. Descartes said. 'I think, therefore, I am.' It is an imperfect formula at best, but it would have been a better statement... had he said, 'I Will, therefore I am'"

Thus do we find that the Ego, or "I" is, in its last possible human analysis, Will. And, thus do we find that Will is in the nature of Potential Infinite-Manifestation of All-Activity—the Essential Beingness of all Being—the Plastic Essence which may mould itself into any and all forms—the Essence of Activity which may manifest how and as it pleases, under The Law always.

As we said in Lesson XII, of The Arcane Teaching: Running back from cause to prior cause, and to still more remote precedent causes of his desires, the Individual finds himself at last confronting the Cosmic Will. Retracing his path back to the present, he finds himself confronting his Personal Will which is moved by Desire. In other words, he finds a Chain of Desire extending from the Cosmic Will to the Personal Will—a chain of countless links, having a beginning in Will, and ending in Will— an Endless Chain, because it is a Circle. Thereupon he learns the first lesson of the Arcane Secret of the Excluded Middle, and thenceforth strives to realize *the union of the two ends of Will*. From the realization of this Union arises the Individual Will— the Positive Will of the Ego. In this process the Law of Cause and Effect is not violated, but Will is made the Cause of

Will— the Cause and Effect merge. When this is attained—then does Man indeed become the Master!

Lesson VI. The Excluded Middle.

In closing the preceding lesson, we referred to the Secret of the Excluded Middle. This is one of the most ancient and fundamental formulas of the Secret Doctrine or Arcane Teaching of the ancient occult fraternities. It was regarded as the Keystone of the Mystic Arch. Those who grasp the inner spirit of this Secret are, as the Aphorism informs us, "well on the road to Mastery." Let us refer you to Aphorism XX, at this place.

The Aphorism informs us that: "When a man attains Individuality-Egohood-he enters upon the plane of Will, and rises above the plane of Desire. Desire and Will are the opposite poles of the same principle—the Centre of Balance being Reason. On the plane of Will, though one remains under Law, yet he may learn to use Law instead of remaining passive to it.

He may learn to oppose Law to laws. He may learn to create Desire by Will. Furthermore—and this is the greatest of all—he may learn to Will to Will. He may learn to complete the Circle of Will. He may learn the Secret of the Excluded Middle. When this last Secret is learned, man is well on the road to Mastery." We have seen, in the Arcane Teaching, that from the Cosmic Will, which is the Principle of Will, the Cosmos has been evolved. We have seen how this evolution has progressed under the Law of Orderly Trend and Logical Sequence, the active principle of which has been Desire, which is but the negative pole of Will. We have seen that there is an unbroken chain of Sequence extending from the Cosmic Will to the "I" which latter is but a focalized Centre of Will in the great Cosmic Will.

At the personal or individual end of this unbroken chain, we find the "I" or Individual Will But we find that this Individual Will is conditioned, restricted, bound and hampered by the accumulated sheath of evolutionary growth, to the extent of even doubting its own identity or nature. The idea of separateness has crept in, and the "I" fails to realize that it is identical in nature and substance with the great Cosmic Will, in which it is a Centre or Focal Point. So entangled is it in the bonds of Personality—so deluded by the illusions of the "John Smith" nature and characteristics; that it imagines itself to be a thing apart. It feels the personal conscious on all sides, and actually imagines that it, the "I," *is* really this bundle of mental states, impressions and ideas that belong to "John Smith." It has exchanged its Cosmic Birthright for the humble Mess of Pottage of Personality.

The Hindus tell a tale of one of the great gods—Indra—who, following a caprice, incarcerated himself in the body of a pig. He took unto himself a pig mate, and raised a brood of little pigs. He lost all sense of his own identity, and was thoroughly hypnotized with the idea that he *was* a pig. The fellow-gods, grieved at his illusion and his pitiful state, called upon him to come out of the pig-state, telling him that he was a great god and not a swinish creature wallowing in the mud. He grunted out a denial, saying: "I am a *pig*, not a *god*—let me alone!" They persisted, and he continued to repel them. They killed his pig-mate, and his little pigs, but he squealed out his sorrow and rage, and tried to destroy the gods in his wrath. Finally they killed his pig-body, as a last resort, and lo! Indra, the god, stepped forth in all his glorious power, and laughed in astonishment when he realized the extent and degree of his late illusion." By this parable, the Hindu teachers impress upon their *chelas* the fact of their Real Self.

A well-known occult writer. in her little compilation of the ancient teachings, entitled "Light on the Path," says: "Seek in the heart the source of evil (the illusion of Personality) and expunge it. It lives fruitfully in the heart of the devoted disciple, as well as in the heart of the man of desire. Only the strong can kill it out. The weak must wait for its growth, its fruition, its death. And it is a plant that lives and increases throughout the ages. It flowers when man has accumulated unto himself innumerable existences. He who will enter upon this path of power must tear this thing out of his heart. And then his heart will bleed, and the whole life of the man seem to be utterly dissolved. This ordeal must be endured; it may come at the first step of the perilous ladder which leads to the path of life; it may not come until the last. But, O disciple! remember that it has to be endured, and fasten the energies of your soul upon the task. Live neither in the present nor the future, but in the eternal. This giant weed cannot flourish there; this blot upon existence is wiped out by the very atmosphere of eternal thought. ... Each man is to himself absolutely the way, the truth, and life. But he is only so when he grasps his whole individuality (personality) firmly, and, by the force of his awakened spiritual Will, recognizes this individuality (personality) as not himself, but that thing which he has with pain created for his own use, and by means of which he purposes, as his growth slowly develops his intelligence, to reach to that life beyond individuality (personality). ... Seek it by making the profound obeisance of the soul to the dim star that burns within. Steadily, as you watch and worship, its light will grow stronger. Then you may know you have found the beginning of the way. And when you have found the end, its light will suddenly become the infinite light."

The Paraphernalia, of Personality is the "Middle"—the connecting links between the Cosmic Will and the Individual Will—the One Being and the "I." By excluding it, the "I" is merged in consciousness with the Cosmos—he attains Cosmic Consciousness. But this *exclusion* is only relative—it is merely an exclusion in consciousness, but a realization that this middle is fictitious and illusory in reality. When it is so regarded, then the "I" while remaining an individual, yet realizes its real nature and identity with the Cosmic Will, and is able to act according to the degree and strength of the recognition. This process of exclusion is slow and gradual—it begins with an intellectual conception of the Truth, which then gradually evolves into a greater and broader experience and realization as the Neophyte progresses along The Path of Attainment.

By excluding the Middle or Personality, it is not meant that the Individual should cease using his personal instruments of expression and life. On the contrary, *he only then begins to use them*. For, previous to this realization, the things of Personality *have used him*, instead of he *using them*. As the old occult Aphorism informs us: "All things are good for the Individual to use—but none of them are good enough to *use the Individual*. The advanced occultist first learns to set aside the things of

Personality—learns to do without them—learns that he does not need them to remain "I." Then, having freed himself, mentally, from them, he returns and uses them, intelligently and properly, and positively. This the difference between Mastery and Slavery. As Carpenter, the English poet, sings:

"To die—for this into the world you came.

Yes, to abandon more than you ever conceived as possible:

All ideals, plans—even the very best and most unselfish—all hopes and desires, ...

Modes of life, habits, predelictions, preferences, superiorities, weaknesses, indulgences, ...

in one word: To die—— For this into the world you came.

All to be abandoned, and when they have been finally abandoned,

Then to return to be used—and then only to be rightly used, to be free and open for ever.

Be not torn by desire: ...

Slowly and resolutely—as a fly cleans its legs of the honey in which it has been caught——

So remove thou, if it only be for a time, every particle which sullies the brightness of thy mind

Return into thyself-content to give, but asking no one, asking nothing;

In the calm light of His splendor who fills all the universe, the imperishable indestructible of ages,

Dwell thou—as thou canst dwell—contented. ... In place all are to be used.

Yet in using be not entangled in them; for then already are they bad, and will cause thee suffering.

When thy body—as needs must happen at times—is carried along on the wind of passion, say not thou, 'I desire this or that';

For the 'I' neither desires nor fears anything, but is free and in everlasting glory, dwelling in heaven and pouring out joy like the sun on all sides.

Let not that precious thing by any confusion be drawn down and entangled in the world of opposites, and of Death and suffering.

For as a light-house beam sweeps with incredible speed over sea and land, yet the lamp itself moves not at all,

So while thy body of desire is (and must be by the law of its nature) incessantly in motion in the world of suffering, the 'I' high up above is fixed in heaven.

Therefore I say let no confusion cloud thy mind about this matter;

But ever when desire knocks at thy door,

Though thou grant it admission and entreat it hospitably, as in duty bound,

Fence it yet gently off from thy true self,

Lest it tear and rend thee."

The Formulas already given the Neophyte, in connection with the intellectual perception of the Truth of the "I," and the Secret of the Excluded Middle, as well as the Formulas to follow, will bring about a gradual unfoldment of the realization of Cosmic Consciousness, and Recognition of the Identity of the "I" with the Cosmic Will. The following exercise, and others akin to it, will aid the Neophyte in unfolding into this consciousness.

Exercise.

The Neophyte, placing himself in a restful, calm, peaceful position and condition, should then *meditate* upon the great Cosmic Will, Essence, or Spirit. He should picture it as a great Ocean of

Spirit, upon which and in which he rests as an Established Focal Point or Centre. He should picture the resistless force and power of this great Ocean of Spirit, and feel its waves and movements. He should realize that its thrill is perceptible in his inner being, and that in every way he is *of* it, and *in* it. Realize that you are Spirit (Will) and nothing but Spirit (Will). Realize that there is no real separation between you and the great Ocean of Spirit— and that there can be no such separation. In your meditation, mentally wipe out the paraphernalia of Personality—Exclude the Middle of Personality and let Spirit join Spirit—Will join Will. Realize that you are a Centre of Force in the great Ocean of Will—a channel for the expression of as much Cosmic Will as your growth and capacity will allow. Realize that as you grow and unfold, you will become a greater and still greater and grander channel for the inflow and outpouring of the

Cosmic Energy and Life. Complete the Circle of Will. Bring about the Union of Spirit. Learn to Will to Will, by realizing that you *are* Will.

Lesson VII. Mastering the Opposites.

The manifestation of Egohood by the individual who has learned the Secret of the Excluded Middle—who has learned to Will to Will—evidences itself in a variety of forms and phases. In the Mastery of The Opposites, however, we find one of its most important phases, and one which also influences other forms. The individual who wishes to mould his mind by his newly awakened Will, and thus acquire Poise and Balance, must first learn the art of mastering the Opposites in the instinctive and emotional regions of his mental being. In acquiring this art he also does much in the direction of gaining Poise and Balance, and in neutralizing Rhythm.

We have seen in The Arcane Teaching that "every quality, attribute or condition has its opposite." We have seen how these Pairs of Opposites are, in reality, but the different and contrasting poles of the same thing. Just as Heat and Cold are the same thing—just as Hard and Soft are the same thing—so Love and Hate are seen to be but the contrasting poles of the same thing. And, in the same way, and from the same reason, all contrasting emotions, states and feelings are but the opposite poles of a fundamental emotion which depends upon the Will for its expression and outward activities.

All activity proceeds from and through the Will. The Will is involved in all action. There can be no action without Will.

Through the stimulus and incentive of desire, feeling and emotion, the Will is called and directed into activity. But the Will itself must not be identified with the desire, feeling or emotion which inspires it to action. Just as the water in a glass may be colored by a chemical dissolved in it, and yet in itself remain as much pure water as it was in the beginning, so is the Will colored and apparently changed by the influence of the emotion or feeling operative in and through it. The Will is clear and colorless like the water—its emotional color being not of itself. The Will experiences the color of the emotion or feeling, but never is the latter. The Will is always the vehicle for the emotion or feeling—its vital energy so to speak. The Will is the body of action, which clothes itself in the garb of emotion and feeling in order to make itself manifest.

To the ordinary person, it would be an impossibility to divorce feeling and emotion from the Will—for if that were attempted there would be nothing left apparent or manifest in any way. The residuum would be like the abstract conception of motionless, cold, unmoved, pure intellect, independent of any object of thought. To such persons pure will is merely a name corresponding to nothing in their experience. This because in such persons *the Will is unconscious of itself*. When the Ego-Consciousness is attained—when the "I" knows that itself and the Will are identical, then *the Will becomes conscious of itself*. In this latter state, instead of its consciousness remaining centred on the emotional and feeling plane—the instinctive plane of the mind—it is raised up to its rightful seat, upon the throne of the Real Self, and it assumes the sceptre of power and authority which really belong to it.

When the Ego-Consciousness is acquired to a certain degree, the "I," realizing that it is in its inmost nature nothing more or less than Will, sees that the Opposites of Emotion and Feeling are but things *belonging to*, but not *of* itself, things objective to its subjective Self. It sees them as but garments which it may put on and off, as it suits its fancies or interest. It sees them as but the several masks of character which it may place before its face, and then take off and exchange for another, as may seem best or desirable. From the moment when this realization comes to the individual, even in the faintest degree, then that individual has begun to move toward Freedom, and has started on the road to the Mastery of The Opposites.

Contrast the condition of the man who is still hypnotized with the belief that his emotions and feelings are *himself*—that he *is* the character he is playing, with its emotions and feelings and incidents of personality, on the one hand; and on the other hand, the individual who realizes that he, himself, is Will in his real nature, and that the character assumed by him, together with its incidental qualities, feelings and emotions, is but an objective something which he may put on or off, destroy or change, as he may see fit. Can you not see that there is a difference as wide as the poles in the contrasting being of these two men? Can you not see that one is the Master of the Opposites, and the other the obedient Slave?

The Liberated Ego—the Emancipated Self—knows its real nature, knows that it is no emotional creature bent now this way and then that by the power of inherited or acquired feeling—knows that it is the Lord of its own being, capable of using emotion as a means of expression when it suits itself, and likewise repressing it when it is best to do so; of using or discarding feeling when it suits its purpose. Nay, more—capable of *changing* the feeling or emotion from one of its poles to the other—changing love to hate, like to dislike, pain to pleasure, sorrow to joy—backward and forward, at will, and solely because it Wills to do it, and it suits its Will so to do. When the Ego realizes that it is the Lord of itself, instead of a subordinate and slave to its feelings and emotions, or personal traits and characteristics, then alone is it Free. It then feels the spirit of the "Kasidah":

"Do what thy manhood bids thee do, from none but self expect applause; He noblest lives and noblest dies who makes and keeps his self-made laws.

All other Life is living Death, a world where none but Phantoms dwell, A breath, a wind, a sound, a voice, a tinkling of the camel-bell."

The following exercise will tend to bring about a heightened realization in consciousness of the Mastery of the Opposites. It is adapted from an ancient Arcane Formula, modern figures-of-speech being used.

Exercise.

Let the Neophyte place himself in a condition and position of rest, calm and repose. Let him meditate upon the real nature of the "I." Let him cast off the illusion of the personal self, and its attributes, as indicated in previous exercises. Then let him imagine himself as rising above the lower planes of personality toward the higher planes of Egohood—as in a balloon which is rising above the surface of the earth into the higher regions of purer rarified air. Let him then throw overboard from the mental balloon all the likes and dislikes; loves and hates; prejudices for and against anything and everything whatsoever, either good or bad; in short the entire collection of inherited or acquired feelings and emotions which have formed the garment or body of personality for so long. As the mental balloon rises higher and higher let him throw off even the more subtle feelings and emotions, until finally he finds himself divested of every iota of personal character he ever possessed, and his Ego is as naked as a new-born babe. Then, after a few trials of this exercise, will come to him a new sense of power and might—a new realization of his real nature in Will. Then will he realize that the Pairs of Opposites of the Personality are but masks and clothing of the character he has been playing. Then will he feel like the Hindu god when he emerged from the body of the pig whose personality he had assumed. Then he may gradually return to the earth and resume the garments he has thrown off—but as a Master and Owner, not as a Slave to them as heretofore. This exercise will quicken the perception of Egohood, and will aid in the Mastery of the Opposites.

The following exercise will also be found very useful in the same direction.

Exercise.

Let the Neophyte place himself in a position and condition of calm, restful repose, and then meditate upon the fact that contrasting and opposing feelings and emotions are in reality but the opposite poles of the same thing. Let him, in imagination, try the experiment of changing the polarity of some emotion—of inducing the state of love where hate has been dominant, or vice versa. Let him shift the polarity of his feelings and emotions at will, backward and forward. He will thus discover that the feelings and emotions are far from being fixed and constant, as he had supposed, but are capable of being shifted about at Will. This exercise will result in giving the individual a wonderful power over his feelings and emotion, and preventing them from dominating or ruling him. By shifting the polarity one may change a painful feeling or emotion into its opposite. Distressing feelings may be changed in polarity, or balanced with their opposites, and much pain be obviated. It is not necessary always to shift entirely to the opposite pole of the emotion or feeling—many adepts merely change the polarity to the opposite in a sufficient degree to establish a balance and thus create a condition and state of poise and equilibrium, which results in peace of mind— which quiets the stormy sea of passion, emotion or feeling. This condition of Poise and Balance is the true state of the advanced occultist. Equally balanced between the Pairs of Opposites one finds a peace unknown to those who polarize in either extreme. When one fully realizes that he is Master of the Opposites, and may shift the polarity of emotion and feeling at Will, then he himself is able to establish the condition most conducive to his satisfaction and happiness.

Such a one is well on the road to Mastership.

Lesson VIII. Neutralizing Rhythm.

In the Arcane Teaching we have seen the evidence of the universality of the Laws of Rhythm, Cyclicity and Balance. In the realm of the emotion and feelings these laws are as fully manifest as in the physical world. The Arcane Teachers instruct their Neophytes in the art of mastering, controlling and applying these laws, instead of assuming a negative attitude toward them. Instead of meekly bowing and yielding to these laws, the advanced individual either neutralizes such activities as he deems to his disadvantage, or else transmutes or applies the laws to his own advantage and progress. Instead of allowing himself to be overwhelmed by the laws, as by a great oceanwave, he rises on the crest of the wave and rides to safety on it.

The laws may be harnessed and made to work for the individual, instead of being allowed to overwhelm and master him.

The general principles stated in the preceding chapter on Mastering the Opposites are equally applicable to the Mastery of Rhythm, Cyclicity and Balance. When the Ego realizes that its real nature is centred and focalized in Will, then it is able to neutralize the opposites. And, in the phenomena of rhythm, cyclicity and balance the underlying principle is that of the Opposites. For, in rhythm we find a movement to-and-from between the two poles of the opposites. In cyclicity there is a circular movement imparted by reason of the poles, or opposites, of centre and circumference, in fact many cyclic movements are merely forms of rhythm, as we have seen in the Arcane Teachings. And, in Balance there is evidenced the presence of the two poles or opposites, the weights of each tending to maintain the balance or compensation. And, Poise, that great attainment, is accomplished by preserving the right relation between the poles or opposites. So, you may see, that in the Mastery of the Opposites the Neophyte really acquires the mastery of Rhythm, Cyclicity and Balance. The principle of Polarity underlies everything.

The Law of Rhythm is best described in the words of the Aphorism, which informs us that: "Everything moves to-and-from in Rhythm, between its two poles. Everything rises and falls in Rhythm, within the limits of its nature. Everything advances and retreats in Rhythm, within the limits of its power."

On the plane of emotion and feeling the Law of Rhythm is constantly in evidence. We find that we swing like a pendulum between the extremes or poles of our feelings or emotions. To-day we are sad—tomorrow we are joyful; today we are gloomy—tomorrow we are bright and hopeful; today we are slothful—tomorrow we are active and energetic. A study of our emotions and feelings will reveal to us the fact that these mental states are like the ocean and have their tides, in and out, high and low, flood and ebb. We find action and reaction ever evident in our emotional life.

Moreover we find that when we indulge in an extreme degree of any emotion or feeling we have a tendency to fly to the opposite pole of that feeling or emotion. The law of reaction follows the action. The reaction may arise either from a revulsion occasioned by a sense of impotency or powerlessness to attain the object desired or hoped for; or else from a satiety resulting from the attainment of the object of the desire and the discovery that it was not what we had expected of it. We need not point to special examples of this, for the experience of every one who reads these words will supply the necessary examples.

Love, hate, or anger, if carried to an extreme point, have a tendency to fly back to the opposite pole with a startling rapidity. And, likewise, extreme elation is very apt to bound back to its extreme opposite and cause us to experience extreme depression. This is so common that the mere mention of the fact is sufficient to prove it to anyone. In the same way many know that fear and courage have a tendency to react into each other, if either be carried to an extreme. Many a man manifesting extreme courage will find himself swung suddenly back to a state of dire fear. In the same way, and from the same law, many have found themselves in a state of extreme fear, and then suddenly when they could proceed no further they would experience a sudden bound of desperation carrying them to a state of extreme recklessness and daring. The experience of soldiers have shown the bravest men suddenly possessed of a pitiful fear—the reaction from the courage; and, likewise, we see the manifestation of occasional bursts and spurts of reckless daring and startling foolhardiness from notorious cowards. We, personally, know of a case in which a man who was a self-confessed coward, was suddenly overcome with such a revulsion at his own lack of courage that he sprung to the fore and performed a deed so startling, daring, and reckless that he won a special mention in the report of the battle and was ever afterward regarded as a man of the highest courage.

Persons who dwell principally on the plane of the emotions live in a state of alternate heaven and hell. Now enjoying to the fullest the upward swing they revel in the ecstasies of emotional feeling until they feel as if they were indeed gods.

Then comes the backward swing which plunges them into the hell of depression, melancholy, remorse, regret or feeling of impotence and uselessness. The more emotional the person, the higher and lower in the scale of feeling does he travel. Those who are willing to pay the price of these extremes—the toll of feeling—are of course free to do so. But the individual who finds himself resting on Will, his real nature, grows impatient and restless under the force of the play of his emotive nature, and is forced to take steps to master and rule that part of his being. Instead of swinging backward and forward between the poles of emotion and feeling, he seeks and acquires the balance and poise of the focalized will.

The first step in the direction of neutralizing rhythm lies in the realization of the existence of rhythm itself. When one comes to realize that the hot fit is certain to be followed by the cold— the high by the low—the exaltation by the depression—the courage by the fear—the activity by the slothfulness—and *vice versa*, then does he cease to identify himself so closely with either of the poles, and, on the contrary, grows to regard them as mere natural incidents of his mental nature. He values them at their true worth, and *refuses to allow his Will to become involved* in his emotion and feeling. He knows that his depression will be followed by a stage of reaction, and so he refuses to take his depression seriously. Likewise, knowing the truth, he refuses to allow his exaltation to excite him unduly. In short, he centres more and more upon his Will nature, and from that position he stands aside, as it were, and watches calmly the swing of his feelings and emotions between their two poles. In a way, *he detaches himself* from the swing of the rhythmic emotions, and lives on the plane of Will. This mental state may be figuratively pictured as the individual resting on the plane of Will, and watching the swing of the emotional pendulum beneath him, on a lower plane, without allowing his Will to become involved.

The Neophyte may acquire this immunity from the effect of emotional rhythm by *focalizing on his Will* when he is threatened adversely by the emotional feeling. He will acquire a mental "knack" of rising above the plane of emotional feeling, or to the plane of Will, and there calmly watching and observing the storm of emotion, without being influenced by it. It is like one sailing in a balloon above the storm clouds which are thundering, and flashing lightning, beneath him. On the plane of Will there is Peace and Power undreamt of by those still on the emotional plane.

But this immunity to rhythmic emotion does not come to the Neophyte all at once. It is a matter of time, practice and growth. It is aided by the steady practice of *refusing to take the emotional swing too seriously*. Refuse to admit it as being *yourself*—deny away its reality. See, and think of it, always, as something connected with your mental being but *not in any real way You, yourself*. Stand aside and watch the play of your emotional nature, and before long you will be able to laugh at its antics. You will see how essentially unreal it is when compared with the mental life on the plane of Will Once even partially freed from the bondage of emotion and feeling, you will never willingly return to the old thralldom.

This does not mean that you should never *use* your emotional nature. On the contrary, you will find it advantageous to *play out the part* often, for the energy aroused by the emotions are strongly motive, and will enable you to accomplish much if it is properly applied. But, remember always, never allow yourself to become enmeshed and involved in the emotional storms or activities. Handle the emotions as a Master does an instrument but never yield yourself up to your emotions as a passive slave or instrument, any more than you would yield yourself up to the power and influence of some entity outside of yourself.

You have a part to play in the world—a part which is as much of a "character" as that assumed by the actor. And, in order to play it *well* you will find it necessary to throw into it feeling and emotion, just as the actor throws these into his part. But the best actor always maintains a basic knowledge that he is merely *acting*, and his emotional activity is merely the result of previous thought and trained art. *Art in the management of the emotion consists in selecting the emotional activity adapted to the accomplishment of the task or work on hand, and the restricting of all other emotions.* Instead of being a blind tool and instrument of the emotional nature, you should use the latter rationally—selecting that which is desirable and helpful, and restraining the rest. Beware always of the reaction and return swing of the emotional pendulum of rhythm. When it swings back from a desirable emotion, do you then mount to the plane of Will, and from there view it smilingly and with equanimity.

Take what you want, and neutralize the rest.

Lesson IX. Cyclicity and Balance.

The swing of the rhythmic pendulum is always at right angles to its central line of suspension—always to-and-fro, backward and forward, from a fixed center of gravity which is directly under its point of suspension. A similar law is evident in the movements of a body revolving in a circle, in which is manifest the power of the central point which holds the body from flying off into space, and also the power which causes the body to continue in cyclic revolution instead of falling toward the centre. In fact, the cyclic motion is merely another form of rhythm and is dependent on the latter, just as rhythm, itself, is dependent on the existence of the Law of Opposites, or Polarity.

Polarity, or The Opposites, is the fundamental cause of both Rhythm and Cyclicity.

All active movement expresses itself in rhythmic motion, between its two poles or opposites. But this rhythmic motion is not necessarily always in a straight line, as in the case of the pendulum. In fact, the motion of large bodies, and also of races, history, events, etc., is generally in a circle. This results from the attraction and repulsion of objects and forces outside of the swinging thing, which tends to draw it out of its backward and forward swing, and which gradually converts the straight line of the swing into a circle. Consequently, on all sides, and in all things we find the Law of Cyclicity in full operation.

As the Aphorism states: "Cyclicity is akin to Rhythm, and arises by reason of it. All events tend to move in Cyclic Trend—in constant circular movement of continuous recurrence. The only escape from Cyclicity is found in the process of transmutation into Spirality. This is accomplished by *advancing the Central Point of Motion*. The conversion of the Circle into the Spiral is one of the highest forms of mental Alchemy."

It is evident to all who will examine the subject that the mental life of the average person is merely the constant traveling 'round and 'round in a recurring circle—the circle gradually widening from childhood to the prime of life, and then narrowing from that time to old age and death. The average person is held firmly bound by this Law of Cyclicity, and while he finds the circle widening or narrowing as the case may be, he never makes any real progress. It is always a constant swing around the same old central point—a process similar to the travel of the squirrel in the treadmill of his cage—a constant traveling which results in his getting nowhere.

It is only when the individual is able to convert the circle into the spiral, that he is able to advance. All real advance is accomplished in this way. Many acquire Spirality "by accident," as it were. They find that by the assertion of the Ego—by the use of the inner Will, they are able to advance the Central Point of Motion. Advanced Occultists are able to *consciously* advance their Central Point of Life Motion, and thus to do intelligently that which the average person does to a lesser degree under the unconscious influence of circumstances.

It is most difficult to render simple and plain the Arcane Formula regarding this form of Mental Transmutation, for it is so bound up with the conscious use of the Will that it cannot be understood except by those who have felt the realization of the Will, Consciousness. It may be described in this way, however; The average person merely *desires* to advance. This desire exerts more or less influence on the Will. When, however, a person has learned to Will to Will, he is able to accomplish far more than he could by the mere power of plain desire. By his conscious Will he is able to project his Ego a step or more in advance in the Cosmic scale, and thus establish a new Centre of Cyclic Motion. By the increasing power which comes to him gradually by this conscious use of the Will, the individual establishes a habit of Spiralic Progression which replaces the old simple Cyclic movement.

The Neophyte by cultivating the habit of constantly *willing an advance at each circle*, will find that though his life still maintains its circular movement, yet at each return to a given point will he advance a little higher in scale and plane. Just as a traveler ascending a mountain must needs go round and round it, each time a little nearer the peak, so will the traveler along The Path of Attainment find that at each circling the old paths will be below him.

The study of the succeeding chapters of this book will give the Neophyte additional instruction and suggestions in the direction of the use of the visualizing power of the mind to bring about desired conditions. Visualization may be employed in this matter of converting the Circle into the Spiral, as well as in the minor matters of life.

The distinguishing mark of the advanced Occultist, or individual who has found the Real Self, is Poise or Balance. This is always a mark of power, just as its opposite is always a mark of weakness.

As the Aphorism says: "Poise is Power. Poise results from Balance. Balance is secured by adjusting and maintaining the Centre between the Pairs of Opposites. By Balanced Poise the Master neutralizes Polarity and Rhythm, by resolving them into Unity. In the Heart of the Storm is Peace. In the Centre of Life there is Poise and Power. Seek it ever, O Neophyte—for in it thou shalt find thy Self."

The old Occult Masters were wont to illustrate the Balanced Life of the Advanced Ego by the figure of the acrobat walking the tight-rope, a feat which has descended to us from antiquity.

They would picture the Initiate traversing the Razor-edge Wire of Life, balancing himself by the Balancing Pole of the Opposites. Now shifting the weight on one side, and now on the other, he is able to walk the Path in safety. Having the confidence of the Awakened Ego he trusts to his own power and the use of the Balancing Pole.

The untrained person attempting the feat would be home over by the pull of one emotion or feeling, or another, and would be dashed to ruin. But the Balanced Ego walks in confidence and safety, because of his mastery of the art of Balance. Pitting one emotion against another he neutralizes the one which threatens to pull him down. By Mental Alchemy or Transmutation, he is able to transmit a dangerous pull into a part of his balancing process. His axiom is "Action and Re-Action are equal," and this principle he applies in all the emergencies and crises of life. He always manages to have a push or a pull to counteract a push or a pull in a different direction, and thus balance and poise is maintained.

Balance and Poise may be attained by entering into a realization of the real nature of the Ego—that the Ego is based and focalized in Will—that the Ego can, and should, always act from the plane and position of Will rather than from the plane and position of Emotion and Feeling. In fact, the entire instruction of this book, up to this point, has been in the direction of leading the individual to a consciousness of his real nature, which, if once acquired, must inevitably result in perfect Balance and Poise.

The facts stated, the instruction, the exercises, all will aid in the acquirement of Balance and Poise. Toward this goal, all of our efforts have been directed.

Balance results from Mastery. Mastery results from Knowledge and Practice. You have been told the truth. Make it your own. Realize what you are. Practice the methods of the Formulas.

Then, and then only, will you enter into that consciousness of Peace, Poise and Power, which comes to him who hath acquired Balance. As we have said in the Arcane Teaching: Oh, Neophyte, in the Centre of Life shalt thou indeed find Poise and Power. In the Heart of the Storm shalt thou find Peace. In the Centre of the Cosmos shalt thou find thyself. He who finds the Centre of Himself, finds the Centre of the Cosmos. For, at the last, they are one!

Lesson X. Mentalism in a Nutshell.

In the Arcane Teaching we have shown that the fundamental principle of Mentalism, in all of its forms, is the fact that the Cosmos itself is One Universal Mind, and that the Manifested Cosmos may be likened to a great Universal Brain, in which the forms of things and life are but as thought-forms in the human brain. There is Mind in everything, and everything is in Mind. Consequently, just as Thoughts become Things in the Cosmic Brain, so is it possible for a strongly concentrated and focalized Mind (Will) to materialize into objective form things and conditions on the material plane.

Just as the Cosmic Will manifests the Cosmic activities and forms, so may the Individual Will materialize activities and forms on its own plane. There is but one difference between the Cosmic will and the Individual Will—the difference in degree. All Will, from the Cosmic Will to the feeblest Individual Will is identical in nature, although widely differing in degrees of power. In fact, the Individual Wills are but *focalized centres* in the great Cosmic Will, varying greatly in power and manifestation. This being so, it follows that the same laws, and principles are applicable in all manifestations of Will, from the highest to the lowest.

In the Arcane Teaching we have described the principles and laws underlying the manifestation of Mentalism, and there is no occasion for entering into this phase of the subject in this little book. Instead, we shall proceed at once to give you the Formulas for the actual demonstration and manifestation of these principles. We refer you to the Arcane Teaching for the explanation and the theory. In this chapter we shall give you "Mentalism in a Nutshell," condensing into its limited space the essence and substance of what could be expanded into several books.

Formula for Positivity.

In the laws of Mentalism there is a fundamental principle that the positive always dominates the negative—the negative is always subordinate to the positive. Everything has its keynote of positivity. And that keynote depends upon the degree of Will-Consciousness. When one becomes well polarized in Will Consciousness he is intensely positive to those around him— not only to persons but also to environment and conditions.

This positivity is, of course, dependent upon the degree of Will manifested by the individual. Remember, we say the *degree* of Will, not the amount or quantity of Will. The average person, when he thinks of Will Power is apt to think of a large amount of quantity of Will which must be manifested by the individual in order to produce its effect. This is erroneous. There can be no such thing as *quantity or amount* of Will. This is a fact known to all advanced occultists. Will is not a material substance occupying space in the way that matter or force occupies space. It cannot be measured by spatial dimensions. One cannot think of a yard or pound of Will. Nor can he conceive of Will being measured by the units used in the measurement of electricity or other forms of force. There is a standard of measurement of Will, but not a measurement of quantity or amount—it is altogether a matter of *degree*.

The degree of Will manifested by the individual depends upon his degree of focalization or polarity in the Cosmic Will itself. The greater the realization of one's relation to the Cosmic Will the greater is his capacity for manifesting Will Power. Consequently all efforts toward developing positivity in Will Power must be based upon the fundamental realization. The Formulas given in the earlier chapters of this book will give to the Neophyte the key to the Secret of Mentalism.

The Arcane Formula for the manifestation of Will Power consists simply in the development of the realization of Egohood—of the fact that the individual is a *focalized centre of force and Will in the great Cosmic Will*. The higher the degree of this realization the higher degree of positivity will the individual possess. Fasten this truth in your minds: *The Will Power of the individual is not something created by him, but is, in reality, the power of the Cosmic Will in which he lives and moves and has his being. The individual has no Will Power in himself, but all the will he manifests must flow through his organism from the Cosmic Will. The individual is merely the focal point of Will—a channel through which the Cosmic Will may act*. Ponder well these words, O Neophyte, for in them is contained the whole Secret of Mentalism.

Will Atmosphere.

The Neophyte should create for himself a Positive Will Atmosphere, or Aura, which will tend to serve as a protective armor shielding him from adverse influences from outside, and also tending to render his positive power felt by those with whom he comes in contact. The Positive Atmosphere is occasioned by the vibrations in the Mind Stuff with which all space is filled just as the brain is filled with mind-stuff of its own particular quality. The Cosmos is a World Brain, remember, and the Cosmic Mind Stuff is everywhere. Vibration in the Mind Stuff is just as real as vibration in the ether, or in the air, or in matter of any and every kind.

The Positive Atmosphere is created by a pure act of Will, aided by Visualization. The Neophyte should first realize that he is Will itself. Then he should Visualize (mentally imagine or *see*) the Mind Stuff in his immediate vicinity becoming charged with the positive power of Will. It will aid him to think of himself as surrounded for a distance of about three feet with an egg-shaped aura or atmosphere of highly charged Will, radiating from him and vibrating with an intense energy. As a matter of occult truth, this phenomena is really existent, although the ordinary senses cannot perceive the vibrations or aura. Treat yourself every day, or oftener, with the intent to increase the degree of your Positive Atmosphere. The more clearly you can *visualize*, or imagine, the existence of this aura or atmosphere, the greater will be your degree of positive personal atmosphere.

The Neophyte must not allow himself to be deceived in regarding the Imagination as an unreal, fanciful thing—*it is a mental activity of wonderful occult power*.

The Neophyte will soon discover that he has acquired a new positive personal atmosphere, and that those with whom he comes in contact will *feel* a something peculiar about him, and will tend to become negative to him, unless they, too, understand the principles involved. As time passes, and practice renders him more perfect the Neophyte will move about among ordinary people just as a highly charged magnet or electric wire. It is difficult to describe this, but those who will practice to acquire it will soon become conscious of their newly found strength.

In order to focalize more fully, the Neophyte may hold in his mind the mental image, or statement of "I am a Centre of Positive Will."

Personal Positivity.

The Neophyte may occasionally find that he is in the presence of persons more positive than himself, owing to their past training or experience. In such cases he should at once determine that they shall not "overlap" him (the occult term used in such cases). He should determine at least to meet the positive persons "*edge to edge,*" if not indeed to "overlap" *them*. This is accomplished by at once *denying* the positivity of the other person (silently and mentally, of course) by the assertion "I deny your Positivity over me." At the same time the Neophyte should focalize on his own Will-Consciousness, seeing himself as a focal centre of Will, and having the Cosmic Will back of him. He will soon find that he will rise in the scale of positivity, and the other will sink a degree below him.

If he finds himself oppressed by a sense of negativity while mingling with a crowd, he should assert his Egohood in the same way. The greater the realization of one's self as a Focal Centre of Will, the greater the degree of Personal Positive Atmosphere will be manifested.

Visualization.

In this chapter we shall speak of Visualization, in a number of places. Visualization is the creative process employed by occultists desiring to manifest Mental Images on the Mental and Material Planes. Visualization consists in *forming and holding a Mental Image of things and conditions as you wish them to be in actuality*. The Mental Image tends to create for itself a material and objective form and existence—it is the mental pattern around which the material conditions tend to group themselves. It is, in fact, the seed-form of the thing itself.

The prime factor in Visualization is to endeavor to create as clear as possible a Mental Image of the thing or condition desired, *as if it were actually existent at that moment*. These three rules of Visualization should be observed: (1) *See yourself as you wish to be.* (2) *See others as you wish them to be.* (3) *See conditions as you wish them to be.* Around these visualized ideals, do the material realities form and crystallize.

Statements.

All occultists have recognized the value of Statements, or "affirmations" as some call them. These Occult Statements are positive assertions of the existence of the conditions which you wish to bring about. They tend to aid the Visualization to a great degree, and besides have a power of their own. There is an occult power in the Spoken Word which is not necessary to explain here—the assertion that the power exists is sufficient for the particular purpose before us. Always use Statements as in the present tense. Do not say to yourself, "Such and such a thing *will be bye and bye,* but boldly assert "Such and such a thing *is existent and in actual being, now, this moment.*

There is also a good occult reason behind this, which it is not necessary to discuss in detail. The power of the Positive Occult Statement must be experienced in order to be appreciated. Make your statements *earnestly and positively*—avoid all halfhearted statements, for they result in half-hearted results. In making your statements, do not use a tone of entreaty, or of asking a favor—speak in a tone of command. Of course, these statements should not be made aloud to other people. They have the best effect when made in a state of meditation and concentration. Use them in connection with visualization, and you will find that they will tend to energize and vitalize your Mental Images.

Denials.

Occult Denials are a form of Occult Statements. They have a most positive effect when rightly used. With the individual focalized in Will, he is able to exert much occult power by boldly *denying out of existence* the obstacles and difficulties which beset his path. It is marvelous, at times, to see how the obstructing things evince a tendency to disintegrate and disappear from one's mental world, which is followed later by a response of like kind and degree in the material world. Do not be afraid to say: "I deny this or that obstacle. It has no power over me. I deny it out of my world. For me it does not exist." Make your denials as positive as your statements. Command, not beg or entreat.

Mental Alchemy.

Mental Alchemy or Mental Transmutation bears a striking analogy to Material Alchemy or Transmutation, in the sense that in both there is a marked change in form and nature of the substances or things operated upon. Conditions and things, like material objects, may be transformed and transmuted at the Will of the Alchemist. Mentalism, in its most striking forms, is Mental Alchemy. In the crucible of the Cosmic Mind or Brain things may be, and are transmuted and changed in their outward form and character. Nothing in the Cosmos can be destroyed—but everything is capable of *change*. Remember, first and always, that Mental Alchemy means change. You do not destroy things—you merely *change* them.

Mental Vibration.

In all forms of Mentalism there is in evidence the phenomena of Mental Vibration. Vibration is not confined to the gross material substance of the universe, but is equally in evidence in the Mind Stuff with which all space is filled. Mind Stuff is the elementary material of which the great Cosmic World Brain is composed. When one thinks, feels, or wills, there is manifest vibration just as truly as in the vibration of the atom or the tuning-fork. Each kind of thought, feeling or emotion has its own rate of vibration, or keynote.

When a certain rate of mental vibration is manifested it tends to reproduce similar vibrations, and consequent similar mental states in the minds of those coming within its field of induction. Just as a tuning-fork will cause similar vibrations in the objects in the room, so will a mind sending forth vibrations tend to reproduce those vibrations in other minds in its vicinity, or under certain, circumstances, at long distances.

This being so, it follows that if an individual will carry, in his mind a positive, persistent idea, backed up with an application of his Will, he will be able to impress that idea upon others, with more or less effect. He will be aided in this by the practice of Statements and by Visualization, for both of these practices tend to send, forth mental vibrations of a high degree of strength and power.

Thought Waves and Currents.

There are waves and currents in the great ocean of Mind Stuff, just as there are waves and currents in the ocean or in the air.

Thoughts, feelings and emotion manifested by an individual will tend to create waves or currents in the Mind Stuff, which will flow out in all directions influencing and affecting others in their field of force, particularly if those others happen to maintain a degree of mental vibration corresponding to that of the traveling wave or current. Every one sends forth these thought waves or currents, usually unconsciously and without direct intention, and consequently with comparatively slight effect. Those who understand the laws of Mentalism are able to consciously direct, concentrate and focus the Will upon those whom they wish to influence, and consequently their thought waves and currents travel direct to their mark, and create a much greater effect.

Thought Forms.

Thought-forms are concentrated thought waves or thought bodies usually projected from the mind by, concentrated thought and Will, and which, when coming in contact with others, have almost as great an effect upon them as if the sender were present in person exerting his Will and mind upon the person or persons. Occultists who have acquired concentration and focalization are often able to send forth thought-forms of so high a degree of power and strength that they produce upon others the mental impression that the sender, himself, is actually present in person, so strong is the impression created. In some of the methods which we shall now describe, the production of these thought-forms will be described.

Practical Methods.

We have said but a few words in describing the above mentioned various phases of Mentalism. We have not thought it necessary to go into detail regarding the theory of the phenomena. Those who read this book will have read elsewhere much of theoretical detail, and besides will have grasped the fundamental and underlying principles of Mentalism from what we have said in The Arcane Teaching. We think it preferable to pass on directly to the practical methods contained in the Formulas, rather than to dwell upon the theoretical side of the subject.

In connection with the methods herein described, we would say that while anyone may obtain some degree of success by practicing them, still in order to obtain any marked degree of success it is necessary for one to have first developed the Will-Consciousness, or some degree of Egohood. The Will being the motive power back of all forms of Mentalism and Mental Alchemy, it follows that he who is able to focalize and polarize his Ego in Will itself will be able to bring to bear the very highest degree of power in the phenomena of Mentalism.

Therefore, we have devoted the greater part of this book to pointing out the methods whereby one may develop the Will-Consciousness and Egohood within him. For when this one thing is attained, the rest is but a matter of detail. Let us now proceed to a consideration of the Practical Methods. We shall condense these in as few words as possible. The student must read carefully every word so that he will enter into a full understanding of the subject and methods.

Concentration.

The Neophyte must develop and cultivate the art of Concentration. Concentration means "bringing to a centre"— and Mental Concentration is really a focusing of the Will by means of attention. Concentration may be developed by practice. Learn to shut out distracting thoughts and ideas for a few moments, holding the mind "one-pointed" upon the thing or idea before you. Then, after an interval, concentrate upon something else. After you have subdued the wandering tendency of the mind, gradually, you will find that you have acquired a new power of mind which will enable you to direct and apply a focalized mental power upon whatever idea or thing to which you may direct it. We could fill page after page with detailed exercises in concentration, but after reading them you would find that the essence of the whole thing consists *in fixing the attention* upon *anything*, and being able *to hold it there*. This is attained only by practice. And the practice may be had by fixing and holding the attention upon *anything*, for a few moments at a time, until you grow more and more proficient by practice. Remember, concentration does *not* mean "*staring*" at a thing—it consists of fixing and holding the *mind*, not the *eyes*. Begin practicing, and you will soon acquire the knack. It is altogether a matter of the use of the Attention, by means of the Will. All the rest is mere detail and "trimmings." It will do you far more good to *invent* methods for yourself, than to blindly follow some set lesson mapped out by others. Use your own minds, and you will gain thereby.

Mental Imaging.

The Secret of Mental Alchemy may be stated as consisting first, last and always, of the Art of Mental Imaging, reinforced by the Will. Take up your lead-pencil and mark the above statement, so that you will see it easily when turning over these pages. While to the beginner the subject of Mentalism may seem a very complicated one, the advanced occultist knows it to be the extreme of simplicity. *Mental Alchemy, under whatever same it may masquerade, may be found to consist, at the last, of simply the power to create strong, clear Mental Images, and to project them into the outer world by means of the concentrated Will.*

Read over the above italicized words several times, and fix them firmly in your mind. You will find that all that you ever have read on the subject may be "boiled down" to the above stated principle. The rest is a mere matter of detail. This single statement is "Mentalism in a Nutshell."

Whether in the matter of the effect of Mentalism upon persons with whom you are in direct personal contact; or else in the case of persons or bodies of people remote from you in distance; or in the case of the changing of material environment and circumstances—the principle is ever the same, *i. e.*, the projection of your Mental Image into objectivity, and the materializing of that picture by the operation of the Law of Attraction.

The ancient teachers used, as a material object-lesson to their pupils a simple contrivance which we now know in a perfected form as the "Magic Lantern," either in its simple form, or else in the "moving picture apparatus." The teachers would project upon a plane surface the reflection of a design or picture which was passed in front of a concentrated light—the reflection being reproduced on a large scale on the plane surface, at a greater or lesser distance.

The teachers would explain to the Neophytes that the concentrated light represented the focused Will; the slide containing the picture represented the Mental Image held in the mind; the plane surface represented the objective world. As a matter of fact, the analogy between the Magic Lantern and the phenomena of Mentalism is almost exactly parallel, to a certain degree and extent. The pupils of the ancient teachers were bidden to fix this symbol firmly in their minds, and to recall it *always* when practicing or manifesting any of the phenomena of Mentalism. And we, likewise, urge all of our students to fix firmly in their minds this symbol of the Magic Lantern, and always to recall it when they practice Mentalism. *By holding this idea in the mind, the student will be able to give an increased force, power and reality to the projection of mental images*. Do not pass this by, lightly and carelessly—it is most important to you. If this book contained merely this one bit of instruction, it would be well "worth your while" to study it.

With this symbol still in mind, we see that the power and strength of the projection depends materially upon the strength and focused force of the light in the lantern. If the light be weak, or dim, or flickering, the reflection will be likewise. And, if the rays of the light be not focused and concentrated properly, the force and power of the light will not be properly directed and applied. Therefore, in Mentalism, you must rest as fully in the Will-Consciousness as possible, and also must hold the Will firmly concentrated upon the task before you.

Likewise, if the slide containing the picture—the Mental Image—be poorly and faintly drawn, the reflection will also be faulty; in fact, the fault will be more apparent, for it will be magnified according to the distance it is projected. Therefore, cultivate the art of Mental Imaging, and endeavor to train your imagination to see clearly that which you wish to project into the objective world for the purpose of materialization. Train your imagination to form and hold *plain, clear pictures of the things and conditions which you wish to materialize in the objective world*. Upon this one thing depends much of the efficacy and success of the processes of Mentalism. *If you cannot fill in the details of your Mental Picture at first, at least draw firm, strong general outlines, and as you begin to materialize objectively you will be able to add the details.*

Materialization of Thought.

There are certain laws in operation in the Cosmos, by reason of its very nature, which tend to *materialize thought-images*. The very Cosmos, itself, is a materialization of the *ideas* in the Cosmic Brain. And, by the Law of Analogy, the same thing is true on all planes. "From one, know All"—"As above, so below"—these are the axioms. There is a force in operation which has been called "The Law of Attraction," by which "like attracts like" on all planes. And on the mental plane, the "likes" are materialized into corresponding "likes" on the material plane. *Everything that is, first existed as an idea or Mental Picture*, either in the Cosmic Brain, or in the brain of some living creature as well.

There is always a mental plan behind and in every material form, shape or condition. The student should know this fact from a study of the Arcane Teaching, and by submitting the idea to the test of experience and reason. And, when this principle is clearly understood, the process of Thought Materialization through Mentalism becomes quite plain and understandable.

When the truth of Thought Materialization becomes fully understood, the student learns to *avoid making Mental Images of the things which he does not wish to materialize*, on the one hand; and *to make Mental Images of the things which he does wish to materialize*, on the other hand. When he realizes that mental things tend to materialize objectively, he has grasped a fundamental and important occult truth, *and he governs himself accordingly*. We urge every student to fix this idea firmly in his mind, for until he realizes that Mental Images and the Materialization thereof, *are but stages of the one process*, he has not grasped the working principle of Mentalism. When this fact *is* grasped, then the rest is merely a matter of practice, development and application.

Aids to Mental Imaging.

The careful student doubtless will have recognized by this time that the process of Statements and Denials are but forms of aids to Mental Imaging. When the Occult Statement is used, there is created a Mental Image, consciously or subconsciously, and consequently there is given an additional urge to materialization. And in the same way, the Occult Denial tends to erase or wipe out the Mental Picture in one's own mind; in the minds of others; or in circumstances and environment; of conditions or things which are not desirable. (We have stated that in addition to the above effect there are peculiar virtues and properties in the Spoken Word, of which we shall not speak further in this work, as it belongs to another phase of the general subject.) Do not undervalue the Occult Statement and the Occult Denial—they are powerful factors in Mentalism, in the direction of strengthening and *vitalizing* the Mental Images.

General Application.

The average student reading this book will doubtless expect that we will now enter into a detailed description of the various forms of the application of Mentalism, in the form of Mental Imaging and Thought Materialization. But we have no such intention. If this work were to be extended into several volumes for the sake of money-making and humoring the popular taste and demand, we might do so. It would be easy to fill several volumes with detailed description of various forms of application—but to what purpose? The keen analytical student would soon discover that what had been done was simply to build various structures around the one vital and underlying principle of Mental Imaging and Projection. We prefer that our students shall *think and work* for themselves, and not be mere blind followers of any teacher or teachers—even of ourselves. *There is no room for lazy minds in the ranks of true occultism.* Mentalism cannot be given or taken in sugar-coated capsules, one before each meal, like quack medicines. It must be thought out, *and worked out* in actual practice. So, if you wish your Mentalism in capsules, tabloids, or sugar-coats—you must go elsewhere for it—the field is full of occult nostrums, as many of you have found out.

What we shall do, in place of the above, is to give you a Formula by which *you can work out and manifest every form of mentalism for yourself.* No matter how complicated the form may be, it may be worked out by this Formula. We shall not attempt to prove this to you—you can best prove it by actual practice in your own experiments or occult work. We cheerfully stake our reputation as practical occultists upon its efficacy. Try it for yourself, and see what you can accomplish by it. The Formula has borne the test of ages, and the experiments and practice of many of the best occultists of the past and present. Consequently we do not hesitate to stake our reputation upon it.

The Arcane Formula.

The first thing in applying this Arcane Formula of Mentalism, is for the student to lay aside all other theories of Mentalism, for the time being. Forget all about Thought-Force, Mind-Waves, Mental Currents, and the rest of it—these are mere details, and are of no value in the real work of Mentalism. Forget all about theory, for the time being, and then proceed to get down to actual work.

Then, fix firmly in your mind the symbol of the Magic Lantern, with its concentrated light of Will, and its painted slide of the Mental Image. Regard the objective world, or persons, things, and circumstances, as the great plane surface upon which you wish to throw or project your Mental Images that they may materialize objectively. Get this picture clearly in your mind. See your "I" as the Light in the Lantern—with its concentrated Will focused directly upon the Mental Image slide of the Lantern. *Hold this idea in mind whenever you practice Mentalism.* Always stand behind your mental images, as the Light in the Lantern.

Then, having your Mental Image impressed upon your imaginative lantern slide, direct and *point your lantern tube upon whatever object in the outside world you wish*. If it is a person whom you wish to impress with your thought, mentally direct and focus your mental Magic Lantern upon him, just as you would upon a plane surface—*whether he be far or near*. All "treatments," as they are called in certain circles, are based upon this principle. The Mental Image is projected by means of the highly concentrated Will. If a number of persons are to be impressed, they may be considered as present in a group, or else the lantern tube may be turned first upon one and then upon another, and so on. If general conditions or environments are to be "treated," image them as a whole, and focus your lantern tube directly upon them, producing a projection of gigantic proportions. Surely, these directions cover the whole process. Read them over, again and again, until you grasp them thoroughly and fully.

In the cases of persons whom you may wish to impress, you will find that better results may be obtained by either imaging them as seated or standing before you, in full short-range of your mental Magic Lantern; or else, by imaging yourself as in the other person's presence, in his own place, turning your mental lantern full upon him. In the case of persons actually in your presence, proceed in the same way. **Places,** present or absent, may be "treated" in this way, in order to dispel undesirable conditions or vibrations. The vibrations of places may be entirely changed in this way. **Conditions** may be "treated" successfully by turning upon them a strong Mental Image of the changed conditions you wish to bring about. The entire category of the phenomena of Mental Transmutation or Mental Alchemy may be successfully undertaken by the use and application of this Formula. You will find that this Formula is applicable to all manner and kinds of condition. A little analysis of each and every case will show you that the Formula is applicable to it.

Let not the simplicity of this method cause you to discard it in favor of some more technical, complicated or metaphysical theoretical method. This method overrides all theories of the metaphysical schools—and analysis of the latter, divested of the surrounding theories, will show the underlying principle of this method in full operation in each and every one of them.

Why not discard and tear off the encumbering theories and "explanations" and avail yourself of the advantage of employing the essential method underlying all of the forms and theories.

Truth, at the last, is always found to be simple. And, in the case of this Formula, the very simplicity of the operation is a convincing proof of its truth, particularly when a little experiment and practice will prove its availability in all cases. Analyze all other forms of "mental treatment," or Mentalism, and see whether the principles of this Formula are not involved in them, and form their very essence. The beauty of this Formula is its simplicity and its capacity for universal application. It may be applied under a thousand forms or disguises, but the principle remains unchanged.

In conclusion, remember that "Mentalism in a Nut-Shell" is the idea conveyed by *the symbol of the Mental Magic Lantern, with Concentrated Will as the Light; Mental Image as the pictured slide; the Projected Idea as the picture thrown on the screen; and the Objective World, of persons, things and conditions as the plane surface on which the picture is thrown. Add to this the fact that*

Mental Images Materialize in response to the Law of Attraction, and you have the entire story of Mentalism.

Re-read your books on this subject; listen to the teachings of the cults and the schools. Then when you have finished with them, ask yourself calmly if the Mental Magic Lantern does not give you the best symbol of the best methods of each and all of them, reduced to the ultimate analysis and divested of useless fringe, trimming, theory and detail.

Then, practice Mentalism along these lines. The rest is a matter of patience, practice and persistency. We have given you the first and the last word in the practice of Mentalism.

FINIS.

BOOK THREE
THE ARCANE III.

VRIL: VITAL MAGNETISM

This is the third part or the series "The Arcane Teaching" (the other two are "The Arcane Teaching" and "The Arcane Formulas".

In this, the author analyzes VRIL, the universal principle of vital-energy, life-force, or vital magnetism, as it is sometimes called.

In many of the ancient occult treatises we find frequent reference to "Vril" not only in its sense of the principle vital energy, but also that sense of inherent usable energy which we seek to express the term " human magnetism".

LESSON I. THE NATURE OF VRIL

IN the Arcane Teaching, the term "VRIL" indicates the universal principle of vital-energy, life-force, or vital magnetism, as it is sometimes called. The term itself is believed to have had its origin in the language of ancient Atlantis, tradition holding that the Atlantean root v*ri,* meaning life, is the source of the word Vril, the latter expressing the idea of the vital principle or life-energy. This original root term is believed to have influenced similar elementary terms in the Sanskrit, and through this that great source of tongues, the Latin, from which our own language is largely derived. In many languages we find words indicating manly vigor, energy, virility, which undoubtedly owe their origin to the original Atlantean root term *vri* from which out" term is derived.

In the ancient Greek we find the term *veros,* meaning "a hero." the Sanskrit we discover *vira,* meaning " a hero," and the ancient Irish v*ear,* meaning "a man." The Gothic wa*ir,* and the Anglo-Saxon w*er,* each meaning " a man," as well as the Latin word v*ir,* meaning " a man," (from which our terms "virile, virility,' originated.) also appear to have been derived from the Atlantean term v r i, or "life." It was very natural to identify the concept of "man" with "life." In our own language the terms "virile " and "virility " indicate life-force or vital-energy, particularly in the sense of procreative power, the usage of these terms bearing out the above stated theory of their origin. Bulwer, who was well-versed in occult tradition and terms, used the term "vril " in one of his novels, to indicate a mysterious form of energy employed by a newly discovered and highly advanced race of people, upon whose doings his story was based. It is almost certain that Bulwer borrowed this term from some of the ancient occult writings, with which he was so familiar, and that the ancient Arcane term " vril " was known to him.

In many of these ancient occult treatises we find frequent reference to "Vril" not only in its sense of the principle vital energy, but also that sense of inherent usable energy which we seek to express the term " human magnetism. In such writings we find the term employed to explain many of the phenomena of occultism, Nearly, if not all, of the schools of occultism, in all lands and in all times, have taught the existence of this wonderful principle of energy. Persian mysticism the term *glama* is used in the same sense; in Hindu occultism we find the word *prana* serving a similar purpose, Mesmer seems to have stumbled upon this truth when he taught the existence of the universal fluid," although he was far from the truth in his deductions therefrom. In the revival of interest in occult science in western lands, so noticeable in the past generation, and which continues to the present time, we find frequent references to human magnetism, animal magnetism, "vital magnetism." And in the schools of " magnetic healing" which attracted so much attention about ten years ago, we heard much of "the magnetic fluid." The existence of the principle of Nature which we call "Vril " in the Arcane Teaching, has been recognized by many schools of thought throughout human history. Many names have been given to and many theories have been advanced to account for its existence, and to explain its purposes and effects, We shall not attempt to go into the history of this idea, nor lo consider the many attempted explanations above referred too We prefer to go to the fountain head, and present the original Arcane Teaching regarding the principle of Vril.

In the Arcane Teaching, then, the term "Vril" is used in several senses, general and particular as we shall see as we proceed, the first place, Vril is held to be a great cosmic principle of very fine energy permeating all forms of matter, and immanent in thought processes as well, being employed by the principle of mind in its work of thinking, But Vril is not identical with mind. Mind is held to be a prior manifestation of the Infinite, From the mental principle arose Vril and the grosser forms of energy, and then the forms of matter fine and gross, In this original sense Vril is perceived to be a great universal principle from which proceeds a multitudinous manifestation of activities. Vril, in this phase of existence, cannot be defined any more than any universal principle can be defined. We have no words with which to define or explain it.

It is only when we descend to the consideration its manifestations that we are able to explain or define it in our finite terms.

In the second sense of the term, Vril is the principle of inner vital power or energy found to be immanent in all forms of specialized matter, inorganic or organic. It is this recognition of universal immanence that has led science to advance the new theories that Life is present in all forms of matter, even in the crudest and grossest states, phases and forms of matter.

Haeckel boldly asserts that the atoms of matter possess something akin to life, and manifest the capability of perceiving something like sensations, *and the ability to respond thereto.*

Haeckel says: "The two fundamental forms of substance, ponderable matter and ether, are not dead and only moved about by extrinsic force, but they are endowed with sensation and will (though naturally of the lowest grade); they experience an inclination for condensation, a dislike for strain; they strive after the one and struggle against the other."

Haeckel also says: "The different relations of the various elements toward each other, which chemistry calls "affinity," is one of the most important properties of ponderable matter; it is manifested the different relative quantities or proportions of ponderable matter; it is manifested the different relative quantities or proportions of their combination in the intensity of its consummation. Every shade of inclination, from complete indifference to the fiercest passion, is exemplified in the chemical action of the various elements toward each other, just as we find in the psychology of man, and especially in the life of the sexes. Goethe, in his classical romance, 'Affinities,' compared the relation of a pair of lovers with the phenomenon of the same name the formation of chemical combinations, The irresistible passion that draws Edward to the sympathetic Ottilia, or Paris to Helen, and leaps over all bounds of reason and morality, is the same "unconscious" attractive force which impels the living spermatozoon to force an entrance into the ovum in the fertilization of the egg of the animal or plant-the same impetuous movement which unites two atoms of hydrogen to one atom of oxygen for the formation of a molecule of water. This fundamental unity of affinity in the whole of nature, from the simplest chemical process to the most complicated lave story, was recognized by the Greek scientist, Empedocles, the fifth century B. c., in his theory of "the love and hate of elements.' It receives empirical affirmation from the interesting progress of cellular psychology, the great significant of which we have learned to appreciate in the last thirty years, On those phenomena we base our conviction that even the *atom* is not without a rudimentary form of sensation and will, or, as it is better expressed, of feeling *(aesthesis)* and inclination *(tropsis)*-that is, a universal 'soul' of the simplest character. The same must be said of the molecules which are composed of two or more atoms. Further combinations of different kinds of these molecules give rise to simple and, subsequently, complex chemical compounds, in the activity of which the same phenomena are repeated in a more complicated form."

Science now admits, nay, positively affirms, that the principle of Life is immanent in, and manifest through, all forms of material things, inorganic as well as organic, We are not now concerned with the idea of the presence of mind in all of these forms, except inasmuch as mind is always an accompaniment of life. Life is gene rally defined as the quality of sensation and will manifested in forms of matter. But a closer definition is now being advanced science. The latest conception is that *Life consists in the power of independent action and movement-that* is, in the ability to act and move from inner and inherent power, and not from power or force applied from without. It is this very *power* to act and move which the Arcane Teaching holds to be the second phase of the existence of Vril, A body may possess sensation and will -ability to feel, and ability to exercise volition and yet not be able to act and move. Feeling and will are mental states or qualities but the power which acts and moves is something different from mind, for it is what is called vital-force, life-energy, or Vril. A man may f*eel* the sting of an insect, and may then *will* to brush aside the insect. But unless (by the exercise of his will, usually, but sometimes by reflex activity) he sends a current of vital-force, life-energy, nervous energy Vril, in short his muscles will not contract nor will his hand move. Moreover, without Vril he cannot even perform the processes of thought, and come to a decision regarding the brushing away of the insect.

Vril is the force which operates the machinery from the crudest movement up to the highest exercise of the brain cells of the philosopher or mathematician.

Vril, then, in its second phase of manifestation or existence, is the inner power of action and movement of all material forms of the universe, It is by the action of Vril that the *ions,* electrons, corpuscles, or particles of elementary matter are attracted and repelled, , and by which they engage in the wild whirl around each other which resembles the movement of the planets around our sun, which attraction and repulsion and consequent "whirl " combine to form what we know as the *atom* of matter. Likewise, it is Vril which causes these atoms to be attracted and repelled, and to manifest constant vibration, thereby forming the combinations which give to us our eighty elements of matter. And it is by Vril that the molecules (formed of two or more atoms) manifest their varying degrees of cohesion and other molecular qualities, properties, and attributes, and thus give us the distinctive qualities of matter in all of its various forms, Vril, then, is the fine energy of force which enables material things to move of their own power*the power 'Within them.* Vril *is,* in itself, this *power within,* which enables particle or atom of matter to move to and fro; which enables the atoms to form their combinations; which causes the molecules to manifest their qualities; which enables man to bend his arm and direct his pen at the behest and command of his will, urged thereto by his feelings or desires, and supervised by his intellectual reasoning.

Moreover, Vril is at the heart of the great mystery of science Gravitation; that force which operates over infinities of space without the measure of 'arid in spite of obstacles and interferences. Gravitation, which contradicts all the minor laws of physics, is seen really to be Vril, life-energy, and vital-force, in its second phase of manifestation. Vril, in the second phase of manifestation, pervades all space it is immanent in the universal ether, Wherever *anything* is, *Vril* is, in its second phase of manifestation. The above is quite inadequate to give a complete idea of the existence and nature of Vril, but it is sufficient for our purposes at this time.

LESSON II. VRIL IN ORGANIC LIFE

Vril in the third sense of the term, or the third phase of its manifestation or existence, is the life-force or vital-energy of all organic forms of life of all living creatures. From the single cell or moneron in the slime of the ocean-bed, or the lowly quasi-organic forms of green sediment or deposits on rocks and old trees, to the highest forms of animal and man life, Vril is ever present and operative.

Just as protoplasm is the peculiar phase of matter which serves as the body of living organisms, so is this phase or form of Vril the peculiar force or energy which always accompanies organic life, In fact it is the distinctive property or attribute of organic life. When science is forced to decide whether or not a thing is "living" in the ordinary sense of the term, it is the possession or non-possession of this form of Vril which serves to decide the matter and make the distinction. It is this third phase of manifestation of Vril which forms the subject matter of our present consideration in this book.

Vril, in its third phase of manifestation, is the energy which performs the functions of life in the living organism. It is the power by which the living creature carries on the processes of digestion, assimilation, excretion, nourishment, repair, and elimination. It is the power by which it moves its body by conscious will, and by which the subconscious movements of the cells and organs of the body are performed. Vril causes the heart to beat, and the arteries and veins to carry and propel the blood in its outward and inward course causes the intestines and other canals to manifest their peculiar peristaltic action. It is the power by which the will moves the hand and fingers, and by means of which these words are written. We are accustomed to thinking that the *will* causes these movements, and so it does, but only indirectly. The will is a mental phase; it chooses to make the movement, after which it releases or projects the Vril along the channels of the nerves to the muscles. The muscles then contract, and the movement is effected, The will is like the operator managing one of the great cranes in a modern steel works, who touching a button here, and a lever there, swings the mighty instrument in any direction, causing it to descend upon a great mass of steel, lift it up, and swing it to any desired point. But the man and the machinery could never cause the crane to do this work if there was not available the *power* (electricity or steam) subject to the control and direction of the operator. Vril in the human body is like electricity in the trolley car-it is *that which that makes things go"*

While Vril is distributed all over the human body-even the tiniest cell having its share it is found principally in the two great nervous systems, and is stored up in the great reservoirs of the brain, the spinal-cord, and the various plexi or ganglia of the nervous system. For the purposes of simple conception and easy thinking, we may regard this phase of Vril as the "nervous fluid," or nerve-force, of physiology, remembering always, however, that it is no more a "fluid" than is magnetism or electricity, and that it is not a mechanical force. It is much nearer to mind-power than it is to ordinary physical force, and yet it is different from either.

Its place is between mind-power and physical force, while somewhat resembling both.

All attempts to identify Vril with mind-power or physical force must fail, for it is a thing of itself a distinct manifestation of nature or that which l i es behind nature.

There is manifested in some quarters a disposition to consider "vital force" or "vitality " as a distinct entity or "soul" which energizes the physical body, and the same disposition may be manifested by students in their consideration of the third phase of Vril, This is an error, and all the best authorities positively condemn it as such. For instance, Huxley, in speaking of the principle of "vitality," says: "Considered apart from the phenomena of consciousness, the phenomena of life are all dependent upon the working of the same physical and chemical forces as those which are active in the rest of the world. It may be convenient to use the terms "vitality,' and 'vital force' to denote the causes of certain great groups of natural operations, as we employ the names of "electricity ' and "electrical force', to denote others, but it ceases to be proper to do so if such a name implies the absurd assumption that either "electricity" or "vitality" are *entities* playing the part of efficient causes electrical or vital phenomena."

In the same way, it is erroneous to consider Vril as an *entity* or soul, directly and immediately causing the activities and movements of the body. Vril is not the soul, spirit, or mind, of the person any more than it is his physical body, but is a mighty natural force operating upon the body under the control of the conscious or subconscious mental faculties, Its activities manifest in and by means of the physical bodily forms and structure, it is true, but they are inspired and directed by the mind, conscious or subconscious. The physical form may and does *carry* its charge of Vril, but does not *produce* the latter.

Vril *energizes and moves* the physical structure, but does not *cause* it. In a similar manner, while Vril is active in every process of thought, it is not produced by thought; and while it energizes thought processes, it does not *produce* thought in the sense of *causing* it.

Mind (in the ordinary sense); Vril, either as a principle or in its manifestation; and Matter, either as a principle or in manifestation; are *the three coordinate manifested principles* of the Infinite, and depend upon each other for their activities.

This is the teaching not only of modern science, but also of the ancient Arcane sages.

In the previous volumes of this series devoted to the Arcane Teaching, we have seen that Matter exists forms far more tenuous, subde, and fine than any known to the senses of roan; and also in forms far more gross than the imagination of man can picture, In the same teaching we may see that, even more subde than the finest forms of matter mentioned, there exist etheric substances infinitely rare, tenuous and refined. The same is true regarding the teaching concerning Vril. Not only do we see Vril manifesting in the inner movements of the *ions,* atoms, and molecules of matter, and again in its finer phases of animal and human life, but the teaching is that there are forms and manifestations of Vril so much higher than the latter that the ordinary human mind would be unable to conceive of them. But the principle of Vril is ever the same, in high or low manifestation, Much that is called "psychic phenomena "is explainable only by a knowledge of the existence, principles and laws of Vril, as set forth in the Arcane Teachings, Even the ordinary processes of thought are performed by the aid of Vril in a manner not as yet understood by ordinary men, or even by the physical scientists. remains for the occultist to state and understand the finer forces of nature, as manifest in the processes which we call "thought."

Many of us confuse the idea of "thought" with that of "mind," but the occultist and scientist know better than this. Mind, in itself, is a great principle the exact nature of which cannot be grasped by the ordinary mind. Thought, on the contrary, is a manifestation of mind, assisted by Vril. The material scientist who perceives the operation of Vril in the processes of thought, and who recognizes the relationship between these processes and that of the physical world, is right so far as he goes, for the activities of Vril are employed therein, just as they are in many physical and chemical processes for reasons which we have already stated. But he makes a wrong induction who holds that, by reason thereof, thought is merely "a secretion of matter," or "a byproduct of matter." He fails to realize that Mind is the original cause of thought, and that it employs Vril in its thought processes just as it employs the fine matter of the brain-cells in these processes. It is only when we recognize the co-existence and co-ordination of Mind, Vril, and Matter, that we are able to perceive the real underlying causes of the phenomena of thought.

Physical science is also error when it attempts to limit the activities of "vital-force" or "nerve-force" (which are but names for the activities of one phase of Vril) to the particular human body in which it is generated or stored, Science loses the opportunity to satisfactorily account for much perplexing phenomena, by insisting upon this antiquated and narrow conception. That which is generally termed "psychic phenomena" is explainable only when the fact of the "long-distance" effect of Vril is perceived and admitted. Likewise, many of the metaphysicians and pseudo-occultists are in error when they attempt to account for certain psychic phenomena by the hypothesis of "mind action" alone. *The mind cannot produce effect at a distance without the employment of the power of Vril,* any more than the wireless-telegraph operator can produce his long-distance effects by his own will unaided by the power employed in his wonderful instruments.

The physiologist who leaves Vril out of his calculations is no more at sea than is the modern metaphysician or "mental scientist" who omits it from his theories, explanations, and experiments, Without the power of Vril there could be none of the phenomena of mentalism, made so popular by the new schools of mental science and the great revival of interest in ancient occultism which has distinguished the present generation. The mental scientist who understands the nature and methods of employment of Vril, is enabled to double successes. He uses Vril, of course, unconsciously and unknowingly, in all of his experiments and work but he wastes more energy than he uses. 1t is only when he understands the nature of Vril, and the methods of its employment in his mental science work, that he can hope to project his mental power effectively and efficiently, Yet so carried away with their metaphysical theories are some of these practitioners, that they iterate and reiterate "all is mind." and deny even the existence of such a principle as Vril.

Those who assert that "thoughts are things" are right so far as they go but they do not go far enough. A thought cannot be generated without Vril. Neither can it be projected to a distance without a peculiar employment of the force of Vril. The earnest belief and active faith of many practitioners of mental science causes them to unconsciously energize their thought with Vril, spite of their denials of its existence, if they would lay aside some of their prejudices, and investigate the subject of Vril, they could and would be enabled so to energize their thought that their power and success would be redoubled, The narrow metaphysician is as much in error as is the narrow materialist. It is only when *the triangle of being* Mind, Vril, and Matter-vis recognized, that one's full powers and energies may be manifested.

LESSON III. THE MECHANISM OF VRIL

The student should bear in mind that Vril is never *manufactured* in the human body.

There is just so much Vril in existence a certain amount or quantity and this amount or quantity never can be added to, nor subtracted from, by the organism of man. Just as the instruments employed in electrical science gather up, store up, and transform into various forms and phases the electricity already in existence in nature, without creating or destroying a single particle thereof, so does the organism of man gather from the principle of Vril that which it requires; so does it store up a reserve supply of Vril; so does it transform Vril into the various forms and phases required for the purposes of the organism; and so does it use Vril in its activities. But the Vril so gathered, stored, and transformed is never created by the organism; nor is the Vril so used ever destroyed. The seeming creation is merely the absorption of the Vril needed, from the universal supply thereof; and the seeming destruction is merely the return of Vril to the universal supply thereof, Vril is never created nor destroyed it merely undergoes transformation of phase, form, and use.

The mechanism of the human body involved in the absorption, storage, transformation, and use of Vril, is that which is known in ordinary physiology as "the nervous system." Very few persons know the facts concerning this most wonderful mechanism of the human organism, which is employed as the mechanism of the activities of Vril. In order to understand the activities of Vril, the student should have at least an elementary knowledge of the human nervous system. Accordingly, we invite you to a brief consideration thereof.

The nervous system of the human being is divided into two great systems, vis, the cerebro-spinal system and the sympathetic system. The cerebro-spinal nervous system consists of that part of the general nervous system which is composed of the brain and the spinal cord, together with the nerves which emerge from the latter. Its functions are those connected with the processes of sensation, volition, and the higher processes of thought, conveys to the reports the organs of feeling, seeing, smelling, hearing, and tasting. It manifests consciousness and the phenomena thereof, It attends to the functions of thought. It is the channel and mechanism of action. Through it the individual receives knowledge of the outside world, and communicates information to the outside world, It has been compared to a telegraph system, the brain being the great central station, the spinal column being the cable running from the central office, and the nerves being the connecting telegraph wires running to the minor stations of the body.

The brain of man consists of three parts, known, respectively, as the medulla oblongata, the cerebellum, and the cerebrum. The medulla oblongata is situated at the upper end of the spinal cord, and is an enlargement of the upper portion thereof. It is a reflex centre of a high order. It controls, to a certain extent, certain functions of the sympathetic nervous system, and therefore the activities of the heart, lungs, blood-vessels, and the abdominal organs, its activities are out of the ordinary field of consciousness, and belong to those of the subconscious mind. The cerebellum, sometimes known as "the little brain," lies just above the medulla oblongata, and like it is a reflex centre of a high order. Its purpose is to co-ordinate the muscular movements of the body, and to function along the line of acquired reflexes.

When we have learned to perform certain regular muscular movements so that they become habitual, we have really passed their execution on to the cerebellum. As we all know, when we first learn to perform a new and difficult task, such as walking, riding, skating, writing, or running a machine, we must pay conscious attention to it, the cerebrum being the part of the brain then employed. But when we have mastered the rudimentary motions so that they may be performed with very little conscious attention, the cerebellum takes charge, and the actions are thereafter performed almost automatically and unconsciously by reason thereof, In habitual muscular activity the cerebrum merely initiates the motion, and then the cerebellum takes it up and continues it subconsciously.

When the cerebellum is injured, the gait is affected and the individual often loses the power to perform many of the usual reflex actions.

Professor Halleck says of the importance of the reflex activities mentioned: "Thus the mind is not only saved trouble of attending to every little movement, but much time is gained, After the child has learned the difficult art of balancing himself on his feet, walking becomes largely a reflex act. At first the child must centre his whole attention on movements to balance the body. The man can think out the most complex problems while walking, because the reflex nervous centres are superintending the balancing process. Few men remember which end of the collar they button on first, or which shoe they put on first; yet the reflex nerve centre, if left to itself, has an variable order in executing these movements."

Professor Gordy says: "The cerebellum is the organ for many acquired reflexes. All that seems necessary for the mind or consciousness to have to do with it is to set the machine well going, so to speak, when some part of the nervous mechanism relieves consciousness of all further work in the matter."

The cerebrum, or "large brain" occupies the greater part of the entire cavity of the skull. It is the headquarters of consciousness, to which the nerves of sensation report. A blow that affects the cerebrum produces unconsciousness. The nervous connection with the cerebrum must maintained, else the sensation is not felt. Injury to the cerebrum impairs the faculties of thought and of memory. From this and other reasons, science knows that the cerebrum is the part of the brain most closely related to consciousness and intelligence, But its quality and functions vary materially its various parts. The" cortex," or thin rind or outer covering of gray matter, is held to be the seat of intellectual activity and consciousness. Moreover, there exists in the cerebrum, what is known as "Focalization of functions," that is to say that certain parts or areas of the cerebrum are devoted to special functional activity. For instance, there is the "motor zone," from which are sent out the orders to transmit Vril so as to move any part of the body.

Science has so definitely located these zones that "it is possible for a surgeon to find the small centre which moves the vocal cords, directs a thumb, or winks an eye." Then there are the "sensory tracts,' which receive impressions from the senses. The various sense centres have been located with a surprising degree of accuracy.

Science has not as yet succeeded localizing the intellectual areas definitely, although phrenology has done something in that direction.

The spinal cord is continuous with the brain, the two forming parts of the same system. The spinal cord occupies the canal in the centre of the spinal column, or "backbone." It is composed of gray matter and white matter. It is almost separated into two parts by fissures, but there always remains a ridge of connecting nerve matter something like the connecting bar in the letter H. From the spinal cord emerge thirty-one pairs of spinal nerves, springing from either side of the cord, each nerve having two roots, an anterior and a posterior. An authority says of the functions of these nerves and roots: "the foot were pricked, the sensory impulse would enter the spinal cord by the posterior root. The spinal ganglia would set free a motor impulse, which would leave for the foot by the anterior root of the nerve. If the posterior root of the nerve supply of the foot were cut, the foot might be crushed without a sensation of pain, but a motor impulse could be sent as before; if the anterior or motor root were cut, the application of a hot iron would cause as much pain as ever, but the sufferer could not move the foot an inch from the Iron, no matter how great the pain. A large part of the body is absolutely dependent upon the integrity of the spinal cord for the transmission of sensory and motor impulses.

If a person's back is broken, that part of the body supplied by nerves attached to the spinal cord below the seat of injury is paralyzed. Such an unfortunate might watch the amputation of his own leg with as little feeling of pain as if the limb belonged to another person. No act of will would suffice to move such a limb."

The above authority also says, regarding what is called "reflex action ": "Reflex nervous action is the result of that power resident in nervous ganglia, which often unconsciously causes many muscular and vital movements. The spinal cord is largely made up of such masses of nervous matter, which have sometimes been called 'little brains.' If one were to prick the toe of a sleeper, the sensory nerve at that point would report the fact to one of the lower spinal nerve masses, This ganglion, without waiting to hear from the brain, would issue a command to the motor nerve, and the foot would be immediately withdrawn. Unless the thrust were severe, the sleeper would not awake, nor would he be conscious of pain or of movement of his foot. This nervous action is called "reflex,' because when the sensory nerve conveys an impulse to the ganglion this impulse is at once sent without the action of the will, reflected back by a motor nerve. Thus the mind is not only saved the trouble *of* attending to every Little movement, but much time is gained".

The nerves emerging from the spinal column divide and subdivide and finally reach every part of the body. Like the wires *of* a great telegraph system they reach every point, important or insignificant. Without these nerves thus reaching every part of the body, some parts *of* the body would be without connection with the brain and would be cut off from the supply of Vril, or vital-energy. These nerves serve to convey sensation from a part to the brain, and to carry in return a motor or movement impulse and supply of Vril from the brain to the part. The nerves are classed as follows: (1) afferent nerves, which carry a stimulus from some part of the body to the central nervous system; and (2) efferent nerves, which transmit the motor impulse, or incentive to movement, from the central system to the part. The sensory nerves are afferent nerves; motor nerves are efferent nerves, Bet there are other nerves of both afferent and efferent classes, in addition to the sensory and motor nerves just mentioned. As an authority says: "In addition to these there are nerves which regulate the size of the blood vessels and the nourishment of the body, control. the secretions, and perform various other offices connected with transmitting stimuli, which are neither sensory nor motor." The nerve-cells are tiny knots of bunches of nerve matter, connected with nerve fibres. They are of various shapes. A *ganglion* (which, as we have seen, performs reflex action) is a group, confederation, or aggregation of nerve cells. Each ganglion may be called a "tilde brain," for it resembles the brain in many respects, The spinal ganglia receive sensory impulses and in return send forth motor impulses to action.

The second great division of the general nervous system is that known as *the sympathetic nervous system.* This great nervous system has control of the involuntary processes, such as nutrition, growth, repair, elimination, digestion, respiration, circulation. It is situated principally in the thoracic, abdominal, and pelvic cavities, and is distributed to internal organs, It consists of a double-chain of ganglia on the sides of the spinal column, with scattered ganglia the head, neck, chest and abdomen. These ganglia are connected with each other by filaments, and are also connected with the cerebro-spinal system by motor and sensory nerves. From the ganglia, numerous branches of fibres reach out to the various organs of the body, the blood-vessels, etc. At various points in the body, the sympathetic nerves meet and form nerve-masses called plexi, of which the solar plexus is the principal and largest one.

The solar plexus is a great mat of sympathetic nerves, situated in the epigastric region, on either side of the spinal column, immediately back of what is generally known as "the pit of the stomach." It is composed of both gray and white brain matter, similar to that which composes the brains of man, and is quite a complex centre. It plays an important part in the subconscious processes of the body, and is very sensitive a blow over its region has been known to produce death, and in a celebrated prize-fight of some years ago it was the place to which the "knock-out blow" was directed.

Its importance is being realized by science, more particularly during the past few years. By some authorities it has been called the "abdominal brain." is the great storehouse of that form of Vril which supplies the organs of the body which are concerned with nutrition, general vitality, the reproductive system, the circulation, and the nerves themselves. Moreover, it serves as a reserve storage battery from which even the brain may draw power times of necessity, and which, after effecting a slight transformation, it may use effectively.

It must remembered that ordinarily the processes of the sympathetic nervous system are performed subconsciously and without calling on the conscious mind for aid or guidance. But the sympathetic nervous system may be and often is affected by the action of the conscious mind acting upon it along the lines of "suggestion," and often causing it to perform its work improperly and poorly. In the same way, however, the conscious mind may suggest to the subconscious, and thus affect the sympathetic nervous system in the direction of helpful ideas and impulses. The conscious mind of the trained individual may reach any of the organs of body, and not only may send them currents of Vril and thus strengthen and build them up, but by moving the involuntary muscles supporting them may even give them internal exercise, The man or woman who understands the art of suggesting to the subconscious mind, and of directing currents of Vril to the parts of the body, may keep his or her system in perfect condition and functioning power, and thus reach an old age of health, vigor, and virility.

By this method not only an additional nervestimulus may be given to every part of the body by means of both sets of nerves (cerebro-spinal and sympathetic) but the circulation of blood may also be so directed by the will, and when charged with Vril may invigorate any or all parts of the body, at will. AH of these features of the use of Vril by means of the trained will, will be considered during our treatment of the subject in this book. At present our only purpose is to explain the mechanism in, by, over, and through which Vril operates in the human organism.

LES SON IV. VRIL IN PHYSICAL MANIFESTATION

VRIL is in physical manifestation every activity or function of the body, From the slightest movement of the cell to the more complex activities of the organs of the physical body, Vril is seen to be in manifestation and activity, The subconscious planes of the mind of the individual have control of the majority of the physical activities and functions, the conscious mind not being drawn into the activity. But in these subconscious processes Vril is ever the active force and power by means of which the work is performed. The subconscious mind without the power of Vril would be like a man without arms, hands, or tools, who would seek to perform skilled manual labor.

On the other hand, Vril without the directing impulses of the subconscious mind would be like the arms, hands, and tools, apart from the directing power of the brain of the workman. It is by the power of Vril that the acorn grows into the oak, and the blade of grass forces its way through the hard soil. It is by the power of that the single reproductive cell of the parents develops, grows, and evolves into the babe at birth, and later into the adult man or woman. There is, of course, always mind behind these activities, but there is also always Vril power to perform the work of that mind.

Science teaches us that the body is composed of a multitude of single cells, which forming in groups of greater or less size and degree of complexity, constitute the organs and parts of the body. Each tiny has its own degree of mentality, and each its own little charge of Vril. These cells are as tireless workers as the bees in a hive. There is constant activity in the realm of the cells. Day and night, without haste and without rest, these little cells are being born, are performing their life tasks, and are dying, being cast from the system and supplanted by new cells which have evolved from them. Every cell is, to an extent, an independent entity an individual. But this individuality is often merged with that of other cells, and a co-operative cell-community is formed for the purpose of performing that portion of the common task of the socialistic commonwealth of the body.

Some of cells are stationary, while others are operating under a roving commission. Some are on the scouting line, while others are engaged in actual warfare with the invaders of the body. Others still are held as a reserve corps, awaiting a special call to action, great body of cells performs the work of the day-laborer, and does the drudgery of the community, Others are engaged in the processes of thought, and are consumed by these activities, millions of cells giving up their lives to produce a single piece of continued thoughtwork, Some of the cells perform the work of carriers, conveying new material in the blood to all parts of the body, where other cells build it up into physical form the carrying cells are the hod-carriers and the brick-carriers of the system, while the building cells are like the bricklayers, carpenters, and other artisans.

Other cells are busily engaged in carrying away the debris, worn-out tissue and dead cells, to the great crematory of the lungs, where the waste matter is burned up by the oxygen and cast off through the exhaled breath, Other cells perform the odd jobs of scavenger work, and carry waste matter to other parts of the system, where it is cast off in excrementitious form. Other cells attend to the work of digestion, purification, assimilation; the chemical laboratories of the system being very extensive and complicated. Other cells are as living instruments and telegraph wires in the nervous system, and receive, send, and transmit the messages of the system, acting, as well, as transmitters of the additional supply of required in various parts of the body. The standing army and pol ice-force of the cell community are very large, These protectors and guardians of the body protect the system from the invading germs, bacteria, and other foreign organisms which have found entrance to it. They attack the invaders, and either devour them or else cast them forth from the system through the ordinary channels or by means of boils, pimples, and other eruptions.

The large force of cells employed in the great chemical laboratories of the system is kept very busy at all times. There is oxygen and food-substances to be used by cell-groups in all parts of the body, There is carbonic-acid refuse, and burnt up material to be cast off.

There is food to be converted proper form and condition to nourish the system.

There is gastric juice, saliva, pancreatic juices, bile, milk, procreative fluids, to be manufactured constantly.

To give one an idea of the number of cells so employed, the authorities have estimated that in each single cubic inch of blood there are at least 75,000,000 of the red blood cells alone, not to speak of the white corpuscles and the other classes of cells.

Seventy-five million in one single cubic inch think of that! And each one of this army actuated by mind, and carrying its tiny charge of Vril!

And we should remember that at every moment of our ·lives, from birth to death, the great army of cells is constantly at work building, repairing, renovating, replacing, every portion of our bodies, In a few weeks our bodies are almost entirely made over. It requires an enormous amount of energy and power to perform this work and that power is always Vril-power, for there is no other power that can do the work, or by which the work can be done. There is a constant using up of Vril-power, and there must need be a constant replenishing of the store of Vril in the body.

In addition to the expenditure of Vril in the processes of the cells, we find that there is also an enormous expenditure in the voluntary activities of the individual. Each individual is like a great piece of machinery, moves about, walks, runs, or leaps, He moves his arms and legs, his hands, his fingers, and his entire body, in the activities of waking-life. Every motion of the body, even the slightest, causes an expenditure of Vril-power, and each expenditure must be paid for by a decrease the store of Vril in the system. Each item of expenditure must be counterbalanced by a renewal of the supply, else there is physical deterioration and loss of energy to the individual. Many persons are so prodigal of their Vril, and so ignorant or heedless regarding the renewal of the supply, that they become depleted in vitality, virility, and general nervous energy, and become physical wrecks or else subjects of the so-called neurasthenia or "nervous prostration " which so sorely afflicts the modern race. This result is not caused by excessive thinking, as so many suppose, for the brain will stand an immense amount of regular, arduous labor without manifesting evil results. It is the emotional excesses (emotion consuming an enormous amount of Vril), and the "waste-motion," which tends to this depletion.

Moreover, the average man or woman who suffers from nervous breakdown is not aware of the need of the system for calm repose and relaxation for the purpose of recharging the system with Vril. Even in sleep these persons keep their nervous system and muscles at a tension, and exhaust their supply of Vril just as the careless housewife exhausts the household supply of water by allowing the faucets to dribble and drip, The prevention of this waste of Vril is a very important matter, second only in importance to the knowledge of the proper methods of acquiring a more than ordinary supply of Vril in order to meet the requirements of modern life in a civilization which is seemingly bent upon burning up nerve-energy. The ordinary person, pursuing the even tenor of man's natural 1He, has very Little need of instruction along these lines, for he neither wastes nor expends in work more Vril than is normally supplied to the system by means of the impulses of the subconscious mind. But the man of the large cities of to-day persistently wastes an abnormal amount of Vril, as well as expends in work an also unreasonable amount, and unless makes up the deficit by the methods made known by a study of the subject, he will suffer by reason thereof.

It is deemed extremely probable, according to eminent thinkers along these lines, that in the course of the evolution of the race, nature will adapt the supply of Vril to the increased needs of the race, and the whole matter will adjust itself accordingly. But nature works as slowly as it works surely, and it will be some time before it feels the necessity of automatically adjusting the conditions to meet the unnatural requirements and expenditures of modern life in our large centres of industry. Until then, man should help nature along, as he has in many other ways, and by preventing the unnatural waste, and increasing the supply of Vril by methods such as we shall describe in this book, he will be able to maintain an equilibrium and balance, with consequent preservation of health and energy. He may even go still further and by increasing his supply of Vril he may so charge himself with this life-energy and nerve-force as to become a very dynamo of energy, activity, and power.

The man or woman doing this will possess a mighty advantage over the majority of the race at this time. Such a course will mean increased efficiency, increased power, and increased success and, let us hope, increased happiness.

LESSON V. THE TRANSFORMATION OF VRIL

We have seen that Vril, in its second phase, is inherent all forms of atomic matter, and consequently in all forms of matter resulting from combinations of material atoms, As all matter is composed of material atoms, it follows then that Vril is to be found *all* matter. But there is a vast difference in the forms and the conditions in and under which it so appears. Just as matter is the same whether appearing in the form and condition of the diamond or hardest steel, or in the form and condition of bread and butter, so in the same way it may be said that Vril is the same *in* principle whether it appears in the granite rock or in the air. But it is likewise true that just as steel and diamond cannot be used by man as a source of physical nourishment in the same way that bread and butter can be so used, so Vril in the granite rock is not available to man in the same way as is Vril in the air, the water, and in protoplasmic food material.

While all things nature are, at the last, one in substance and principle, nevertheless the laboratory of nature forms many combinations and imposes many conditions upon these things, thereby fitting some things to one purpose and other things to other purposes. Here is where science steps in and insists upon the practical side of things as opposed to the "pure principles" of metaphysics. As an authority once said: "Those who like to study the puzzles as to what mind and matter really are, must go to metaphysics. Should we ever find that salt, arsenic, and all things else, are the same substance with a different molecular arrangement, we should still not use them interchangeably." And so to the man who may object that "Vril is Vril," we would remark that, while "matter is matter," he would do well to select protoplasmic forms of matter for food, rather than diamonds or steel the same principle applying to Vril in its application to human requirements.

Nature has so wisely arranged matters that the supply of Vril, in its second phase, is found in its most usable form for man in the precise combinations which meet the requirements of its transmutation into the third-phase condition, in which alone man may use it in those very forms of substances which man employs in his physical economy for other purposes. Vril, in the precise combination required for transmutation for man's requirements, is found (1) in the protoplasmic substances which man naturally partakes of as food and nourishment; (2) in a lesser *degree,* in the water which man drinks. in order to preserve his fluid-balance and to eliminate from his system the waste matter: and (3) in a high degree in the atmospheric air which man breathes Into his lungs for the purpose of obtaining oxygen to serve in maintaining bodily heat, and to bum up the waste-matter of the system, both in the cell itself and in the lungs. Thus, we see, man may know nothing whatever regarding the principle and uses of Vril, and yet will be compelled by nature to partake of those very substances to which it inheres.

Under normal circumstances the individual will secure sufficient Vril by the "hit or miss" system of eating, drinking, and breathing practiced by him, without any particular instruction on the subject, But, as we have said, the unusual conditions in which modern man lives, particularly in the large cities, are such that there is a greater waste and a greater use than Nature has intended or provided for, and, accordingly, the man who so dissipates one of Nature's greatest forces must replace and replenish it by extraordinary means. He must bring his intellect to the aid of his subconscious mind, and supply that which in the ordinary course of his life he may fail to secure. This is in no way contrary to nature, is merely aiding nature in her work. We see instances of this in other features connected with the physical well-being of man. For instance, man in the natural state does not need to be urged to exercise, for his ordinary vocation and day's work supplies him with all the exercise he requires. But the man whose work keeps him indoors and at the desk does not obtain the normal amount of exercise or out-of-doors experience, and accordingly he is compelled to walk for his health and to practice various forms of "artificial" exercise. The natural man does not need to take a vacation and indulge in fishing, boating, golfing, for his physical well-being, while his brother in the city is advised to do that for recreation which the natural man does from necessity, The example of an eminent statesman felling trees for exercise and recreation, while the woodcutter finds nothing but "work" in the same employment, is another illustration of this fact.

So in this little book we shall have something to say regarding the means and methods whereby one who is deficient in Vril-force may obtain that which he needs and which he cannot get the ordinary way. The man leading the natural life in the woods and with sufficient physical exercise to bring into action the Vril-absorbing functions, not need this instruction it is not for him. But it is highly important that the average individual who reads this book should take advantage of the simple, natural, rational system and methods herein advanced. This ancient teaching is highly practicable and applicable to modern conditions. We may apply these teachings of a past civilization to the requirements of our own, with great benefit.

LESSON VI. VRIL IN FOOD AND WATER

ORDINARY physiology does not recognize the element of Vril in food, but concerns itself with much important discussion of "calorics," "proteids," "food-units," all of which is very well and proper, for a scientific knowledge of food elements and the values thereof is important. In the state of nature man instinctively selects the class and variety of food best adapted for his needs. The centuries of human experience have built up an almost infallible instinct in this respect which man may safely follow under normal conditions. But so artificial are the conditions under which the majority of us live that instinct is almost stifled, and a most unnatural system of nourishment prevails. Accordingly, instruction upon this point is much needed by the race. But we have no intention of discussing this phase of the question of nourishment or food.

The work has been well done by many others and the information concerning the same is at the call of nearly every person, Our purpose is to consider food merely from the standpoint of its Vril-containing properties.

There is a vast difference in the amount form of Vril in the various forms and kinds of foods. The foods rich in proteids contain much Vril in a form readily available to man. The carbohydrates are also charged with considerable Vril. The fats contain but little Vril in a form available for man very Little real energy, but much heat-producing material.

But man in his unscientific methods of obtaining nourishment fails to secure either the best food-value or the greatest amount of Vril from any class of foods, Modern science, as well as the ancient teachings, informs man regarding the wasteful methods employed by him, and the methods which will obviate these.

Human food material may be divided into three general classes, as follows: (1) Proteid or nitrogenous foods, such as meats, nuts, peas, beans, etc., which are the plastic foods or tissue-builders of the system; (2) the carbohydrates, such as sugars, starches, gums, etc., which are both tissue-builders and heat-producers; (3) the fats, such as animal fats, vegetable oils, butter, etc., serve principally as heat-producers.

Various authorities have many differing theories regarding the proportions in which the various food-elements should enter into the ordinary diet. But all agree that a variety is needed, and that a well-balanced diet consists of articles of food from each class, in about the proportion usually observed in the usual menu of "middle-class" families, The very poor often are unable to obtain many articles of nourishing food, while the very rich often neglect the truly nourishing foods in favor of the "fancy dishes." The average gives us the best selection. A well-known authority was fond of stating that in his opinion the well balanced diet was clearly represented by the sentence: "Bread and butter, beefsteak, potatoes, eggs, and milk," and that variations of the menu would be equally well balanced, providing the same general rule was followed.

It was one of the favorite theories of the ancient occultists that all "sex foods" contain more Vril than other classes of food. By "sex foods" is meant such animal or vegetable products as contain either the reproductive cell or seed, or else serve to nourish the young animal or plant. In the first mentioned class we find eggs, nuts, fruits, grain, com, berries, which contain the "seed" of reproductive life. In the second class we have milk, cream, butter, the fruit-juices, syrups, The theory was that nature gave in concentrated form the Vril needed by the young growing· animal or plant. While modem science has not as yet adopted this idea of the ancient occultists, there are indications that such recognition and approval is not so very far off.

The growing popularity of nuts and fruits as articles of diet, the increase of interest in the milk diet, the increasing use of fruit-juices, show that human experience is verifying the ancient theories.

But we are only indirectly concerned with the question of "what kind of food." Our principal concern in this book is rather ((*how* food should be eaten." The ancient occultists laid great stress upon the importance of the proper mastication of food, and modern science is becoming very much interested in the subject, actual practice the old occultists practiced many of the fundamental principles that are found in the modern popular theory called "Fletcherism," except that they did not carry the matter to such an extreme as some of the modern teachers on the subject.

The ancient teachers held that all food should be thoroughly masticated until it was reduced to a pulp and was then almost unconsciously swallowed. They carried this to such an extent that they even followed the plan of mastication when a mouthful of milk was taken, and when the softest foods were placed in the mouth. They did not have the knowledge of the chemistry of foods possessed by modern science, but their experience taught them that food masticated this way gave the greatest nourishment, and, what to them was equally important, that this way the nerve-ends of the tongue and mouth absorbed a supply of concentrated Vril from the food. They held that the nerves of the tongue and mouth alone were capable of performing this office, and that after the food passed down the throat there was no possibility of the absorption of Vril from it.

The ancient occultists held that so long as there remains "taste" in the mouthful of food, there is Vril to be found in it. When the "taste" disappears, the Vril has been absorbed. Consequently they ate slowly, and masticated each mouthful carefully so as to extract the greatest amount of "taste" from it. They claimed that this method of eating not only served to extract largest amount from the food, but also gave to the person eating it fullest epicurean pleasure. They claimed that they obtained a pleasure from eating that the glutton could never experience or even conceive.

Accepting this as true, it is further evident, by reason of the physiological principles involved, that food so eaten is thoroughly saturated with saliva and more easily digested by the stomach and intestines when finally swallowed, and that there is consequently but a trifling amount of waste, and a freedom from overloading the stomach. By giving the stomach only an easy task to perform, we are enabled to employ the energy and blood (generally used in the processes of digestion) for service in the bran.

The occultists were always "clear in the head," and never suffered the feeling of over-eating and brain-lethargy, neither did they acquire dyspepsia or other disorders of the digestive organism. The student will do well to experiment with this plan of eating, or at least partially adopt it in his everyday life. We promise that if he does this, he will before long experience a new feeling of energy, health, vigor, vitality, and virility, which will prove to him the soundness of the method.

We have no intention of prescribing a dietary for students of this book. Such information must be looked for in works on the subject of nutrition and diet. But in order to answer the very natural questions which frequently arise in this connection, we would say that the ancient occultists, as a rule, lived very simply and followed the rule of " eating to live " rather than "living to eat." Yet such is the law of compensation to be found throughout nature, that they obtained far greater pleasure in their nourishment than did the gourmands and gluttons of their times. This principle is true throughout all nature avoid excesses and thus experience the true normal satisfaction in all of nature's functionings. He who would seek satisfaction in excess but defeats his object: while he who religiously avoids excess attains that which the extremists miss.

The ancient occultists, while avoiding artificial systems, and while keeping as close to nature as possible, found that their natural instincts (freed from excesses of any kind) inclined them toward a diet of nuts, fruits, milk, eggs, grain, butter, juices, vegetable oils, all of which, it will be noticed, come under the classification of "sex foods," as previously mentioned.

Even the vegetable oils, such as olive oil, are found to have some association with "seeds" or the material surrounding the same. Milk, butter, and the fruit juices come under the category of nourishment for the sprouting seed, or growing young thing, We are of the opinion that the ancient occultists did not deliberately select this dietary from any specially preconceived theory, but that, on the contrary, they found by experiment and experience that this class of foods served their purposes better than any other, Of course the very natural explanation is seen in the fact that nature bends special energy toward supplying the embryo with the most nourishing and the most vitally-powerful material this being true in both animal and plant life. It is very probable that this theory will be worked out in detail, in the light of modern science, by some scientific investigators in the near future, In the meantime, we may do well to take this leaf of experience from the book of life of the ancient occultists, even in the absence of a detailed theory.

The ancient occultists also held that water contains a certain amount of available Vril, which man may extract to advantage by scientific methods of drinking. Accordingly they drank only in small sips, allowing the water to remain in the mouth a few moments before swallowing, during which time it came in continued contact with the nerves of the tongue and mouth. They held that after being swallowed, the water yields no Vril to the body, and serves merely the very useful purpose of the irrigation of the system and the carrying away of refuse material; that no one could ever experience the real pleasure of drinking except in this way, So long as available Vril remains in the water, the tongue and mouth experience a peculiar feeling or sense of satisfaction and gratification, which is unknown to those who *pour* the water down their throats. The increasing use of "straws," o. "sippers" by modem persons in drinking lemonade, iced-tea, and other liquids, would seem to indicate that this satisfaction or gratification is becoming known, even though its reason is not suspected, In this way the very *essence* of the water or cooling beverage is absorbed, and the person feels correspondingly refreshed. The plan may be employed to equal advantage in drinks, although ancient occultists refrained from hot drinks except for the purpose of occasionally "washing out" the stomach intestines, or of correcting some physical indisposition, the latter, however, being quite rare among them by reason of the life they led.

We trust that in the spirit of investigation and knowledge, at least, the student will experiment with the above indicated methods of eating and drinking, in order to demonstrate to his own satisfaction the advantages obtaining the Vril contained in food and water. In connection with the methods of breathing which will now be taken up, the aforesaid methods will be found to afford a method of cultivating and preserving physical well-being which will be far ahead of the more complicated systems advised and exploited by the teachers of hygiene and physical culture. The advantage lies in the quick results obtained, as well as in the fact that one does not have to seek for material outside of the everyday things of nature, All that is required is that one manifests his appreciation of nature's bounty in a rational manner. It is merely an "intelligent return to nature."

LESSON VII. VRIL IN THE AIR

As we have said in a preceding lesson, Vril is found in a high degree in the precise combination required for transmutation into human vital energy and nervous force, in the atmospheric air which man constantly breathes into his lungs. But science does not admit this anymore than it does the existence of Vril in food and water. To science, air is merely a combination of oxygen and nitrogen with a mixture of carbureted hydrogen and carbonic acid, a trace of ammonia, and a suggestion of the four newly discovered atmospheric elements, vis, argon, crypton, metargon, and neon or, more strictly, oxygen and nitrogen holding a mixture of several other substances in small proportions. But the occult teachings have always held that in the atmospheric air of the earth there is to be found Vril in a high degree of potency, and in a condition which renders it very easily absorbed and assimilated by the nervous system of plants, animals, and human beings. It would seem that the special combination of oxygen and nitrogen produces a condition in which the element of Vril is easily liberated under certain conditions, in such form as to be easily transmuted and absorbed.

To the physiologist the sole purpose of breathing is that of oxygenating the blood and burning up the waste matter of the system. So important is this function that man is unable to exist for more than a few minutes without fresh air. Without correct habits of breathing, no living creature can hope to live the average lifetime of its kind. So much importance does modern hygiene attach to the subject of correct breathing, that a vigorous attack is being made upon the old-fashioned habit of keeping houses and rooms tightly closed, and a campaign of "open air cure" is under way under the leadership of enthusiastic physicians.

But highly important as is *this* function of breathing, it is no more important than the twin-function attached to it by the Arcane teaching. The latter .is the function by means of which the human system absorbs, transmutes, and stores away a supply of Vril from the atmospheric air in the course of ordinary breathing, When it is known that at least eighty-five per cent of the used in the human body is obtained directly from the air, the importance of breathing, in relation to this function, may be appreciated. Not only does the human system obtain Vril directly from the air, but it obtains it indirectly also from the same source. For instance, the Vril in the food has originally been obtained from the air. Also it is known that inherent charge of in water has been in some way absorbed from the air. Water that has become "stale" may be given new energy by being poured cup to cup such a way as to allow it to pass through the air. And it is a matter of common knowledge that distilled water lacks a "something " that can be given it only by passing it through the air in the manner above described, -that "something" is Vril.

The Arcane teaching is not explicit in the direction of explaining the exact physiological process by which the system acquires its supply of Vril from the air in the ordinary process of breathing. AH that is said on this score would seem to indicate that the sympathetic nervous system plays an important part in the absorption and transmutation, and that the various ganglia and plexi of the system act as storage batteries or reservoirs from which the entire nervous system draws regular supply, and its emergency supply in case of unusual need. Moreover, all the occult teachings insist that the preliminary absorption of Vril is dependent to some extent upon the passage of air through the nasal passages and the continuation thereof, and that "mouth-breathing" some way fails to produce the same result, is thought probable that some the delicate nerves which are involved in the sense of smell may in some way have a secondary part to play in the preliminary function of the absorption of Vril.

It is a fact acknowledged by physiologists that persons who breathe through the mouth are not nearly so healthy as those who habitually breathe through the nostrils. This fact is known to the savage races, many of whom take great care in forcing their infants to acquire the habit of nostril-breathing and to avoid mouth-breathing, Children afflicted with adenoids (a growth or swelling produced by the overgrowth of the adenoid tissue in the roof of the pharynx, which interfere with correct nasal breathing, are usually deficient in physical and mental vigor. The slight operation required for the removal of the growth works almost a miracle, the former sufferers manifesting from the start increased physical vitality and mental energy. In many other ways the report of modern physiology agrees with that of the ancient occult teachings regarding the matter of nostril-breathing as compared with mouth-breathing.

Occultists who practice breathing methods for the purpose of the absorption of Vril frequently moisten each nostril before beginning their exercises. This plan is held to increase the power of the nerves of the nasal channel, and to increase the sense of smell as well. Some of the Oriental occultists draw water by suction up through the nasal passages, allowing it to escape through the mouth by means of the canal connecting the nose with the throat, This plan, by the way, is said to be a preventive of nasal disorders such as catarrh. The nostrils should always be kept clear of obstructions, and a healthy condition preserved.

Another fact known to the ancient occultists which also is unknown to modern physiology is that *the individual may largely influence the power of absorption of Vril by the action of the mind, in the form of ideation and use of will-power-* that is to say, by the familiar process of visualization or the forming of a mental picture, backed up by the use of the will. To those who may be skeptical as to the effect of the mind over a physical function of this kind, we would say that in the first place the absorption of Vril is somewhat different from the ordinary physiological function, and in fact may be considered rather as a psychophysiological process than a purely physiological one. Vril is not a material substance, but a form of energy of a very subtle nature, filling a space in the scale between matter and mind, and being in a way associated with both, Therefore it is not unreasonable to suppose that mind may exercise an effect in its absorption. In the second place, it is a well-known fact that the mind may and often does have a very marked effect over the ordinary involuntary processes and organs of the body. The history of psychic healing establishes 'this fact, and moreover it is known that certain men have developed the power of moving and affecting the involuntary muscles and the sympathetic nervous system by pure acts of will.

It is known that thoughts and mental images held in the mind of a person may react upon his physical condition, not only in a general way but even as regards a particular organ or part, Thus thoughts and mental pictures diseased lungs or liver, or a weak heart, often result in the manifestation of the exact condition previously pictured in the mind, The subconscious mind, operating upon the sympathetic nervous system and guided by the harmful auto-suggestion of the person, frequently adversely affects the organ question and impairs its normal functioning. the same way the mental picture of a healthy, normal condition backed up by a strong will to manifest such condition very often results in the materialization of the ideal. This is the essence of psychic healing the very heart of mental science and of what is called "the new thought," which is attracting so much attention at this time.

It may be seen that if the mind is capable of influencing the functions of the body in any way whatsoever (and there is a mass of testimony regarding the same, which is unquestioned and indisputable), there is nothing to prevent it from influencing the delicate psychophysiological functions involved in the absorption and transmutation of Vril.

The gastric juices of the stomach are increased by thoughts and mental pictures of favorite foods; the liver is quickened into activity by good spirits and a happy frame of mind; the reproductive organism is peculiarly affected by the imagination; the saliva flows in response to the thought or memory of some pleasant taste: in short, all the bodily functions seem to be more or less under the influence of the power of the mind, and particularly of the imagination backed up by the will. It is known that the nervous system often gets "in a jangle " by reason worry and fear. Excessive emotion affects the nerves and often the brain itself. What is there then to seem strange in the idea that the part of the nervous system which is employed in the process of Vril absorption may be encouraged to increased activity by the action of the mind in its phases of ideation and volition? In fact, it would seem very strange if this were not found to be so, when we consider the general principle of the action of mind upon body. When this is understood, we may see the real reason and explanation of much in "psychic phenomena" that has heretofore perplexed us.

LESSON VIII. VRIL AND THE BREATH

OCCULTISTS in ancient and modern times have bestowed great attention upon the matter of the influence of the breath upon psychic power and physical well-being. Under various theories they have laid 'down complex rules and announced fantastic methods of breathing for the purpose of increasing one's vitality, physical energy, and psychic power. As is nearly always the case, we find here an example of the bit of truth surrounded by the mass of rubbish the centre of fact surrounded by the fringe of superstition. Let us consider the matter in the spirit of fairness and understanding, but with the sole purpose of discovering the .core of .truth and exposing the error with which it is surrounded.

In the first place physiology teaches that correct and normal habits of breathing are necessary to perfect health, and tend to restore health to those who have lost it. It is an elementary truth of physiology that the quality of the blood depends largely upon correct habits of breathing. Unless the blood be properly oxygenated, the waste matter of the system is not properly consumed, the result being that the system is clogged and poisoned by broken down tissue and other debris. Moreover, in such case the cells of the body suffer from the lack of a sufficient amount of oxygen which under normal conditions they receive from the blood. Again; the processes of digestion depend to a certain extent upon the presence of oxygen in the blood, and an absence of oxygen reacts materially upon the digestion and assimilation of food, and consequently upon the welfare of the entire system. Not only this, but the nervous system, also, and even the brain, depend upon the condition of the blood for the nourishment and stimulus which is necessary in their processes, In short, unless the blood be sufficiently oxygenated, the entire system suffers and is unable to function normally and naturally, And, as the oxygenation of the blood is accomplished only by correct habits of breathing, it is seen that the whole system is dependent upon proper breathing. The natural man breathes properly by reason of his habits of life, but the man of our complex and artificial civilization has lost the natural method, and few men or women breathe as nature intended they should. So much for the physiological aspect of the question.

In addition to the physiological side the case, as above stated, there is also the side which ordinary physiology ignores, but which is of equal importance to the more familiar side -the phase of breath which is concerned with the absorption of Vril. We have seen that the natural man absorbs sufficient Vril his ordinary breathing, without knowing anything about the matter his instinctive mentality regulates the matter, and co-ordinates the work of breathing for oxygen and breathing for Vril, to such a nicety of degree that a perfect harmony exists, and the observer may fail to even notice the existence of the dual function because of the perfect unity thereof, But the civilized man of the nervous strain and unnatural rush of life in the large cities, not only does not receive the normal amount of oxygen, but also fails to absorb the normal amount of Vril, This is especially deplorable by reason of the fact that while absorbing much *less* than the normal amount of Vril, he uses and wastes much *more* than the normal amount.

With such a man .it is indeed a burning of the candle at both ends, and the result is seen in the nervous wrecks and shattered constitutions that are evident on all sides.

It will be seen by the student that before we can consider the special methods of absorbing Vril by breathing, we must first take up the matter of the establishment of natural, normal methods of breathing, which will not only result in one absorbing the normal amount of Vril but will at the same time give him the proper amount of oxygen as indicated by the authorities of physiology. So, in indicating the normal natural process of breathing, we not only aid the student in increasing his Vril supply, but at the same time establish him habits which must result in an improvement of his general health and state of physical wellbeing. This is as it should be, for the various phases of the physical being are more or less interdependent, and harmony between them is always desirable.

To many, the idea of instructing the race in correct habits of breathing may seem ridiculous. And so would it be if the race lived normally and naturally. The animal needs no instruction in breathing, neither does the barbarian unspoiled by contact with civilization, the infant born under desirable conditions, or the young child properly reared at least before it makes the acquaintance of the school-desk, But when it is remembered that physiology informs us that the great majority of civilized persons breathe incorrectly and contrary to nature's evident plan, then we think it may be admitted that instruction along these lines is not unreasonable *or* unnecessary.

Physiology informs us that there are three general forms of breathing practiced by the race of men, which forms are known by the following names, v *iz.:* (1) Clavicular Breathing; (2) Intercostal Breathing; (3) Abdominal Breathing, The distinctive features of each are described as follows:

CLAVICULAR BREATHING. This form of breathing is also termed ." collar-bone breathing." It is the form of breathing common to many persons, particularly women, and is considered by the best authorities to be the very worst form of breathing known to the race. It necessitates the expenditure of the greatest amount of effort with the least return a maximum of energy with a minimum of result. It is held accountable for many diseases of the lungs and throat.

Persons practicing it habitually, often have harsh, discordant voices. It is found frequently in connection with "mouth-breathing." this form of breathing the person raises the collar-bone and shoulders, and pulls up the ribs, at the same time drawing in the abdomen. This movement allows only the upper part of the chest to be inflated and only the upper part of the lungs to be filled. But a small quantity of air is admitted to the lungs, as only the upper and smaller portion of the lungs is employed. One may easily convince himself of the folly and inefficacy of this form of breathing, by trying the experiment of raising his shoulders and endeavoring to take a full breath. Then let him drop the shoulders and take a full natural breath, and notice the difference. This experiment is the best possible argument against this injurious method of breathing which is too often habitual with men and women who work over desks, sewing-machines and type-writers.

INTERCOSTAL BREATHING. This form of breathing is also sometimes called "rib breathing." It is a compromise, at the best. While an improvement over clavicular breathing, it is inferior to "abdominal breathing," and far below the standard of the "full breath."

In it the upper ribs are inflated, the abdomen drawn in, and the diaphragm pushed upward. It employs the middle part of the chest and lungs, neglecting the lower and upper, It is a favorite method of breathing with many men. Women seldom practice intercostal breathing but pass on to the clavicular breathing mentioned above. It is only a half-way method at the best.

ABDOMINAL BREATHING. This form of breathing is often referred to as "deep breathing," or "diaphragmatic breathing." It has been highly recommended by a number of eminent authorities of late years, and many of the health magazines have made a leading feature of it, Systems and methods of teaching it have been widely advertised, and large prices have been often obtained for a little simple instruction decorated with frills, and dressed up with fancy titles and terms, The principle of abdominal breathing is, however, really quite simple, and its benefits will repay the student who acquaints himself with it and practices it until he has fully mastered it, But we feel that it is but a part of a larger method known as "the full breath" which we shall describe a little further on.

To understand abdominal breathing we must first acquaint ourselves with that wonderful piece of physical mechanism known as the "diaphragm," The diaphragm is defined as: "an inspiratory muscle, and the sole agent tranquil respiration, It is the muscular septum between the thorax and the abdomen, assists the abdominal muscles powerfully in expulsion, each act of that kind being accompanied or preceded by a deep inspiration, also comes into play in hiccough and sobbing, laughing and crying." In simple terms, the diaphragm is a strong plate-shaped muscle which divides the chest and its contents from the abdomen and its contents. At rest, it is arched upward in the centre, like the inside of an inverted bowl, the " sky," or as an arched dome appears to us from below. Viewed from the chest the upper side or surface of the diaphragm would seem like the round top of a man's Derby hat, or the rounded top of a hill. In normal breathing, the diaphragm is flattened out by the arched dome pressing downward. This movement causes the diaphragm to bear downward on the contents of the abdomen, and the abdomen is pressed outward in front and at the sides. This movement occurs in abdominal breathing.

In abdominal breathing, the lower part of lungs is filled, the diaphragm is pressed down and the abdomen is pressed out in front and at the sides, as above described. It is difficult to correctly describe the exact motions of abdominal breathing, but the student may acquire the same by practice, using the above description as a basis. By" bearing down" on the abdomen by lowering the diaphragm and pressing out the abdominal muscles, the lower lungs are given space and free movement, and the deep breath is instinctively inhaled. A little practice will enable anyone to demonstrate this for 'himself or herself, much better than by reading pages of printed instruction.

FULL BREATHING. The best authorities agree that the best possible form of breathing is that which *is based on abdominal breathing, but which also includes the filling of the middle and upper part of the lungs as well.* By what may seem to be a striking coincidence, it is noted that this particular form of breathing is that which was taught by the ancient Arcane teachers to their students as a means increasing the absorption But the coincidence is quite a natural one and it would be indeed strange had it not occurred, For this full breathing " method is the true, natural, normal method of breathing which natural man instinctively employs. It not only fills every part of the lungs, and exercises every part of the chest not only secures the greatest possible amount of oxygen and Vril -but also obtains the greatest returns from the least comparative effort. It is an example of the universal economy of nature just as marked as is the economy of the form of the wax cell of the bee's honeycomb.

In full breathing, all of the respiratory muscles are called into play; the entire area of the lungs is used; the entire machinery of the respiratory organism is exercised, strengthened and developed. There is every evidence that this, and this alone, is nature's normal method of breathing. Moreover, it is known that the hardiest races of men have practiced this form of breathing. We know this from the modern instances, and because the statuary of ancient Greece shows that muscular development of the abdomen and chest which comes from this form breathing. It is first word of nature to man regarding breathing-it is the last word of science to man on the same subject. It is the best natural method; it is the best scientific method.

Full breathing is not an artificial system or method of breathing but is rather a return to natural normal methods and habits, But, nevertheless, it will require some practice on the part of many students hereof, by reason of the fact that they have lost their natural instinct in the matter, and are under the dominion of the " second nature" of false habit. Before the instinctive habit may be resumed, the effect of the false habit must be overcome, and this usually takes time. The best, and indeed almost the only way of counteracting and defeating any objectionable habit, is to practice its opposite and this rule applies here with great force. The only way to get rid of the old habit is to practice the new. And the only way to acquire the new is to practice it. So, from both angles, the importance of practice is seen.

EXERCISE: The following exercise will serve to develop the full breath, if conscientiously practiced: (1) Standing erect, or sitting in a natural position, inhale slowly through the nostrils, and according to the method of " abdominal breathing " fill the lower lungs, press down the diaphragm, and push out the abdomen in front and at the sides; then in a continuous effort (2) fill the middle part of the chest and lungs, as in intercostal breathing, pressing outward the mid-ribs, breast-bone and chest; then in the same continuous effort (3) fill the upper portion of the lungs, as in clavicular breathing, lifting the upper portion of the chest, slightly raising the collar-bone, slightly drawing the abdomen and thus raising the diaphragm, as heretofore explained.

It will be noticed that this method of "fun breathing " is really a combination of the three forms of breathing previously described, beginning with the abdominal, proceeding to the intercostal, and finishing with the clavicular method. But the student is cautioned against proceeding as if there were three distinct and separated stages of the process. *There is but one continuous process,* rising gradually from the lower part of the lungs to the middle portion, and then to the upper portion. A uniform continuous muscular movement is effected, the several regions being called into action in a rising sequence. *All disconnected, spasmodic, jerky motions should be avoided.* A little practice will result in the acquirement of the continuous inhalation.

The inhaled air should be retained for a moment, and then exhaled naturally and easily, No attempt should be made to unduly *retain* the breath, as is taught by some schools of breathing, There is nothing to be gained by the retention in the lungs of stale, exhausted air; besides which, there is always more or less of *strain* in this forced retention, as the whole process is unnatural, natural normal breathing there is no sense of strain or effort, when once the habit is acquired, or rather re-acquired. The infant or young child manifests no effort or strain in breathing, and neither should the adult.

Some teachers announce a variety of methods of breathing, which upon examination are found for the most part to consist of fantastic and fanciful processes, designed evidently to impress the student with the novelty, and presumably great virtue, of these newly invented methods, There is only one safe and sane rule, and that is to *go back to nature*. The "full breath " is nature's own method. If you doubt this, watch the motions of a sleeping, healthy child, or sturdy infant.

LESSON IX. SECRET OF VRIL ABSORPTION

IN many treatises upon psychic breathing, or other occult teachings in which the breath is employed in the process of the absorption of Vril (under some one of the names applied to it), we find many fanciful methods of breathing given, great stress being laid upon the supposed merits of each. A Little close analysis will show that these methods are divided into two classes, *viz.:* (1) methods in which the breath is inhaled, retained, and exhaled, in some fanciful manner often according to the count of so many moments to each step in the process, or else in some fantastic accompaniment. Another variation of this class of methods is that of inhaling through one nostril, exhaling through the other, and then reversing the order of nostrils. The best authorities hold that there is no virtue whatsoever in the fanciful form of these methods, outside of the suggestive effect upon the imagination of the person, the auto-suggestion causing some benefit by reason of the belief of the person setting into effect the activities of the subconscious mind, and accordingly of the physical organs by means of the sympathetic nervous system. These methods are but variations of the principle underlying "faith healing," and their results are obtained in the same way. (2) The second class of these fanciful methods consists simply of combinations of well-known physical-culture movements, with an emphasis laid upon the use of the breath in their performance. These exercises, of course, have their value in the direction of promoting physical culture, the breathing phase being merely incidental and secondary.

It will be seen that the above explained fanciful methods, while possessing no special value in themselves, nevertheless may result in good, if practiced in moderation and if excess is avoided. There are some exercises given, however, which we feel lay undue emphasis upon the retained breath, and upon the length of time employed in inhaling and exhaling. In our opinion there is a possibility of a strain in such practices, and we do not recommend them, particularly when it is remembered that they have no real physiological or psychical value.

We have heard of teachers of some of these systems teaching classes of persons to inhale very slowly, and to retain the breath until a feeling of giddiness arose, the peculiar "swimmy" feeling thus experienced being held to be proof of the development of some high psychic state. The slightest acquaintance with elementary physiology, however, should teach one that the dizziness is not a psychic state, but arises from the poisoning of the body by the carbonic acid gas generated in the system, which under natural conditions would have been expelled, and also from the fact that the body and brain are crying out "Oxygen ! send us oxygen, or we perish! " In short, instead of a state of psychic power being attained, there is really a state of partial asphyxiation induced.

The Arcane teachers do not teach any of the above mentioned fantastic or fanciful methods. On the contrary, they hold that there is no better way of absorbing Vril, under ordinary circumstances, than the "full breathing" method of nature. They hold 'that the man or woman who acquires or re-acquires the habit of proper natural "fun breathing " will usually absorb a normal degree of Vril. But they hold also that an additional amount of Vril is often needed by those living under conditions which tend to deplete them of their Vril by excessive use or excessive waste. They accordingly teach methods by which additional Vril may be absorbed according to the desire or need of the person. But this method of absorption does not consist of any fanciful physical method or exercise, but *depends upon the use of the mind* connection with the natural normal process of breathing. The Arcane method is psycho-physical, rather than physical. Those of our students who have studied the previous works of this series will understand the power and effect of the mind upon the physical functions, without our going into the matter in detail in this place.

The secret of the Arcane method of Vril absorption consists of the fact that *the nervous system may be spurred to redoubled efficiency by the action of the mind directed upon it.* In Lesson X of "The Arcane Formulas, or Mental Alchemy," which lesson is entitled "Mentalism in a Nutshell," is explained the method of psychic "visualization" or the forming and holding of the mental image of things and conditions which one wishes to realize objectively and in material form.

The same lesson is explained the use of the will in the materialization and objectification of desired conditions. On page 97 of the said book and lesson, you will find the following paragraph:

"The secret of mental alchemy may be stated as consisting first, last and always, of the a r t of mental imaging, reinforced by the will"

While to the beginner the subject of mentalism may seem a very complicated one, the advanced occultist knows it to be the very extreme of simplicity, *Mental alchemy, under whatever name it may masquerade, may be found to consist, at the last, of simply the power to create strong, clear, mental images, and to project them into the outer world by means of the concentrated will.* You will find that all you have ever read on the subject may be "boiled down' to the above stated principle. The rest is a mere matter of detail. This single statement is "mentalism in a nutshell."

We have quoted from the earlier work of this series in order to emphasize the fact that the power of psychic visualization, backed by the power of the will, is the secret of Vril absorption, as it is of all psychic or psycho-physical phenomena. The first step in Vril absorption is the realization by the student that there exists in the atmospheric air a universal supply of Vril such phase and condition as to render it easily assimilated by the nervous system of man and other living creatures. The second step is the formation of *a clear mental picture* of this universal supply of Vril. Of course, Vril having no definite shape or form, color or outward appearance, the mind cannot form a picture of it as a thing of form, color o:1" other tangible attribute. But the mind *can image* it, as it would *image* a space filled with electrical power, magnetism, or ether, The mind must enter into a consciousness of the *presence* of Vril in space, all around one, and in every atom of air that is breathed. This *consciousness of that presence* must be gained before further progress is possible it must be dwelt upon mentally until the mind grasps its reality and becomes conscious of its presence, just as one is conscious of the presence of space itself, In the degree that this consciousness is gained, so is the degree of manifestation possible.

The next step is the realization and mental imaging of the faculty of the nervous system to absorb such amount of Vril as is required, in response to the mandate of the will. The mind must visualize the nerves as absorbing the Vril from the air, just as .it can visualize the lungs absorbing oxygen from the same source. The one must be seen to be as real as the other. Of course the nerves will absorb Vril in the ordinary way whether or not one is conscious of the process-in fact, this is the way that the average person absorbs Vril -but in order to *increase* the absorptive power the system, the mind must be employed in the manner above described. This process imparts to the absorptive function an increased efficiency, just as thought-force is known to increase the efficiency of the stomach, liver or other organs of the body.

The final step is the use of the will in the direction of *commanding* the system to absorb a greater amount of Vril. After the reason recognizes the possibility of this process, and the imagination pictures it as being performed, then the will may be directed to the task of demanding its performance. To those to whom this may seem a strange statement, we would say that the majority of our physical actions are evolved in just this way. With the exception of a few elementary instinctive actions which are performed almost automatically, the young animal, and particularly the young human child, first realizes that a movement may be made, then sees it being made by the imaginative or ideative faculties, and then deliberately *wills* it to be made. The child follows this process in learning to use its legs in walking; in using its hands in taking hold of a thing .and guiding it to its mouth; and afterward in directing its hand to write, use the knife and fork or perform similar offices.

The story of evolution as told by Lamarck and his school tells us that the life-forms have gradually developed new functions in this way, the physical organ evolving in response to the mental picture and desire, In forming the mental picture until it becomes firmly fixed in the subconscious mind, and then reinforcing and enforcing it by the will, the "nature" of the person develops the faculty of increased power of absorption of Vril, which is manifested in response to the will of the person.

VRIL-ABSORPTION EXERCISE. The following exercise will serve as a general guide to those who wish to increase their power of Vril absorption. (1) Practice the "full breath " (as heretofore described), and, while inhaling, picture in your mind the absorption of Vril first by the nerves of the nasal cavity and the back of the head, and then by the cells of the lungs, at the same time "willing " that the Vril be so absorbed. Or, if it is preferred, it may be stated in this manner: WILL that the system absorb an increased amount of Vril, and at the same mentally picture the process of absorption. Or perhaps a third form will be easier for some: *WILL the Vril absorption, and at the same time "feel" that it is under way.*

After a little practice the student will find that the system will become as responsive to the will in this function, as the lungs are responsive to the will when one decides to take a breath fuller and deeper than usual. And, in the same way, the person will become almost as vividly *conscious* of the influx of Vril as he is of the influx of air in breathing. A little practice will demonstrate this to the student of his own actual experience, much better than can we in pages of written description and statement. Imagine what it would be to attempt to describe the sensation of breathing to a creature that had never breathed, --a visitor, for instance, from some distant star where breathing was unknown, or imagine describing the sensation of seeing color" scarlet," to a man born blind. Or the sensation of the taste of sugar, to one who had never tasted anything sweet. Sensations of this kind must be experienced in order to be understood. The student has the matter in his own hands his experience and actual knowledge depend upon his own practice.

Is not intended that one shall practice this conscious Vril absorption all the time this is not necessary. Moreover, it is not practicable, for the process requires the concentration of attention upon the task, and one requires the attention for other purposes, is sufficient for one to practice this method only when he feels that his Vril supply is depleted, or just before engaging in work that will probably require additional energy. One may absorb additional Vril while engaged in other work, without disturbing his occupation it requires but a moment or two-just as the flying locomotive takes up water without stopping. It will be found to be an excellent plan to practice some light physical-culture exercise the morning before arising, and then to devote a few moments to Vril absorption. This will start one well in the work of the day, When fatigued during the day, a moment's relaxation and practice of Vril absorption will yield great benefit. There are no set rules to be observed in this matter. Each one must use his own judgment, and fit the method to his own inclination and necessities. *Absorb Vril whenever you feel you need it.*

LESSON X. APPLICATION OF VRIL-POWER

WHEN the student has acquired the knack of Vril absorption, he may apply the power of Vril to his physical requirements in many ways. He will have laid up a reserve store of Vril in the solar plexus and other centres, which he may direct and distribute to the various parts and organs of his body, at will, It is possible for anyone, with 'a little practice, to acquire the art of directing the flow of Vril to any particular part of the body. This will be found very advantageous in the treatment of physical troubles and weaknesses.

When any part of the body is found to lack proper vitality, or when any organ shows signs of imperfect functioning, a supply of Vril directed to that part or organ will be found to be highly beneficial in the direction of vitalizing and stimulating the part or organ in question. This is true not only of organs like the stomach or liver, but also of the great nerve centres of the body, including the spinal cord and even the brain itself.

Treatment of the spinal cord in this way will result imparting a new spirit of vitality and energy to the entire system, and is one of the best tonic treatments known to psycho-physiology, The following general directions will serve to give the student the key to the many forms of application possible under The general principle once clearly understood and firmly grasped, the student may apply it as indicated by his own particular requirements and necessities, and in such manner as seems preferable to him.

GENERAL DIRECTIONS. Either sit in a comfortable position, or else recline in an easy position, relaxing every muscle and quieting every nerve. Then concentrate the attention upon the solar plexus (or the region of the pit of the stomach just where the ribs spread apart), and awaken your consciousness of the storage of a reserve supply of Vril at this point. Then *will* that some of this Vril supply shall flow along the nerves to whatever part of the body you wish to energize. If the part to be energized is situated *above* the solar plexus, you must mentally and by an effort of the will, *draw upward* the Vril current; if the part to be energized is situated *below* the solar plexus, you must in the same way mentally *push downward* current. In either case you must accompany the will effort by the mental picture and consciousness of the actual passage of the current. It may take you a little time to acquire the peculiar "knack" of directing the current in this way, but after a little practice you will find it very easy, in fact it will become almost "second nature" to you to send the current whenever you recognize the need of it.

When you feel generally tired, exhausted, or "used up," it will be found beneficial to treat the whole body in this way. In special cases, particular parts or organs may be so treated. A feeling of relief will be experienced in the part treated, in a few moments. In case of headaches, or other *pains,* relief may often be obtained by first *flushing* the affected part with Vril (in the manner above described), and then reversing the process and drawing away the current this plan tending to equalize the circulation and the nerve currents, and thus to restore normal conditions.

Cold feet often may be relieved by stimulating them with a supply of Vril. Stiff muscles or rheumatic joints often are relieved in this way. In fact, one who can so direct and distribute the Vril currents is practical master of his or her own body, and may successfully "treat" himself or herself in this way to great advantage. The brain may be stimulated by sending it a strong current of Vril, or it may be rested by first "flushing " it with Vril and then drawing away the supply and allowing the brain to rest quietly in a relaxed condition of peace and comfort.

GENERAL SELF-TREATMENT. A form of general self-treatment by Vril currents, in the direction of a general vitalization and energization of the entire system, is herewith suggested: (1) Lie in a comfortable position, and concentrate the attention upon the solar plexus, awakening a consciousness of the presence there of the reserve-supply of Vril. Then direct the current downward to the feet first to the left foot and then to the right until you can feel the energy manifesting in them. In some cases a slight tingling may be felt, while in others merely a general "feeling " or subconscious " awareness " is manifest, Then treat the lower part of the legs in the same order; then the thighs: then the reproductive region; then the abdomen and the lower internal organs; then stimulate the solar plexus itself; then the lungs and throat. After having treated the various organs and parts of the body in this manner, reverse the current and cause it to flow down the spinal column, sweeping it repeatedly from top to bottom, allowing some of the current to flow out through the connected nerves. Next concentrate the attention upon the sacral plexus, at the lower part of the spine giving to this region a decided stimulation. Finally, direct the Vril to the nerves and muscles of the neck, and then to the brain, giving the latter a good "flushing," and then withdrawing the current by a reverse impulse and direction of the will. Rest quietly a few moments, and you will arise refreshed and energized, Variations may be applied to this general treatment, but the general order above suggested will be found to be adapted to the majority of cases.

SPECIAL SELF-TREATMENT: In cases of local pain or physical disorder, one may treat himself not only in the above stated general manner, but also by specially concentrated currents of Vril directed by the use of the hands, In this case the Vril flows down the nerves of the arm and hands and into the affected parts with renewed and increased force and effect, Passing the hands over the affected parts, or holding them there, at the same time *willing* that a steady, continuous, and powerful flow of Vril pass through them and into the part, will be found quite effective in many instances. If preferred, the Vril may be forced into the part in this manner by a series of mental " pushes" or "pumping motions." Some prefer one plan, and some the other.

Both should be tried, and the one best adapted to the particular wants of the person adopted and applied thereafter.

TREATMENT OF OTHER PERSONS: The student may treat other persons in the same way as indicated in the above directions for self-treatment. The principle is the same in all cases. The knowledge of the direction and distribution of Vril to the bodies of other persons constitutes the secret of what is popularly known as "magnetic healing." There is no special new principle involved in the treatment of others. Treat the other person just as you would treat a part of your own body. The current of VRIL will flow into the affected part other person and back to yourself.

Always place *both* hands on the other person during the treatment, in order to complete the connection in this way. After the treatment, it will be well for the healer to treat himself briefly, and to recharge himself with Vril by the method previously described. In this way he will never suffer from depletion of Vril, and will avoid "taking on the condition " of the patient which often occurs to psychic healers who are not acquainted with the means of recuperating and protecting themselves.

Interesting experiments have been tried along the lines of charging water with Vril, by holding the glass in one's hands and sending the current into it. Some magnetic healers have made quite a feature of charging water in this way, and then giving **it** to their patients to drink in sips, in addition to the regular treatment. We mention it here merely as a matter of general interest, and as a suggestion for experiment on the part of our students. We feel that, interesting though it may be, it is not a necessary or important part of treatment by Vril, for the reason that the course above outlined should be sufficiently successful without the assistance of such methods.

By reason of the simplicity of the methods suggested and the absence of all attempts to dress the subject fanciful and mystic verbal garb and imagery, there is danger of the average student failing to appreciate the benefits that may be gained by the use of Vril in the manner indicated in this lesson, and of his failing to realize the importance of the information herein given. We warn the student against undervaluing any knowledge or instruction merely because it may be stated simply and plainly. It is no easy matter to reduce teaching of this kind to simple plain terms, and equally simple methods, for this task is really the condensation into a few lines of the experience of many years and of many persons, It is much easier to elaborate the matter in detailed technical style, than to reduce it to terms and methods capable of being understood and applied by all persons of average intelligence, The student must not forget that behind this simple exposition and explanation, and the equally simple methods of application, there is to be found one of the greatest and most wonderful of nature's forces, the real inner meaning of which will probably never be fully known to the mind of man.

The final secret is bound up with the secret of Life itself. The student who masters these instructions and methods is brought in touch with this great force of Life, and is enabled to apply its energies at will. Let him beware of undervaluing the power he is using, simply because it is capable of simple, plain application. And let him beware, further, of allowing familiarity with this power to develop into contempt of it. Nature does not approve of belittling or trifling with her great forces. Triflers who enter the field of psychism or occultism frequently are brought to a rather vigorous realization of the fact that they are but pygmies playing with titanic forces. On the other hand, there is something in nature which seems to approve of the right use of its mighty forces, and which encourages and aids those who employ these forces in the proper spirit and toward worthy ends. And the right use of vital-energy, life-force, Vril, is .always in the direction of LIFE and HEALTH.

LESSON XI. CONSERVING VRIL-POWER

THE Arcane teachings hold that not only does the wise person store up a sufficient supply of Vril to meet sudden and unexpected demands not only does he direct and distribute Vril to meet the requirements of his physical and mental system-but he also avoids unnecessary waste and dissipation of Vril power, and strives to stop all leaks of energy. Such person practices not only industry and thrift in relation to Vril, but also manifests a wise economy regarding its conservation.

Vril waste and dissipation occurs in two ways, vis.: (1) emotional waste; and (2) physical waste. The majority of persons are more or less prodigals along one or both of the above stated lines, They turn on the emotional or physical faucet, and allow Vril to drip and dribble almost constantly pure waste.

Emotional waste is habitual with many persons who fail to realize that in every useless flow of emotional activity they are really dissipating a portion of the life-power and vital energy. Not only does this emotional dissipation result in a drain on the life energies, but, like any other form of dissipation, it results also in killing the healthy and normal emotional expression, replacing the latter with a false emotional activity which is without real feeling and which seeks constant excitement and stimulus as the drunkard seeks drink, and the drug habituate his particular narcotic or stimulant.

One may avoid this emotional waste by watching carefully the formation of emotional habits. As an authority says: "All emotions deepen by repetition. If one allows an undesirable feeling to master him once, he should be on the watch to check that feeling at the start on the occasion of the second manifestation. The man who falls into a rage once, falls into the same emotion easier a second time; the man who keeps cool once under trying circumstances, will be more easily able to control himself the next time. The truth cannot be too strongly emphasized, that a habit of emotional feeling is, at the outset, often the result of an intellectual habit. Summon different ideas to the mind, and notice how the emotion changes with the idea...to repress certain trains of feeling, repress the ideas that give them birth. This will have restraining power, even when the emotional state tends to bring up a consonant idea, just as a fire may suggest putting fuel on it."

Emotional waste may also be prevented by carefully training oneself to control the physical expression usually accompanying the feeling or emotion. An authority says: "By restraining the expression of an emotion, we can frequently throttle it; by inducing an expression, we can often cause its allied emotion, We know that animals, barbarians, and children generally allow motor discharges without inhibition, and that control comes in some way or other with culture." Another eminent authority says: .. Even if we cannot prevent a' feeling from arising, we may possibly prevent it from spreading, by inhibiting the organic movement which accompanies it, and indulgence in which augments it."

An authority says: "Novices frequently make the mistake of thinking that intense expression of emotion indicates not only a character rich in feeling, but also one that will make great unselfish sacrifices for the welfare of others. The truth lies generally in the opposite direction. Many persons expend all their energies in the expression of emotion and have none left for action. Some demonstrative people find it difficult to understand that to feel intense sympathy is not the same as to exert themselves in actually relieving distress. The world could very well spare a million of those who only feel for a dozen of those who *act:*"

In the volume of this series entitled "The Arcane Formulas," we have devoted considerable space to instruction along the lines of mastering and controlling the emotional nature, not in the direction of killing out or destroying that part of one's mental and spiritual being, but rather in the direction of attaining perfect mastery and control thereof. We have therein instructed the student in the art of "mastering the opposites" of feeling and emotion, that he may secure and maintain the true mental, moral, and spiritual balance and poise. We have said therein: "Acquire the mental "knack" of rising above the plane of emotional feeling, on to the plane of will, and there calmly watch and observe the storm of emotion without being influenced by it. This is like one sailing in a balloon above the storm clouds which are thundering and flashing lightning beneath him. On the plane of will there is peace and power undreamt of by those still on the emotional planes. Never allow yourself to become enmeshed and involved in the emotional storms or activities. Handle the emotions as the master does an instrument but never yield yourself to the power and influence of slave or instrument, any more than you would yield yourself to the power and influence of some entity outside of yourself.'

The study of the Arcane teachings, in the preceding volumes of the series, will do much for anyone who has found himself or herself carried away by emotional storms, or cyclones of feeling, which result in Vril dissipation and waste. The principles therein taught, and the methods therein stated, will do much to impart balance and poise, self-control and self-mastery to those who seek "poise and power." Emotion and feeling play an important part in our lives, and when properly employed are good for us to use but, even when normally good, they become bad when we allow them to *use us* to the extent that we become subject to them and under their control. Even "the divine gift of sympathy" may become a veritable curse in this way, and may tend to wreck the mental and physical well-being of a person, without the least benefiting the objects which aroused it originally. We must be strong ourselves before we may help others, As in everything else in life, so in this case we must avoid the extremes or "opposites," and preserve the happy mean in the centre, where alone is poise, power and balance to be found.

Passing from the consideration of this first form of emotional waste of Vril-power, we perceive that the average person manifests an equally harmful waste his physical life. Waste motion, waste nervous strain, excessive nervous tension, and excessive purposeless physical motion is seen on all sides. The majority of persons are in a state of unrelaxed nervous and muscular tension during their waking hours. Their nerves are tense, and the muscles contracted, without any real cause. Their fingers are beating the "devil's tattoo," and they waste nervous energy to no purpose whatsoever. They whittle pencils, chew toothpicks, or masticate chewing-gum. They do not know the meaning of the word *relaxation,* and have no conception of its physical expression. When talking, these persons throw into the task sufficient energy to sustain a vigorous orator through the strain of his greatest effort. When walking, they expend enough energy to carry a giant up a steep. When riding they sit on the edge of the car seat, leaning forward as if they imagined that they were using their energy to help propel the train to their destination, Poise is unknown to these people who are burning their Vril candle at both ends.

Such persons should take an object lesson from a young resting infant, or from a cat in a relaxed position. The child "lets go" to perfection. The cat relaxes every muscle and nerve, and yet so finely organized is it that in the twinkling of an eye when necessity for possible action arises, its muscles become as steel, and its nerves as hair-triggers. The cat crouching before a mouse-hole gives one of nature's best object lessons in the quality of "relaxed power." Here we find the latent hair-trigger nerves, and the potential steel muscles, in a state of perfection.

The only way to relax properly is to withdraw the Vril tension from the muscles. And this is not so easy for those who have contracted the unnatural habits of unnecessary tension. They must first learn how to "let go."

The student wishing to learn how to relax should begin by practicing with the hands, first taking away all tension, and then swinging the hands from the wrists, until they become perfectly limp. Then practice "limbering up" the fingers. Then swing the arms to and fro in the same manner. Then, tense the upper arm and swing the fore-arms freely from the elbow, Then follow the same general course with the legs, until you have them thoroughly "loosened up. Then swing the head about, the neck being made limp. And, finally, lying down, manage to take every bit of Vril-force from the muscles of the whole body, imitating the attitude, position and general condition of the tired baby who has dropped to sleep over its play.

A variation of the "loosening up " exercises may be found in the imitation of a Newfoundland dog shaking himself vigorously this wil1 give you a good general "limbering up." "Stretching" the limbs, in the familiar motion of the lazy hoy, will also be found to give relaxation and rest, and to relieve tension. Conclude the relaxation exercises with the " Bracing-up exercise " given below, which will also be found excellent in case of the tired feeling caused by sitting or standing in one position, or when the brain feels fagged and tired, or when from any mental or physical cause one may feel "stale" and not "fit".

BRACING-UP EXERCISE. Stand erect, and take several natural, easy, "full breaths," combining with them the mental exercise of Vril absorption. Then, holding your arms out front of you, clench your fists and draw them slowly toward your breast, gradually increasing the muscular tension. Then push .your fists out and draw them in (muscles still tensed) several times. Then drop your fists to your sides, and gradually draw them straight up as far as they will go, tensing the muscles as the fists ascend. Repeat several times. Then moving your arms about (with clenched fists) alternately tense and relax the muscles.

A few moments of this exercise will fill the upper part of the body with fresh Vril, and will impart a wonderful feeling of energy and power. Similar exercises, employing the .legs in alternate tension and relaxation, will likewise vitalize and energize the body below the waist. There are no set motions in this exercise, the whole principle being that of alternate tension and relaxation. The benefits of this exercise, or any similar light exercise, will be doubted if one t h row his mind into it.

Picture the benefit to be derived from it and while performing the exercise, endeavor to enter into the consciousness of the action of Vril, and you will, and you will find that the action of the mind will serve to give the Vril a mighty force and impulse in the direction of the exercised parts and their vicinity.

In the field of emotional Vril waste, we find that the emotional states of anger, hate, jealousy, fear, worry, and over-anxiety, and the attempt to vicariously live out the life of another for him or her, are the ones which produce the greatest strain, tension, waste and dissipation. Steady, calm mental work seldom wrecks one, while the above emotional states, and others, expressed to too great a degree, slowly but surely undermine the nervous system, and react upon mind and body. In the same way steady, normal physical exercise or work seldom affects one injuriously, while the unnatural nervous and muscular tension before mentioned, and the nervous physical actions resulting from the presence of the injurious emotions to which we have alluded, frequently strain the physical nature to the utmost. And, as in the majority of cases the emotional waste is manifested in connection the physical waste, each serving to feed the other by action and reaction we may readily see that in waste and dissipation we have the secret of that curse of the age known as neurasthenia or nervous prostration. This is not the result of overwork, as is generally supposed, but is the result of over-worry, undue tension, and 'lack of mental balance and poise, which serve to waste the life-forces, the vital energies, or Vril.

To overcome this trouble it is first necessary to recognize its cause, and t hen to counteract the cause by following the course directly opposed to it. We trust that in this book we have explained the former, and pointed the way toward the latter.

LESSON XII. THE PSYCHIC PHASE OF VRIL

IT is not our purpose to enter into a detailed discussion of mental science, psychic phenomena, or occultism, in this book. In the preceding books of this series we have dwelt upon this subject in some detail, and we must refer thereto the student who is especially interested this particular field of teaching. But our consideration of the subject of Vril would be incomplete did we not at least call attention to the part played by Vril in the phenomena generally classed as "psychic," "mental science," or " occult." Therefore we shall in this lesson point out in a general way the office and function of Vril in such phenomena.

PSYCHIC INFLUENCE. In the various phases of what is known as " psychic influence," or the effect of the mind of one person over that of another, Vril plays an important part. In the degree that the thought projections, thought waves, thought-vibrations (or whatever term may be used), are charged with Vril, so is their effect upon person receiving them. just as the degree of clearness in the sound of telephone depends materially upon the strength of the current operating the system, so does the strength of the Vril current materially determine the power of the thought vibrations sent from one person to another, over a short or long distance, In fact, Vril is the real force or energy in all manifestations of thought-force --the mind merely serving to project that force by the and to color it by the idea or feeling held the mind. The thought sent forth is colored and charged with Vril by the strength of the feeling or desire manifested, in the majority of cases. But the trained mental scientist or occultist uses his direct will-power to accomplish the same result, using precisely the same method that he does in directing and distributing the Vril to parts of his own body, or to the body of another person when he is giving personal psychic treatments as described in preceding lessons. This fact, understood in connection with what we have said on the subject in the other books of the series above mentioned, gives one the complete key to psychic influence, mental science treatments, and other occult phenomena in which mind acts upon mind or body over a distance. The general principle is the same in all of these cases. Persons may be "treated" by sending them thoughts of strength and vitality, or of courage and success, charged with strong currents of Vril impelled by the will of the sender. In the same way, one may send to another direct currents of Vril, and thus increase his or her vitality, energy, force, and power. Telepathic messages may be increased 'in power by charging them with an increased supply of Vril, Thought-forms sent forth in the manner familiar to occultists, may be energized and vitalized by charging them with the dynamic force of Vril, The student who is interested in this phase of the matter should study carefully the lesson "Mentalism in a Nutshell," in the book of this series entitled "The Arcane Formulas."

SELF-PROTECTION. In the same way the self-protection by thought-auras, psychic armor, etc., familiar to all occultists may be wonderfully increased by charging the protective thought-force with a strong current of Vril. The Ideative power of the mind, and the will, are used in this process. By forming a strong mental image of the presence of the protective thought-aura surrounding the body, and which is rendered dynamic by currents of Vril, the occultist may surround himself with an armor of protection that will defy all attacks on the part of others. the same way, one may use Vril in connection with the thought-atmosphere with which he surrounds himself, and which gives the keynote to the attitude of other persons toward him. He may create this mental atmosphere by the character of the thoughts held by him, his mental attitude, or his affirmations, according to the system followed by him and in either case he may greatly increase the power of this mental atmosphere by charging it with Vril according to the general method which we have repeatedly mentioned in this book visualization and will-power, This is the explanation of that peculiar "force" or "power" which we feel emanating or flowing from the presence of strong individuals –a force or power which strikes us with almost a physical impact.

As we have already said, we do not purpose entering into a detailed consideration of psychic phenomena in this book the above mention of Vril in this connection we have given in a few words, and in simple form, an occult secret which should prove very valuable to all occultists who are not already acquainted with it and who have been contenting themselves by merely using *thought* their psychic experiments or work, will be found that this use of will prove to be the missing keystone which is essential to give to the whole psychic arch that strength, unity, and power which it needs, The student will find that it may be added or adapted to any of the many systems of occult practice with which students of the subject may be familiar. It is an "attachment" which may be used in connection with any or the systems, old or new, ancient or modern.

In this matter, as in a number of others in this book, we have given you the spirit of a great occult method or system in a few plain words. We have condensed it, and given you the essence. We have stated the whole thing in a nutshell, Once more we warn you not to overlook the value and importance of the thing by reason of its simplicity and plainness.

FINAL ADVICE

You have now read this book through in a more or less hasty way. You have seen some things which have attracted you, and which you have decided to apply your own work. But you have missed many other things of equal or perhaps greater value. Therefore, we ask that you lay this book aside for a few days, and mentally assimilate that which you have learned from it, Then take it up again, and carefully re-read and re-study it from beginning to end. Much to your surprise you will find that there are many things in it which you have entirely overlooked. Also, that many things will appear to you in a new light and with an added meaning. A week or so later, read and study it for the third time, and you will have a like result. You will not begin to understand the real value of the principles announced in this book in less than the three readings above advised. In this connection you should re-read and re-study the other books of the series, and each will serve to throw light on the others.

The Arcane Teaching is based upon certain general principles which are immanent in every branch and in every phase of it. Each phase blends into the others. Thus does the teaching present a unity and a harmony when each phase is studied and considered in relation to the others.

In conclusion let us use words once before used in this series: "Oh, Neophyte, in the Centre of Life shalt thou indeed find poise and power. In the Heart of the Storm shalt thou find peace. He who finds the centre of himself, finds the centre of the Cosmos. For at last they are ONE!"

FINIS

BOOK FOUR

THE ARCANE IV.

THE MYSTERY OF SEX OR SEX POLARITY

I. THE UNIVERSALITY OF SEX

All the ancient occult and esoteric fraternities, organizations, and schools agreed upon one point—the Universality of Sex. They realized that the Sex principle was manifest through all the Cosmos, and that it was in activity throughout all the universe. The Phallic Cross symbol is found in use in nearly every occult organization or body, and signifies the teaching that the male and female principles are immanent in each and every form of nature's activities and manifestations.

It will be noticed in many of the older writings that the term "gender" is used in preference to sex. This arises from the fact that the primal idea of Sex, as understood in occultism, is that of begetting; bringing forth; procreating, etc.; of which the term "gender" is peculiarly significant and expressive. Occultists realize that the work of procreation is manifest on every plane, physical, mental, and spiritual, and that the "gender" principle is active everywhere, at all times, in all ways. But in this little book we shall use the term "sex" in preference to "gender," for several reasons, the understanding being of course that the term is employed in its widest and most universal sense, rather than as referring to the particular sex manifestation of living things, or the human race in particular.

The Arcane Teaching embraces the well-established occult doctrine of the Universality of Sex. It holds that not only on the physical plane, but also on the mental and spiritual planes, is Sex apparent; that not only in the living, organic forms, but also in the so-called "lifeless" and inorganic forms, is the principle of Sex in evidence. The principle of Sex is bound up with the law of the Opposites, *of* which we have spoken at length in our other works. Sex is a manifestation of the great Law of Polarity which is in evidence throughout the Cosmos. The sexes are counterparts, opposites, contrasting poles of Being. There is always to be found the Male Principle which energizes, procreates, and stirs into activity; and there is always to be found the Female Principle which produces, conceives, and brings forth.

In fact, the ancient Arcane Teachers directed the attention of their neophytes to the fact that even in the fundamental activities of the creation of the Cosmos the principle of Sex was apparent. The LAW was held to represent the Male Principle, acting and moving upon the Infinity of Nothingness and causing the latter to conceive, bear and bring forth the activities, shapes and forms of the universe. It will be remembered that The LAW in itself does not conceive, bear and bring forth, but acts merely as the controlling, energizing spirit which incites into activity the creative powers inherent in the Infinity of Nothingness. The latter is distinctively the Female Principle, for it is acted upon by the energies of The LAW, goes through a period of Cosmic conception, bears in its body the new Cosmos, and finally brings forth the new world in all its youthful vigor and activity. The LAW is the Absolute; the Cosmos is the Infinite. The Absolute is the moving and energizing power ; the Infinite contains within itself the "possibility" of all things -the creative properties which conceive, bear, and bring forth the Cosmos. This idea of the manifestation of the Sex Principle in the Cosmic activities is carried out in the symbology of the ages, and the figurative terms of even our own age show the insistent desire of the mind to express the thought. We always speak and think of "Nature" as the feminine principle, containing in her womb the seed of all shapes and forms and things, and bringing forth all the forms of life that fill the world. "Mother Nature" is the term embodying the idea. How ridiculous it would seem to speak or think of "Father Nature!" And yet the mind instinctively recognizes that there can be no Mother without a Father, and seeks to find the Paternal principle above Nature.

It will be noticed that in all the religions, past, present, living or dead, the Sovereign Power or Supreme Deity is always Male. But, at the same time, this Supreme Male Principle is never pictured or thought of as producing the universe of individuals, shapes and forms, as in the case of our ideas of Nature. The Male Deific Principle is always pictured as performing a creative act of some sort, by word, thought or will, which in some way acts upon another vague and nebulous Something, or a Nothing, and causes it to produce, bear and bring forth. In the ancient religions there was always a recognition of 'the Male and Female Deific Principles. In some cases these were symbolized by Deities, male and female, as for instance the male Osiris, and the female Isis, in the Egyptian mythology. In others there was a personification of God and Nature, male and female in principle. The Hindu religions all recognize this principle of Deific Sex, and their male gods are always pictured as having female counterparts, or mates. Even when their gods are recognized as being principles instead of persons, the female principle will always be found accompanying the male. To the Oriental there is always the Divine Mother, as well as the Divine Father; whether regarded as principle or person.

Sex is manifest in all material forms, from the atom to the highest organized living being. In the particles composing Matter-the atoms, and the smaller particles which go to form the atom—we find the polarity of Sex, manifesting in the activities of attraction and repulsion; love and hate. The atom itself is now held by the leading scientific authorities to be composed of thousands of infinitesimal particles called *ions,* electrons, or corpuscles. These electrons are held to be of two kinds, so far as quality is concerned, namely, "positive" and "negative." These positive and negative electrons whirl around each other, never coming in actual contact but always exerting an attractive or repulsive effect upon each other. The best authorities hold that the atom is formed by the action of numerous negative particles which cluster around a single positive particle, the latter seemingly exerting some kind of energy or force upon the negative particles, causing them to group themselves in certain ways, to form certain combinations, the result of which is the creation of the atom.

The various elements, of different fundamental kinds of matter, are held to obtain their special varieties of elemental nature by reason of the various groupings and combinations of these negative electrons around the one positive electron.

This action of the electrons, of which matter is formed, is in close accordance with the ancient Arcane Teaching regarding the male and female particles of matter, which by action and reaction tend to build up the more complex forms. The moment we recognize that the "positive" is the male principle, and 'the "negative" the female, we may read the modern scientific teachings in the light of the Ancient Wisdom. The word "negative" is a poor one, however, with which to describe the principle of generative activity. But the actions and properties of this "negative" aspect of matter prove that it is really the female principle masquerading under a poor name. The negative pole of an electrical battery is really the "generative" pole. Many of the best authorities are now using the term "cathode" to designate the "negative" pole of the battery, the new term arising from a Greek word meaning "descent; the path of generation," etc. From this cathode or female pole of the battery swarm the corpuscles or electrons; the new "rays" recently discovered by science; and the strange and little understood energies which are tending to revolutionize scientific thought. Always from the negative, cathode, or female pole or element of the battery, come these strange things. The positive, or male pole or element never "brings forth," although it is needed to energize and vivify the complementary element or pole. Is not the feminine nature proven by the strongest kind of analogy, is not the male element likewise seen to be in evidence? This cannot arise from mere coincidence—particularly when we may see that the Sex Principle is manifest throughout all of Nature's activities.

The detached electrons which compose the various "rays" and strange energies which are engaging the attention of modern science, are 'negative" or female. The negative electron - travels through space, either being cast off by its male ruler, or else leaving of its own accord, and flying through space. It repels, and is repelled by, other female particles or electrons, and this action of repulsion creates certain disturbances or activities in 'the field of force. When it comes into the near neighborhood of a male or positive electron, an attractive force is manifested, each being attracted to the other, and leaving their orbits in order to meet the other. Scientists hold that this attraction and repulsion—these unitings and separations—these marriages and divorces —among the electrons, are the cause of the greater manifestations of energy or force, and the creation of matter. When the female electron comes within the influence of the male, it begins to vibrate and circle around the latter, in company with its sister particles. This movement and vibration is held to be the vibration from which arises all forms of matter, and all varieties of force or energy on the material plane. Light, heat, magnetism, electricity, chemical affinity, cohesion, and the other forms of energy, arise from the vibrations caused by the action and reaction of the male and female principles of the electrons.

The polarity to *be* observed in the phenomena of magnetism and electricity is distinctively a sex manifestation, as we have said a little further back. The attraction and repulsion manifested by the several poles of the battery, or magnet, is seen to be closely related to sex phenomena on other planes of activity. A leading dictionary gives the following definition of "Polarity:"

"The disposition in a body to exhibit opposite or contrasted properties or powers in opposite of contrasted directions; the existence of two points, called poles, possessing contrary tendencies: for example; the attraction or repulsion at the opposite ends of a magnet; opposite tendencies in polarized light, etc."

II. THE LAW OF LOVE

Not only do we find manifestations of the creative Sex Principle in the animal and vegetable forms of things, but even in the world of minerals it is in evidence. In the crystallization of minerals there is to be observed a phenomenon closely allied to the processes of reproduction in the lowest forms of animal and vegetable cell life. The cells reproduce themselves by growth and division-the crystals do likewise. From the "mother liquid," the infant crystals begin to form. Once formed, they draw to themselves more nourishment from the mother liquid, and begin to form the nucleus of a new crystal, which is finally split off from the older crystal. In many ways the phenomena of crystalization resemble those of the manifestation of creative sex activity in cell life. And this is to be expected, for if the Sex Principle is universal, then it must be in evidence in at least *a* faint degree in everything. Even in the atoms back of the crystal shape, we may see it in operation, in the shape of chemical affinity. Even in the electrons of which the atom is composed, we may see its presence indicated by the positive (male) electrons, and the negative (female) counterparts — the first energizing, and the latter generating shape and form. And even in the energies and forces of Nature, we see the evidences of polarization, which in the end is a manifestation of *Sex*.

William Marion Reedy, in his brilliant essay entitled "The Law of Love," calls attention to the universality of the Sex Principle, or as he calls it, the principle of Love. He says, among other things: "Prof. Von Schroen's recent alleged discovery of life and sex in crystals need not astonish the world. Man has felt that there **was** nothing inanimate, from the beginning of time. His intuition has always been in advance of his reason. His poetry has led his science everywhere. The oneness of things is being demonstrated in these days; that is all. . . . Biology has resolved life back to the single cell, in which all the senses are converged. . . . Sex is a differentiation of the single cell. Philologists assert that, originally, the name of God in every language was both masculine and feminine. *LIFE* is but force. Matter holds together by force. Matter, therefore, has life. . . .

The star is brother to the clod; the moth is kin to the mastodon. Worlds are made to blossom in space as flowers are fructified by floating pollen. Mingling atoms make suns. Cell seeks affinity with cell. Dust blown from the unimaginable outer rim of silence finds its fellow dust and, engaging in amorous whirl, a nebula is formed, and from that nebula suns and systems of suns. Worlds in contact give birth to worlds. The crystals meet and kiss and mingle and produce other crystals. . . . Love is the only law. Love is spirit, and matter is the child of spirit. All this any man who reads may know,"

Reedy continues: "'Nowhere,' says Balzac, 'is motion sterile. Everywhere it engenders' Number; but it may be neutralized by a superior resistance, as in minerals.' This neutralization, Professor Schroen's discovery disproves conclusively—if he has made the discovery. The motion is in the crystal itself; the instinct whereby it seeks out its mate that it may 'increase and multiply.' . . . Out of the single cell—protoplasm, amoeba, vorticella—in combination, but each seeking its own, comes variation or number and, ultimately, Harmony. The atoms, themselves almost inconceivable, operate upon one another in the workings of these forces. The pollen from the flower finds its way to another, miles away, and fecundates it, as Schmid's father, born in Germany, found his mother, born in Australia, to the seemingly unimportant end that Schmid should come to be. Surely those ancients were not far wrong in deeming the atoms 'themselves endowed with conscious intelligence. There is life in everything and everywhere, and no life without love. As a man lies with a woman to perpetuate their kind, so do all things, infinitesimal and vast, through Nature, bed with each other. The phallus is a mightier symbol than the virtuous wot of. It is found even in the Cross. The sciences are a study of the universal lust. Flower fecundates flower, though one sends its seeds to another on the wings of a wandering and uncertain bee. There is a rain *of* life between the planets. Collisions scatter world-fragments in the far furrows of space, and the fragments are gathered up by other planets and life transferred to them from systems that have ceased to be. In mathematics, numbers cohabit, and the results are glimpses of the secrets of Infinity. In chemistry, fluids and solids mingle to make things new. In physics, the savagery and the tenderness of force, in destruction or reproduction, produces power. Biology shows us the operation of the same affection to the development of life. Differentiation, selection, organization—all these are processes of intelligent amorousness in matter. This intelligent amorousness is the spirit in matter—the 'love that makes the world go round/ that 'holds the universe ensnared.' "

Reedy concludes, as follows: "But where does it end—this intelligent amorousness? There is a limit to the finite. But the finite is part of the Infinite. It would seem that the pursuit of this law of love would bring one only to the Unknowable, pushing it only a little further back. Love may follow where love leads —unto the essence of God even—for God is love. The material aspect of love, dwelt on so far, need not deter us from pushing 'farther North.' To whoso believes in the oneness of Matter and Spirit, there is no Unknowable. The end of the law of Love, and of the spiritual faculties for its perception, can be the knowing of this Unknowable—union with the Infinite. Let us make a flight!'

The Arcane Teachers see the presence of Sex not only in the material forces and the forms of matter, but also in the very mind and spirit itself. The teaching is that every individual has not only evidences of both sexes within himself or herself, in the physical body; but also that each has 'the elements of both sex principles within his mental realm. There are certain mental faculties distinctly masculine in their characteristics, such as the Will, the Logical Faculties, etc. There are also certain faculties which are distinctly feminine in their characteristics, such as the Emotions or Feelings; the Imaginative Faculties; Memory; and Intuition. Every individual, male or female, contains within himself or herself, this dual-nature of mind. The Imagination, Memory and Intuition, are essentially feminine in all of their characteristics — their work is a "bringing forth;" an exercise of the reproductive function on the mental plane. Nay, more, even Desire is feminine in its nature, and operates by coaxing', alluring, and drawing the Will into action. The Will and the Logical Faculties, are essentially masculine, and operate in the direction of energizing, applying' force or energy, and stimulating the other faculties to action.

Moreover, that region of the mind which is known to modern psychologists as the "subjective;" the "subconscious;" the "subliminal," *is* feminine in its activities—it produces .and brings forth—it is procreative in its nature. On the other hand, the "objective," or "outer" mind is essentially masculine in its nature. It creates nothing, but merely acts upon the feminine mentality in the direction of inciting it to activity and reproductive functioning. Intuition is distinctively feminine, and is diametrically opposite in polarization to its companion, Logical Reasoning. We have not the space to follow up this thought in detail, but those who are familiar with the characteristics of the various mental faculties, and regions of the mind, will have no trouble in identifying— and classifying them according to their mental sex.

In connection with the subject of the manifestation of Sex on the mental plane, we may say here that the Arcane Teachers hold that the phenomena of Thought Transference, Telepathy, Mental Influence, Hypnotism, etc., are explainable only by the admission of the existence of Sex in the mind. The workings of Suggestion and Auto-Suggestion are also explained when this principle is grasped. This idea of Sex in the mental faculties and regions gives one the key to Psychic Phenomena. All energizing, or projection, by thought waves, etc., is caused by the activities of the masculine principles of mind being employed; all receiving or impression of the influences so sent forth, is caused by the activities of the feminine principles of the mind. The thought or suggestion sent forth is a masculine effort; its reception is feminine—the result arising' therefrom is essentially procreative or reproductive, and is manifested by the feminine principle, always. The domination of some persons by the Will of others, is akin to the tyranny exercised by the male in many forms of life, not excepting' the human kind. The alluring, fascinating, coaxing, attracting, and drawing activities of Desire are decidedly feminine, and often enmesh the strongest Will, just as the strongest man often surrenders to *a* fascinating woman's wishes. The Will operates by force; Desire operates more subtly, but not the less strongly.

The individual manifesting strong Will Power, exercises his or her masculine mentality while the man or woman manifesting Personal Magnetism, charming and fascinating those with whom he or she comes in "contact, exercises his or her feminine mentality. The Will forces and drives; the Desire, Emotion, Feeling, or "Magnetism," draws and attracts. The feminine is always the finer, subtler force which in the end overcomes the apparently stronger force of the masculine mentality. Each however, the masculine and feminine, has its place, and the best work is performed when they are both strongly developed and actively employed.

An understanding of this subject of Sex in mental action will give the magic glasses through which many of the riddles of psychology may be seen clearly solved. We suggest that those to whom the idea is new, put on these glasses of the new understanding, and read anew their old works on psychology, psychic phenomena, occultism, "New Thought," etc,, and see how clearly illumined many hitherto dark pages have grown.

III. THE EVOLUTION OF SEX

It was at one time believed by many, in fact by all persons, that some of the lower forms of life originated spontaneously; that is, without being reproduced from some parental life-form. It was thought that frogs and other reptiles, worms and small insects, and other lowly forms of life, originated from the dust of the earth, or the slime of the river-bed. But Science has brushed aside all such erroneous ideas into the great dust-bin of discarded theories, and has firmly established the doctrine that: "All life proceeds from Life." Reproduction is universal among the living forms, and reproduction always presupposes the manifestation of Sex in at least an elementary degree.

The lowest forms of life are found in the slime of the ocean bed. These elementary forms are but little more than drops of gelatinous glue, without apparent or perceptible organs, but yet manifesting the activities of life, in nutrition, assimilation, elimination and reproduction. , And Science will later on discover the presence of Sex in even these primitive forms, to account for the processes of reproduction, which will be in accord with the old occult teachings on the subject.

The simplest form of reproduction is that of some of these lowly forms of life, which consists simply of *division*. The minute cell grows to a certain size, and then begins to separate itself into two cells. For a short time these two cells are connected by a minute filament, causing them to resemble a miniature dumb-bell. Then the filament breaks, and the two single-cell creatures become separate individuals. Later on, each one of these cells divides itself into another pair, and so on, generation after generation. Science, so far, has not discovered evidence of sex activities in this process of reproduction, but reasoning by analogy it may be seen that the old occult teaching is correct, and that before this division or separation can take place there must be a process of fertilization of one cell by another, at certain periods, the effect of which is continued through several generations of cells. It has been noted that if the cells are kept apart from foreign cells, the process *of* separation ceases after a certain number of generations, and the particular branch becomes extinct; so that it is reasonable to suppose that the generative and reproductive function must be stimulated from time to time by sexual action and fertilization.

A step higher in the scale is that of the Protozoon which also reproduces itself by subdivision. But before this subdivision takes place, there occurs a union of two separate cells, in what is called *conjugation,* after which the processes of separation or subdivision begins. But instead of merely two separate cells form***ing*** from the original cell, there appears a subdivision ***into*** many cells, the young cells appearing as buds upon the combined parent- cells, similar in appearance to 'the buds of the plant. These buds afterward drop off and pursue their mature individual life, afterward combining each with another cell, and then reproducing as did their parents. It is not held that the two uniting cells are distinctively male or female, but that they possess the quality of dual-sexuality, as do some animals much higher in the scale. When the union takes place, the male element of each fertilizes the female element of the other, and the reproduction follows thereupon.

Maupas says: "The para -or micro-nucleus is a 'hermaphrodite' sexual element, of sole importance in conjugation. The stages of the process are as follows: (1) The micro-nucleus increases in size. (2) Division occurs until 'there are eight micro-nuclei. (3) Of these eight, seven disappear. (4) The remaining one divides again, differentiating, a male and female pro-nucleus. (5) In the next stage, the male elements of the two individuals are exchanged, and the new male nucleus fuses with the original female portion. (6) Finally the individuals, separating from one another, reassume all their original organization before beginning again to divide in the usual fashion."

Geddes says: "Sometimes as many as three or four spores of lowly Algae club together, as if to gather sufficient momentum to make a combined start in life. The young forms of the sun-animalcule usually unite in twos, but Gabriel has observed in some cases a multiple union. In another sun-animalcule two to thirty individuals may unite loosely in what is called plastogamy, but close union of nuclei occurs only between two individuals. So in gregarines, while the usual union is certainly dual, Gruber has observed what may be called multiple conjugation. . . Conjugation of two similar unicellular organisms occurs, as we have seen, very generally in the Protozoa, and is also a common fact in the life-history of simple Algae. . . . opposite cells of adjacent filaments are attracted to one another, and the contents of one cell pass bodily over into the other. In the great majority of cases where conjugation occurs, the uniting' cells are to all appearances similar, but it must be remembered that it does not follow from this that they are physiologically alike. . . . In fertilization among higher plants and animals, the two elements which unite are highly differentiated, alike in contrast to one another and in opposition to the general cells of the body. A consideration of the phenomena in loose protist colonies, which suggest a bridge between unicellular and multicellular organisms, shows how gradually this latter contrast also may have been brought about."

As the scale of life ascends under the impulse of the evolutionary urge, the life forms begin to develop organs by means of which the sexual activities may be better performed. In some cases 'the individuals are sharply separated into male and female in their sexual functioning, although preserving their similar outward appearance, while in others each individual possesses the organs of both sexes, this state being styled Hermaphroditism. This state is quite common among some of the lower forms of living things. The oyster, and other shell fish; the barnacles and allied forms; the tapeworm; the earthworm; and even the members of the snail family, are hermaphroditic. Among some of the higher forms of life, even occasionally in man, this condition is manifested as a reversion, or abnormal condition. But in many of the lower forms this condition is the natural and normal one. But it must be remembered that even in the human race each sex has organs which are rudimentary complementaries to the developed organs of the other sex. The breasts, and prostate gland in the male; and the clitoris in the female, are examples of this. A fish is sometimes male on one side and female on the other. Male frogs sometimes contain well developed ovaries.

Geddes says: "An organism may be said to be truly hermaphrodite when both male and female organs are present, or when, without there being separate organs, both male and female elements are produced. It is then both anatomically and physiologically hermaphrodite, and of this, as we shall see, there are abundant illustrations among the lower animals. Snail, earthworm, and leech are examples of this hermaphroditism, in varying degrees of intimacy."

There are two theories regarding the origin of hermaphroditism, one view holding that hermaphroditism was the primitive condition, and that the uni-sexual, or one-sex condition resulted therefrom by evolution; the second view being that uni-sexuality was the original condition, and that hermaphroditism evolved therefrom. Other authorities hold that both theories may be true, and that the original and secondary conditions varied with different species.

Geddes says : "One view of the matter is that hermaphroditism was the primitive state among the multicellular animals, at least after the differentiation of the sex elements had been accomplished. In alternating rhythms, eggs and sperms were produced. The organism was alternately male and female. Of this primitive hermaphroditism, there may be more or less of a recapitulation in the life-history of the organism. Gegenbaur states the common opinion in the following cautious and terse words: 'The hermaphrodite stage is the lower, and the condition of distinct sexes has been derived from it.' Unisexual 'differentiation, by the reduction of one kind of sexual apparatus, takes place at very different stages in the development of the organism, and often when the sexual organs have attained a very high degree of differentiation.' The first structural stage in the separation would probably be the restriction of areas, in which the formation of two kinds of cells still went on at different times in one organism. In different individuals the opposite tendencies we have already spoken of more and more predominated, till unisexuality evolved out of hermaphroditism. That environmental conditions are effective in changing the hermaphrodite into the unisexual state is suggested by many experiments. And it has been shown in regard to some flowering plants, *e. g,* butcher's broom *(Ruscus aculeatus),* that 'the monoecious or dioecious condition may be evoked by altering the nutritive conditions. Quite different is the view which regards hermaphroditism as a secondary condition, derived from primitive unisexuality. Thus Pelse- ticer maintains that the 'study of Mollusca, Myzostomidae, Crustacea, and Pisces shows that in these groups the separation of the sexes preceded hermaphroditism; various cases in other groups tend to show that this is true universally; and the same conclusion applies to plants. In Mollusca, Crustacea, and Pisces, at least, hermaphroditism is grafted upon the female sex.' "

As an example of the results of perfect and normal hermaphroditism among the lower forms of life, the following instance of the method of fecundation among snails may be mentioned. It must be remembered that the snail has both male and female sexual organs, both perfectly developed and both actively employed in the work of reproduction. The process is stated by Prof. T. R, Jones, F. R. S.. of England, who says : "The manner in which snails copulate is not a little curious, their union being accompanied by preparatory blandishments of a very extraordinary kind, that to a spectator would seem rather like a combat between mortal foes than the tender advances of two lovers. After sundry caresses between the two parties, during which they exhibit an animation quite foreign to them at other times, one of the snails unfolds from the right side of its neck, where "the generative orifice is situated, a wide sacculus, which, by becoming everted, displays *a* sharp dagger-like speculum, or dart, attached to its walls. Having bared this singular weapon, it endeavors, if possible, to strike it into some exposed part of the body of the other snail, who, on the other hand, uses every precaution to avoid the blow, by speedily retreating into its shell. But, at length, having received the sexual wound, the smitten snail prepares to retaliate, and in turn uses every effort to puncture its assailant in *a* similar manner. The darts are generally broken off in this encounter, and either fall to the ground, or remain fixed in the wounds which they have inflicted, After these preparatory stimulations, the snails proceed to more effective advances.

The sac of the dart is withdrawn into the body, and another sacculus is by a like process protruded from the common generative aperture. Upon this last named sacculus, two orifices are seen, one of which connects with the female generative system of the animal, while from the other a long whip-like filament, the male attachment, is gradually unfolded, being gradually everted like the finger of a glove, until it attains the length of an inch or more. Then each of the two snails impregnates the other, and is itself impregnated at the same time"

Even in hermaphroditism however, the female element is predominant, being more largely concerned with the reproductive and generative processes, while the male element apparently exist only for the purpose of energizing, or inciting into creative activity, the female element. And, as the scale is ascended, the male individual becomes specialized apparently for convenience in forming unions with female organism mo ed is sp from the original female. In the generative and reproductive, the mother element is the principal and predominant one.

IV. SEX IN PLANT LIFE

To many persons who have not considered this phase of the subject, it may seem strange to hear scientists assert that the manifestations and, activities of sex are as much in evidence in the world of plant-life as among the animals. The male and female elements are found in every plant, and reproduction is the result of sex union just as truly as is the case among the animals. The flower is the sexual organ, or rather *organs,* of the plant. The female element of the flower produces the seeds of the plant, but only when it is fertilized with the sexual product of the male element. In some cases the male element is found on one plant, and the female on another. In other cases the male and female elements are found in different parts of the same plank; as, for instance, in the case of the Indian corn, in which the "tassel" contains the male dement or flowers, while the "silk" contains the female element or flowers— the "ear" containing the seeds afterwards emerging from the female element or flower after the latter has been fertilized by the male element. In the greater number of plants, however, the flower contains both the male and female elements, and is thus fully hermaphroditic.

In order to understand the activities of sex among the plants, or flowers, let us consider in detail the several parts of the plant sex organs, which we know by the name of "flowers:"

First we have *the* part of the flower known as the *calyx,* which is the *cup* of the flower, which covers its lower and outer parts, and which is generally of a green color. Next we have the *corolla,* which is the *crown* of the flower, which is composed of petals usually beautifully colored, and which to many constitutes the real "flower" itself. The calyx and corolla form a cup-like receptacle in which are found the two essential and distinctive sex organs of the plant, (i) the *Stamen,* or male organ; and (2) the *Pistil,* or female organ.

The Stamen, or male organ of the flower, is an upright, thread-like filament, bearing at its summit two minute sacs, which are called the *anthers,* and which contain a very fine, microscopic dust or powder called the *pollen,* the latter being the active male element of reproduction.

The *Pistil,* or female organ of the flower, is found in the center of the flower, in the middle of the stamens, and which secretes and stores in a tiny cell the female element of reproduction which is called the *ovule.* Crowning the Pistil are found the *style* and the *stigma.*

Some flowers have but one Stamen; others have two; others still have many. Linnaeus was the first great authority to explain the sex activities of plants. He says: 'The flower forms the theatre of the amours of the plants. The calyx is to be considered as the nuptial bed; the corolla constitutes the curtains; the anthers are the testes; the pollen, the fecundating fluid; the stigma of the pistil, the external genital aperture; the style, the vagina, or the conductor of the prolific seed; the ovary of the plant, the womb; the reciprocal action of the stamens on the pistil, the accessory process of fecundation."

Kellog says: "In many instances, the action of plants seems almost to be prompted by intelligence. At the proper moment, the corolla contracts in such a way as to bring the stamens nearer to the stigma, or in contact with it, so as to procure fecundation. In some aquatic plants, the flowers elevate themselves above the surface of the water while the process of foundation is effected, submerging themselves again immediately afterward. Other very curious changes occur in flowers of different species during the reproductive act. The stigma is observed to become moistened, and even to become slightly odorous. Often, too, it becomes intensely congested with the juices of the plant, and sometimes even acquires an uncommon and most remarkable degree of contractility. This is the case with the stigma of the tulip and one variety *of* the sensitive plant, and in these plants it is observed to occur not only after the application of the pollen to the stigma, hut when excited by any other means of stimulation, The flowers of some plants, during and after fecundation, also show an increase of heat, in some cases so marked as to be readily detected with the thermometer. This is said to be especially the case with the *arum* of Italy. In some plants in which the pistil is longer than the stamens, thus elevating the stigma above the anthers, the female organ is often observed to bend over and depress itself, so as to come within reach of the anthers."

Fertilization of the female elements by the pollen of the male element, in plant life, is effected in numerous and various ways. In instances in which the male and female organs are situated on different plants, as in the ease of the willows, etc., the pollen is carried to the female flower by the passing breezes, the transfer often being effected over great distances. But the more frequent method, and the one in operation where the male and female elements are near each other, is that of fertilization by means of insects, small birds, and even small animals like the snail.

Sprengel was one of the first naturalists to discover and announce this "secret of nature." He anticipated the later researches of Darwin, and indeed cleared a path for the later scientist. As Geddes says: "Sprengel laid sure foundations, now somewhat hidden by the superstructures which Darwin and others have built, to Sprengel's eyes, the many ways in which the nectar is protected from rain seemed full of 'intention,' He recognized in the markings of the petals illumined finger-posts to lead injects to the hidden hoards; and he further demonstrated that in some bi-sexual flowers it was physically impossible for the pollen from the stamens to pass to the tips of the carpels. His general conclusion, freely stated, was, that 'since a large number of flowers have the sexes separate, and probably at feast as many hermaphrodites have the stamens and carpels ripening at different times, nature appears to have designed that no flower shall be fertilized by its own pollen.' A few years later (1799), Andrew Knight maintained that no hermaphrodite flower fertilizes itself for a perpetuity of generations. Sprengel's secret of nature had, however, to be set forth afresh by Darwin, who, in his 'Fertilization of Orchids' (1862), and 'Effects of Cross- and Self-Fertilization' (1876), has not only shown, with great wealth of illustration, the manifold devices for ensuring that insects unconsciously carry the fertilizing pollen from one flower to another, but has also emphasized the advantage of cross-fertilization for the health of the species. 'Nature tells us,' he says, 'in the most emphatic manner that she abhors perpetual self-fertilization.' Hildebrand, Hermann Muller, Delpino, and others, have, with consummate patience of observation, further traced out the secrets of nature in this relation; and the student may be referred to D'Arcy Thompson's valuable edition of Muller's 'Fertilization of Flowers,' Sir John Lubbock's 'Flowers in Relation to Insects,' the classic works of Darwin, and P. Knuth's 'Handbuch der Blutenbiologie,' *2* vols., Leipzig, *1892*. Reference must, however, also be made to Meehan's protest that self-fertilization is neither, *so* rare nor so 'abhorrent' as is generally believed. In a great number of cases, cross-fertilization by means of insects does occur; in many it must occur. In another by no means small set of flowering plants,-usually with inconspicuous blossoms, —the fertilizing gold dust is borne by the wind, and falls, like the golden shower on Danae, upon adjacent flowers. In many hermaphrodite flowers, again, self-fertilization does certainly take place; in some this is necessarily so. Indubitable self-fertilization occurs in the small degenerate unopening (cleistogamous) flowers of some plants, such as species of balsam, deadnettle, pansy, etc. These occur along with ordinary flowers, and, curiously enough, are sometimes more fertile than they."

Another authority says : "Fertilization is the fecundation of a plant by the application of the pollen to the stigma. In some cases, the pollen simply drops upon the stigma, which is called self-fertilization. In most instances, however, it is blown by the wind, or carried by bees, or moths, or such-like insects, 'from other flowers of the same species. This is what is called cross-fertilization. Darwin found that twenty heads of Dutch Clover left open to the visits of bees produced 2,290 seeds; the same number defended from the visit of the bees did not yield even one seed."

Plant life affords many curious and interesting instances of ingenious devices arranged by Nature for attracting to the flower the insects needed to fertilize it; the bright colors of flowers, and the honey or sweet fluids contained within many flowers, being intended solely for this purpose. The shape and size of the various parts of the flowers are arranged so as to cause the bee or other insect first to brush against the receptacle containing the pollen, and then to brush the same off into the female parts of other flowers. The subject is extremely interesting, and will well repay one for studying it in detail in the text books on the subject.

V. SEX IN ANIMAL LIFE

In animal-life, as in plant-life, we find the male and female elements of reproduction. In animals, the male element of reproduction is called the *Spermatozoon;* and the female element of reproduction is called the **Ovum.**

The *Spermatozoa* (plural of *spermatozoon*) are the active, moving constituents of the male element of reproduction, and consist of a head, a rod-shaped middle piece, and a long hair-like tail, by the vibratile motion of which they move in a spiral manner. They were formerly regarded as parasites inhabiting the seminal fluid, but were finally discovered to be the fecundating cell or male element of reproduction. They are found in all animals, including man. The size of the spermatozoa varies in different animals. In man they are about one six-hundredth of an inch in length. Their peculiar movements resemble those of the tadpole, the hair-like tail manifesting constant motion from side to side, propelling' the spermatozoon from one point to another. It is composed of protoplasm, the substance which is the base of all physical life. The Spermatozoa develop from a mother-sperm-cell, by the progress of segmentation or subdivision, in a manner analogous to that of the lowly forms of animal life. They dwell in a gelatinous fluid, which mingles with other fluids secreted by the glands, and which thus constitute the male seminal fluid.

Geddes gives the following information regarding the physiology of the Spermatozoa. He says:

"A few facts in regard to the physiology *of* the sperm demand notice, (a) It is specialized as a highly active cell; its minimal size, the usual absence of any encumbering nutritive material, the contractility of the tail, and the general shape, all fit it for characteristic mobility. More than one histologist has likened it to a free muscle-cell, or to a flagellate monad, *(b)* Furthermore, the sperm has very considerable power of persistent vitality. Not only does it often remain long unexpelled in the male animal, without losing its functions, but it may retain its fertilizing power after remaining for weeks, or even months, in the female organism.

In the earthworm, the spermatozoa pass from one worm to another, not directly to the ova nor to female ducts, but to be stored up in special reservoirs or spermathecae. So it is with many animals. The spermatozoa received by the queen bee during her single impregnation, are for a considerable period-even for three years—used in 'fertilizing successive sets of worker and queen ova. Quite unique, however, is the case of one of Sir John Lubbock's queen ants, which laid fertile eggs thirteen years after the last sexual union with a male. The spermatozoa had apparently persisted all that time. Hensen cites the facts that a hen will lay fertilized eggs eighteen days after the removal of the cock, and that in bats, spermatozoa may remain alive a whole winter *in* the uterus of the female. In most European bats, indeed, sexual union occurs in autumn, but the sperms are simply stored in the uterus, for ovulation and fertilization do not take place till spring. In exceptional cases, especially in young forms which were not mature in autumn, pairing occurs in spring. An exactly parallel condition is known in some snakes. Thus Rollinat notes in regard to *Tropidonotus viperinus* that mature females are inseminated in the autumn previous to the egg-laying (in June or July), but in females laying for the first time, copulation probably occurs in early spring, *(c)* Remarkable too, and again suggestive of monads, is the power the sperms have of resisting great deviations 'from the normal temperature. The presence of acids has usually a paralyzing influence, but alkaline solutions have, on the whole, the opposite result. "

The **Ovum,** or female element *of* reproduction, is a small egg-like cell, very small, which is formed in the ovaries of the female, and is afterward passed downward through a duct. Ova are developed from time to time, and pass downward through the duct that they may be fertilized by a spermatozoon or male element.

Geddes gives the following information regarding the physiology of the Ovum. He says ;

"The ovum presents all the essential features of any other animal cell. There is the cell-substance, consisting in part of genuine living matter or protoplasm; and there is the nucleus, or 'germinal vesicle,' which plays such an important part in the ripening, fertilizing, and subsequent division of the cell. Besides the living matter, there are simpler substances, especially in many cases a reserve capital of yolk nutri- erit for the future embryo. The modern masters of microscopic technique have detected many marvels in the egg-cell, into which we cannot at present enter, but it is important to recognize clearly that although the ovum is in a sense simple, being a single cell, it is not structureless like white of egg. About details there is great diversity of opinion, but all are agreed that the ovum has 'organization.' In many instances, *e. g,.* in the minute ovary of hydra, in the ovary of *Tubularia,* or in the ovarian tubes of insects, the ovum is but the surviving competitor among a crowd of surrounding cells, which to start with were all potential ova. This is an often forgotten chapter in the struggle for existence,—the struggle between germ-cells. There is a struggle between potential ova; there is also enormous elimination among the spermatozoa, even after they come, to close quarters with the ovum. Many are almost successful, but in most cases only one fertilizes, *i.e.* survives. And even after the eggs begin to develop there is often elimination apart from enemies, thus it is stated that only about a third of the eggs of the New Zealand 'lizard' *(Sphmodon* or *Hatteria)* ever hatch, *(c)* In the third place, and this is the rarest form, the egg-cell acquires a store of food-material from a special yolk gland, as in many of the lower worms.' "

Fecundation, or reproduction, is caused by the union of the male and female elements— the Spermatozoon and the Ovum. The former enters into and is enclosed by the latter, and the process of the formation, development and evolution of the young life is begun. The union of the two creative cells—the male and the female elements — forms a new and more complex cell, which then develops and evolves into the perfect young of the species to which the parents belong.

In various ways, and by means of various methods and processes, the spermatozoon is brought in contact with the ovum. The act of physical union between the male and female of the higher form of animal life is called coition or copulation—and its sole purpose is that of fecundation and the reproduction of life, It is usually accompanied by a peculiar nervous, spasmodic disturbance, which exhausts the participants to a greater or lesser extent. The spermatozoon comes in contact with the ovum and penetrates the outer covering of the latter, the entrance of other spermatozoa being then prevented by the immediate formation of a thick membrane through which they cannot penetrate.

Geddes gives the following information regarding the physiology of fecundation or fertilization. He says:

"There are various steps in the process which is often summed up in the one word— 'fertilization. (1) There is the process by which the spermatozoa are brought into general proximity to 'the ova. In higher animals this is best termed insemination, and is accomplished by copulation. (2) There is the approach of the spermatozoon to the ovum, but of this little is known. (*3*) There is fertilization in the strict sense—the intimate and orderly union of the two sex-nuclei. . , ,

"The adaptations which secure that the sperms shall reach the ova are very varied. Sometimes it seems almost a matter of chance, for the sperms from adjacent males may simply be washed into the female, as in sponges and bivalves, with the nutritive water-currents. In other cases, especially well seen in most fishes, the female deposits her unfertilized ova in the water; the male follows and covers them with spermatozoa. Many may have watched from a bridge the female salmon ploughing along the gravelly river bed depositing her ova, careful to secure a suitable ground, yet not disturbing the already laid eggs of her neighbors. Meanwhile she is attended by her (frequently much smaller) mate, who deposits milt upon the ova. In the frog, again, the eggs are fertilized externally by the male just as they leave the body of his embraced mate. Or it may be that the sperms are lodged in special packets, which are taken up by the female in most of the newts, surrounded with one of the male arms in many cuttle-fishes, or passed from one of the spider's palps to the female aperture. In the majority of animals, *e. g.*, insects and higher vertebrates, copulation occurs, and the sperms pass from the male directly to the female. Even then the history is very varied.

They may pass into special receptacles, as in insects, to be used as occasion demands; or, in higher animals, they may with persistent locomotor energy work their way up the female ducts. There they may soon meet and fertilize ova which have been liberated from the ovary; or may persist, as we noticed, for a prolonged period; or may eventually perish. When the sperms have come, in any of these varied ways, in close proximity to the ovum, there is every reason to believe that a strong osmotic attraction is set up between the two kinds of elements. . . . The spermatozoa, which seem so well to deserve Ralph's epithet of 'starved,' appear to be powerfully drawn to the well-nourished ovum, and the latter frequently rises to meet the sperm in a small 'attractive cone.' Often, however, there is an obstacle in the way of entrance in the form of the egg-shell, which may be penetrable only at one spot, well called the micropyle.

Dewitz has made the interesting observation that round the egg-shells of the cockroach ova, the sperms move in regular circles of ever-varying orbit; and points out that thus, sooner or later, a sperm must hit upon the entrance. He showed that this was a characteristic motion of these elements on smooth spheres, for round empty egg-shells or on similar vesicles they moved in an equally orderly and systematic fashion. The persistence with which the spermatozoa often force their way to the ova makes it impossible to doubt the reality of a strong- chemotactic attraction. One' illustration may suffice. According to Dr. Sadone's account of the impregnation in the rotifer *Hydatina senta,* the spermatozoa of the male, which are injected into the body-cavity of the female, reach the totally enclosed eggs by boring through the thin membrane at a point where the mature ova are situated—a process not known in any other animals. The oval head of a spermatozoon was seen to attach itself to the membrane of the ovary, the tail continued to make lashing movements, the head was gradually forced through the membrane, and the tail followed, the whole process taking about ten minutes."

In addition to the numerous examples of the various methods and processes of fertilization mentioned by Geddes, as above quoted, we may mention a few unusual examples. Among the most curious is the process of Parthogenesis. In this process, which is the common method among certain of the plant—lice, the male and female copulate in the usual manner, and the female lays eggs, which *in* time are hatched. But the young so hatched from the eggs are not normal insects—they are neither male nor female, but are peculiar sexual creatures which may be called "imperfect females." These imperfect females, instead of seeking 'fertilization from the male, and then laying eggs as did their mother, produce young resembling themselves, by a process of "budding." These "budded" young, then "bud" forth a new generation, and so on until nine generations are born, when a few perfect males and females are produced, and the process begins anew in the normal fashion. Some of the polyps, a low animal form resembling a plant, 'bud" forth young, which then separate and swim about as independent organisms. Instead of developing until they resemble the parent polyp, however, these young, upon reaching maturity, are fertilized and lay eggs, which when hatched produce the original form of polyp, resembling the grandparent. And so on, the generations alternating.

A curious state of affairs is noted in the case of the Bilharzia, a parasitic trematode, the male of which carries the female about with him in a "gynaecophoric canal" composed of folds of skin. Similar to this peculiar case, *is* that of certain barnacles in which the female carries around with her her male mate, secreted in a little pocket-like contrivance. This mate is much smaller than the female, and is very different from the latter in appearance, so much so in fact that it took Science a long time to determine that it was not a parasite. In some cases, the female has been found to carry several of these tiny male mates around with her.

Geddes gives the following additional information on this subject. He says: "A not unfrequent mode of fecundation is by means of spermatophores, or packets of spermatozoa. These may be seen at times attached to the earthworm, or found within the leech and snail. Even in newts spermatophores may be formed, and taken up as such by the females. In the spider the spermatozoa are stored in a special receptacle on the palp, and hence hastily transferred to the fierce female. In cuttlefishes this mode of impregnation is yet more marked. One of the "arms' of the male, much modified and laden with spermatophores, is thrust, or in many eases bodily discharged into the branchial cavity of the female, where it bursts. Such a discharged arm was, on first discovery, regarded as a parasite, and hence received the name of Hectocotylus. A curious aberration from the ordinary relations is where two distinct individuals of a species of fluke (*Diplozoon*) physically combine in almost lifelong union. In many cases again, especially in bony fishes, there is a sexual attraction between male and female, but without any copulation.

The female, accompanied by her mate, deposits ova, which he thereupon fertilizes with spermatozoa. A slightly more advanced stage is seen in the frog. Fertilization is still outside the body of the mother, but the male, embracing the female, liberates spermatozoa upon the eggs, just as these are laid. In the majority of cases, however, special organs for emitting and for receiving spermatozoa are developed, and copulation occurs. The male organ is often an adaptation of some structure already existing, as in many crustaceans, where modified appendages form external canals for the seminal fluid. In skates and other gristly fishes, the remarkably complex copulatory organs, the so- called 'claspers,' are in dose connection with the hind limb. The copulation may be quite external, as in crayfishes, etc., where the male, seizing the female, deposits spermatozoa upon the already laid eggs. Oftener, however, it is internal, and the intromittent organ is inserted into the genital aperture of the female. True copulation may occur without the presence of special organs,-notably in the case of many birds, where the cloaca of the male is apposed to that of the female. The spermatozoa, forcibly expelled by the excited male organs, pass up the female ducts, probably, in part, as the result of peristalsis, but chiefly at least by their own locomotor energy, and one of them may eventually fertilize an ovum. In addition *to* the intromittent organ, and the lower portion of the female duct which receives it during copulation, there may be auxiliary structures. such as true claspers for retaining hold of the females. The limy 'cupid's dart' or 'spicufum amoris' of the snail, is usually interpreted as a preliminary excitant."

VI. SEX IN HUMAN LIFE

There are two aspects of Sex in Human- Life. The first, the physical aspect, is merely a continuation of the thought phase of sex in the life of the animal kingdom, and should concern itself solely with the reproduction of the species. The second, the vital, mental, moral and spiritual, leads to planes of manifestation of which the animal world has no experience, although some of its phases are indicated in the lives of the higher animals in the sense of a prophetical promise.

Strange as it may appear to many, some of the moral and ethical features of sex in human- life are seen to have their roots in the sex manifestation of the higher animal-life. There is much in common between them. As Geddes says: "It is with emotions that we have here most to do; and without raising the difficult question whether animals exhibit any emotions exactly analogous to those which in man are associated with the 'moral sense,' 'religion,' and 'the sublime,' we accept the conclusion of Darwin, followed by Romanes and others, that all other emotions which we ourselves experience, are likewise recognizable in analogous expression in the higher animals. Those which are associated with sex and reproduction are in. deed among the most patent; love of mates, love of offspring, lust, jealousy, family affection, social sympathies, are undeniable."

The love of mates, which in the earliest beginning of the lower life forms is evidenced only by an instinctive attraction, is then seen to gradually evolve into something which may be called "affection," and 'from thence into a steadily ascending scale of "love," until in the highest human development it is evidenced by a mental and emotional condition far above anything witnessed among the lower forms of life. Even far down in the scale of life we may see evidences of the mutual attraction between mates. Even among the insects there may be seen that which is truly called "courtship" as distinguished from elementary sexual acts. Geddes says: "There may even be cooperation in work as in the beetles, such as the *Ateuchus,* where the two sexes pursue their somewhat disinterested labors together. The male and female of another beetle inhabit the same cavity, and the virtuous matron is said greatly to resent the intrusion of another male."

Jealousy plays a prominent part in the life of the higher animals, and even the lower forms manifest it in some cases; as, for instance, among' the fishes the stickle-back battles with his rivals, and finally leads his mate to the nest he has built of twigs and weeds, and after going through 'the motions of a wild- love-dance, pushes her in the nest and thereafter guards her jealously from other males. The battles between rival males of the salmon family are terrific. Coquetry and jealousy have been noticed even among the insects. Snakes manifest great jealousy and love of the company of their mates. If a cobra is killed, its mate often travels to the scene of its death and remains there, disconsolate, for many days. Among birds, there are found all the manifestations of courtship, jealousy, and love of mates. The dove affords a striking illustration. Some birds mate for life, and often mourn away their lives if the mate is killed.

Geddes says: "Mantegazza has written a work entitled 'The Physiology of Love,' in which he expounds the optimistic doctrine that love is the universal dynamic; and from this Buchner quotes the sentence, that 'the whole of nature is one hymn of love.' If the last word be used very widely, this often-repeated utterance has more than poetic significance. But even in the most literal sense there is much truth in it, since so many animals are at one in the common habit of serenading their mates. The chirping of insects, the croaking of frogs, the calls of mammals, the song of birds, illustrate both the bathos and glory of the love- chorus. The works of Darwin and others have made us familiar with the numerous ways, both gentle and violent, in which mammals woo one another. The display of decorations in which many male birds indulge, the amatory dances of others, the love-lights of glow-insects, the joyous tournaments or furious duels of rival suitors, the choice which not a few females seem to exhibit, and the like, show how a process, at first crude enough, becomes enhanced by appeals to more than merely sexual appetite. But it is hardly necessary now to argue seriously in support of the thesis that love—in the sense of sexual sympathy, psychical as well as physical—exists among animals in many degrees of evolution. Our comparative psychology has been too much influenced by our intellectual superiority; but while this, no doubt, has its correspondingly increased possibilities of emotional range, it does not necessarily imply a corresponding emotional intensity; and we have no means of measuring, much less limiting, that glow of organic emotion which so manifestly flushes the organism with color and floods the world with song. Who knows whether the song-bird be not beside the man what the child-musician is to the ordinary dullness of our daily toil and thought? The fact to be insisted upon is this, that the vague sexual attraction of the lowest organisms has been evolved into a definite reproductive impulse, into a desire often predominating over even that of self-preservation; that this again, enhanced by more and more subtle psychical additions, passes by a gentle gradient into the love of the highest animals, and of the average human individual."

The love of offspring, which many seem to consider a distinctively human characteristic, has its roots in the mental and emotional life of the lower forms of life. Even as far down the scale as the worms, we find evidences of the offspring' clinging around the mother animal, and often protected by the latter in one way or another. Some of the lowly forms of life carry their young around with them in brood-chambers, or pouch-like contrivances. The *Clepsine,* a small freshwater leech, always carries its young around with it, attached to the surface of its body. The marine leech known as the "skate-sucker" guards faithfully for several weeks its eggs which it has deposited in an old shell, or under a stone. Some of the spiders carry their eggs around with them in tiny sacks, until they are hatched. Among the shell-fish there are many species in which the young return to the shell of their mother after being hatched. The mother cray-fish gives shelter to her young until they are able to care for themselves. The attention and care given to young bees and ants is well known. Some plant-lice mothers are as solicitous for the welfare of their young as is the mother hen. Among the mammals the young are carefully watched and guarded, in a manner strikingly human-like in many eases. Among the higher mammals it is quite easy and natural to apply the term "parental love" to the interest manifested by the mother and father toward their offspring.

Many authorities hold that altruistic emotions and feelings — the sympathies, and love for others—had their rise in the love of the lower animals for their mates and their young. This becoming more highly developed in the human being, reached out to include the love for more distant relatives; then the love for friends; then the community love for the tribe; then the love for the nation; and finally the love for all mankind, and the human brotherhood; which, in the future, will extend to the love for all living things. Under this theory, all the altruistic and unselfish emotions, sympathies and "fellow feelings," arose from the sexual instinct and love of the lower animal for his mate and young. Geddes says of this :

"The optimism which finds in animal life only 'one hymn of love' is inaccurate, like the pessimism which sees throughout nothing but selfishness. Littre, Leconte, and some others less definitely, have more reasonably recognized the co—existence of twin streams of ego— ism and altruism, which often merge 'for *a* space without losing their distinctness, and are traceable to a common origin in the simplest forms of life. In the hunger and reproductive attractions of the lowest organisms, the self-regarding and other-regarding activities of the higher find their starting-point. Though some vague consciousness is perhaps co-existent with life itself, we can only speak with confidence of psychical egoism and altruism after a central nervous system has been definitely established. At the same time, the activities of even the lowest organisms are often distinctly referable to either category. A simple organism, which merely feeds and grows, and liberates superfluous portions of its substance to start new existences, is plainly living an egoistic and individualistic life. But whenever we find the occurrence of close association with another form, we find the first rude hints of love. It may still be almost wholly an organic hunger which prompts the union, but it is the beginning of life not wholly individualistic. Hardly distinguishable at the outset, the primitive hunger and love become the starting-points of divergent lines of egoistic and altruistic emotion and activity. The differentiation of separate sexes; the production of offspring which remain associated with the parents; the occurrence of genuine pairing beyond the limits of the sexual period; the establishment of distinct families, with unmistakable affection between parents, offspring, and relatives; and lastly, the occurrence of animal societies wider than the family,—mark important steps in the evolution of both egoism and altruism. There are two divergent lines of emotional and practical activity,—hunger, self—regarding, egoism, on the one hand; love, other—regarding, altruism, on the other. These find a basal unity in the primitively close association between hunger and love, between nutritive and reproductive needs. Each plane of ascent marks a widening and ennobling of the activities; but each has its corresponding bathos, when either side unduly preponderates over the other. The actual path of progress is represented by action and reaction between the two complementary functions, the mingling becoming more and more intricate. Sexual attraction ceases to *be* wholly selfish; hunger may be overcome by love; love of mates is enhanced by love for off— spring; love for offspring broadens out into love of kindred. Finally, the ideal before us is a more harmonious blending of the two streams."

It is not our intention to speak of the physiology of sex in human—life in this book. There are many good books written on the subject, which indeed requires a large book to consider in detail Nor shall we discuss the physical side of the love of man and woman in this book, except in the matter of pointing out certain grave errors into which the race has fallen— the prostitution of the creative function to the gratification of sensual lust. We shall speak of this in plain words in the succeeding chapters.

From thence, we shall pass on to a brief consideration of the higher phases of Sex in human-life. Sex exists for the human being not only on the plane of the physical, but also on the vital, mental and spiritual plane. Moreover, there is possible for the human being the conservation and transmutation of the creative energy of the sexual organism. Of this, too, shall we speak. The purpose of this book is to show the evolution of sex from the inorganic life, on to the lower forms of organic life, thence onward to the human life, and then on to the plane of the superman and superwoman.

Sex is like the sacred lotus of Oriental lands —its roots buried in the muddy slime of the river-bed, thence rising through the various currents of the river-water, until finally the air is reached, when lo! the plant blossoms forth' in luxuriant purity, a type and symbol of the Highest spiritual development. Sex has its roots in the mud of material life. It rises through the flowing waters of mentality, and finally blossoms in the clear air of the spiritual nature—pure, cred, divine.

We ask all to read carefully and ponder deeply on what we shall now have to say regarding Sex in Human Life.

VII. THE PHYSICAL FUNCTION OF SEX

The student, casting aside all preconceived notions, and all ideas implanted in his mind by custom and general public opinion, and examining the records of Nature as written in her great book of creation, can make no mistake regarding the true function of sex. He will see all through Nature plainly written the universal law that Sex exists purely and solely for the purpose of creation, procreation, and reproduction. If he be candid enough to acknowledge this to himself, he will see that all other uses and employment of Sex must be abnormal, perverted and unnatural.

It is true that the human race has acquired the habit of employing the physical function of Sex for the purpose of sensual gratification alone, reproduction not being desired or intended in the majority of cases. This habit extending over thousands of years, and being unquestioned by the majority of the race, has led many persons to believe and hold that such practices were perfectly natural and in full accord with Nature. But a careful study of Nature's ways, plans and methods will show any fair-minded and unprejudiced person that the habits and practices of the human race regarding the function of Sex, are unnatural and perverted and have no basis in any of Nature's fundamental laws.

All through the various kingdoms of life we may see that Sex is used solely in the direction of creation, procreation and reproduction. It is the function whereby Nature keeps up her supply of living forms and things. She bends every effort toward the exercise of this function, and often subordinates even the life of the parent to the function of bringing forth the new generation. So carefully does she regulate the instinctive desires, that the females of the animal kingdom will refuse to cohabit except at the proper seasons when procreation is possible. At all other seasons the females will vigorously oppose the males, and the latter seemingly recognize the situation and allow themselves to be driven away. The study of the processes of Sex, in all fields of the great kingdom of life, will show conclusively that the one only and sole purpose of Sex is that of creation, procreation and reproduction.

"But," argue some, "that is all very well for the animals, but man is greater than the animals, and has improved on their habits. Is man no more than a beast, to be governed by their habits and customs?" This absurd argument is accepted as valid by many men who seek not reasons but *excuses* for the practices and habits of life. The truth, as recognized by all biologists, is that man in the primitive state followed the same laws and habits as that of all the rest of the animal kingdom, and refrained from cohabitation except at certain periods when the female was capable of conception. In some savage tribes the custom still exists, and the female will vigorously drive away the insistent male at other times. In this she is supported by the public opinion of the tribe, and others will rally to her defense if necessary. And so it was with primitive man, undoubtedly. The desire and will of the female prevailed, and these desires and this will were operated according to natural instinctive lines.

But when mankind advanced (?) to the stage in which woman was held not as an equal and co-worker, but as a serf and slave, man began to impose his passion upon her at unseasonable as well as at seasonable times, and the prevailing unnatural practices of the race resulted. In no other animal except man has this unnatural practice prevailed. Some writers have excepted certain varieties of the goat, which are said to have become perverted in this respect, but certain it is that the general varieties of animals still adhere to the instinctive laws and principles of Nature in this respect. As for man "improving" on the animals, the "improvement" is along the same lines as the other "improvements" which led to the manufacture of intoxicating liquors, and the use thereof; the use of drugs and narcotics; the barbarous social customs which have sprung up and which make the misery of the many the price of the success of the few. Man has "improved" many things, but some of his "improvements" have been in the wrong direction. And *so* it is with the case in point.

To those who will rise in revolt at this statement, we would put the plain question: If the *physical* Sex functions are not intended for the sole purpose of reproduction and procreation, for what purpose are they intended?

Some will answer that they are intended for "pleasurable gratification;" "manifestation of love," etc., etc. But this only carries the subject back another step. Biologists teach that Nature has made all of the necessary functions more or less pleasurable, gratifying and satisfying, in order that the individual living things may perform the acts of these functions. Eating is pleasurable, but hunger and appetite were certainly not devised merely to give pleasure—they were made pleasurable so that the living things would be impelled to gratify them instinctively and thus carry out Nature's great purpose of sustaining her living things. But men have cultivated the sense of taste and appetite until many individuals are abnormal in this respect—they have become perverts and degenerates in regard to appetite and taste.

The ancient feasts, in which the gluttons would take emetics to relieve their swollen stomachs of their contents, only that they might then proceed to refill them with fresh delicacies, give us a striking example of this fact. And some modern gourmands almost equal their ancient brethren in this respect.

The taste for drink gives us another example of the perversion of a natural instinct.

And so it has become with the function of Sex. Intended by Nature solely for the purpose of creation, procreation and reproduction, men have so perverted and degenerated the natural intent that, like the taste and appetites, they have dragged the Sex function down into the dust. That which should be regarded as one of the highest of Nature's functions and processes, has been made the subject of vileiests and abnormal practices. That function which lies at the very root and beginning of Life, has become the subject and object of abnormal, unnatural and degenerate practices which shock any mind which looks upon Nature in all her manifestations as essentially pure. The instinctive realization of this fact has caused the race to regard Sex in itself as impure. It is not Sex that is impure; but the prostitution and perversion of her natural functions have slimed over her primitive purity.

If Sex were confined to her natural functions, the race would regard the subject of sexuality in an entirely different light. It would then occupy the high place which Nature intended for it. The Fount of Life would be kept pure, and would be the subject of veneration, But so befouled have become the waters of the Fount, owing to the unnatural practices of the majority of the race, that many shudder at the mention of its name, and avoid it as unclean and impure. The race does not realize the cause of this strange degradation of the ; subject of Sex, but the intuitive and instinctive mentality of men and women recognizes the unnatural and perverted state of the subject, and naturally recoils from its consideration.

Were the natural and normal conditions existent to-day, then Sex in human life would be regarded as as pure and worthy as is Sex in the life of the plants. So perverted has become the popular idea of Sex, owing to the unnatural conditions prevailing', that the mere mention of the word is taboo in polite circles. Could this arise from natural use of the function? Is there anything impure in the thought of the birth of the child, and the reproduction of the species?

Is it not apparent that the shame, odium and disgust attached to the subject arise from the instinctive knowledge that the function of Sex has become perverted, unnatural, degenerate, and hence ignoble and disgusting?

It will require but the general realization of the facts which we have just stated, to bring about a change of conditions, a resumption of the normal and natural. Just as are other perversions and abuses of the sexual nature highly condemned, avoided and punished by all right thinking people, so would this particular common unnatural practice be regarded as a per version, once the fact was realized that it is *unnatural*. Man instinctively shrinks from anything unnatural — there is an intuition which warns him off forbidden ground. Man's intuition in this particular instance has been diverted, owing to the perverted habit having been accepted by the race as "second nature." Man feels the repugnance arising from intuition, but not understanding the matter he evinces it toward the subject of Sex in general, treating it as impure and unworthy, instead of raising it up to its proper place of purity and condemning only the perversions of its principles.

Once regarded as *unnatural,* the ordinary promiscuous habit of cohabitation 'for the mere purpose of sensual gratification will be placed in the same category as the other unnatural manifestations of Sex, which cause a blush of shame to mantle the cheeks of every decent person at the mere mention or thought thereof, so unspeakably vile are they. All that is needed is the *realization* of the truth regarding the matter. The instinct and intuition of the race will do the rest. And strange and incredible though this may seem to those who have not noticed the undercurrents of public thought, the day is not far distant when the race will see this thing in its proper light. Many indications *of* this are even now apparent. There are many straws showing which way the wind is beginning to blow.

In conclusion, as in the beginning, ask yourself the vital question: If the physical Sex functions were not intended for the sole purpose of reproduction and procreation, for what purpose were they intended?

Carry this query around with you for awhile, and you will begin to see a new light on this subject.

VIII. SATYRISM

The "Satyr" of classical mythology was a strange creature, half-goat and half-man, with the body and head of a man, the head bearing a pair of rudimentary horns, the legs and feet being goat-like and covered with thick coarse hair. The Satyr was believed to dwell in caves and to roam about in the forests seeking to capture and gain the affections of the Nymphs.

The ancient Satyr and his latter-day prototype are regarded as the embodiment of all that is lascivious, lewd, wanton and lustful. He is always pictured with a brutal, sensual face, and lewd, leering eyes. His short horns, thick thighs, hairy legs, and cloven hoofs give to him a most repulsive appearance, and the suggestion of his perverted nature is apparent at first glance.

The identification of the Satyr with the goat arose from the belief that the latter animal was of a gross, sensual, lewd and lascivious nature, being, in fact, the only animal the male of which forced coition upon the female at unnatural seasons. The goat, in ancient symbolism, was always regarded as the embodiment of perverted and degenerate lust, and this because this particular beast had perverted sexual habits which had only in Man an analogous example.

To-day the term "Satyr" is often used to designate a man whose sex-nature has become perverted, until he has lost all sense of the natural functions thereof, and who lives for the purpose of indulging in lustful sensations and lewd experiences. And it is in this sense that we shall use the term, although applying it to some individuals who would indignantly deny its fitness in their case.

If the indulgence of the Sex functions for the mere purpose of gratifying- lustful sensations and lewd appetites be a mark of the Satyr, then *how* many men *of to-day we Satyrs?* How many men are using their Sex functions as Nature intended them to do—that is, solely for the purpose, intent and willingness to procreate and reproduce their kind, in response to the willing desire of their mates, and at only the appropriate seasons indicated by Nature? And, on the other hand, how many men not only are not willing to comply with the requirements of Nature, as above stated, but actually strive to avoid her dictates, and who prostitute their Sex functions for the gratification of their lewd, lustful appetites, at unseasonable times and often at periods in which every natural instinct revolts at the idea? *How many men are Satyrs, and how few are really Men!*

All men who force their Sex nature upon women, whether wives or mistresses, for the purpose of mere sensual gratification; or except in response to the natural desire of the woman; or with an unwillingness to reproduce their kind; or during the period of pregnancy of the woman;-all these men are manifesting the unnatural, perverted, degenerate actions of the Satyr. It is true that the majority of men act the Satyr in ignorance, believing that what they do is "according to nature" and is right and proper, providing that the rites of wedlock have been celebrated-but the act remains the same, nevertheless, so long as it is persisted in and continued. The mark of the Satyr is branded upon the brows of the majority of men, and women are made the serfs, slaves and instruments of sensual gratification by these human beings bearing the characteristics of the goat.

In order to see the enormity of the thing—in order to realize what the consequences are—it is only necessary to use the imagination and picture the world as it would be were natural and normal conditions to prevail. Let us try to imagine what the world would be *if* men used their Sex functions solely for the purpose of procreation and reproduction, instead of for sensual gratification and lewd sensation.

In the first place the "social evil" would disappear, and with it the horrible "white—slave traffic" which is the burning shame and disgrace of our modern civilization. No more would young girls be ruined to gratify the lust of villains, and then either driven, or actually sold, into a life of shame. No more would the "red—light districts" spread their blot upon the maps of our cities and towns. No more would the vile resorts flourish, in which the bodies and souls of men and women are dragged down to disease and death. No more would unnameable vile diseases fester and eat out the bodies of human beings, rendering the Temple of the Spirit a vile charnel house and cesspool. No more would our sons and daughters be offered up as a sacrifice to the Moloch of Lust.

With the disappearance of the "social evil," the crime of intemperance would largely diminish. All students of the subject are aware that the abuse of Sex is one of the most potent causes of intemperance. Wherever lust reigns, there does the demon of intemperance fatten. The brothel reeks with the fumes of liquor. The libertine plies his victim with liquor in order to cloud her reason and befuddle her judgment. The orgy of lust and lewdness is always begun with the drinking *of* liquor. Destroy the unnatural use of the Sex function, and you will have driven a dart into the very heart of the drink evil. Walk through the "red- light districts," the "levees," the "segregated district" of any large city, and see what a foul, unwholesome, unnatural thing it all is. With this unnatural and perverted use of the Sex function comes an instinctive sense of evil and shame that causes men to throw aside all restraint and to make themselves more bestial than the beasts, on the principle that "one may as well be killed for stealing a sheep as a lamb," or that "one may as well go the full length." The women who fall into the evil often seem to realize their degradation, and throwing aside all self-respect and self-restraint, sink to the depths. There is the instinctive recognition, of the human soul that the thing is wrong at its very heart, that develops the character of the Satyr when one enters upon the wrong path.

The newspaper recital of some of the great scandals, as for instance the murder case in which a certain young millionaire was tried for the killing of a wealthy clubman, reveals the extent to which the indulgence of the Sex functions in an unnatural manner can be carried. Lustful vice is made a fine art. Every device possible to the perverted intellect is employed to appeal to the jaded imaginations and desires of the libertines. Things unspeakable and unprintable, yes, actually *unthinkable* to the sane and normal person, result as a logical sequence from the original perversion. The scandalous reports which break into public notice from the resorts of some of the wealthier society men are almost unbelievable. The unnatural and insane excesses of ancient Babylon, Sodom and Gomorrah, Greece and Rome, are duplicated by the modern Babylons. And unless checked, the ulcerous and cancerous moral contagion will spread, and will in the end bring down our civilization in ruins, just as it has the civilizations of the past. For it will be noticed on history's pages, that this moral degeneracy always preceded the actual degeneracy and final downfall of the great nations of the past.

But, many of you will say, all this is true, but it refers only to the sexual excesses and immoralities perpetrated out of the wedded state: that in the married state there can be no immorality. Is this true? Stop and ask your self the question: How many married men are there who lead the natural normal sex life— who use the Sex functions only for the purpose that Nature plainly intended? How many men are there who allow their wives the real ownership of their own bodies, and who refrain from forcing their unnatural attentions upon their mates in a way which every female animal except the goat would indignantly resent and repel? How many men are there who regard their wives as their real mental and spiritual mates, instead of mere physical organisms for the gratification of their (the men's) lust for sensation and lascivious experience? How many men are there who are *fathers* in the true sense of the word, and who seek to, strive for, and look forward to bringing children into the world as nature intended, "well born," welcome, planned for and loved—- instead of as the result of "accidents" arising from the unnatural practice of prostituting the wife for the gratification of the husband's lust? These are hard questions-but they must be answered at the judgment bar of the soul of each. Each must be his own judge, under the Law. Each must pay the price. But each has the opportunity to reform and live the natural normal life that alone can brim- health, happiness and peace.

It may be objected to that we have placed the blame of this perversion of Sex upon man alone, and have said nothing about the woman. We are aware of this, and have purposely placed ' the blame where we think it belongs. **Woman** in the free state, not dependent upon man for her support, happiness, and right to live, would be in a position to dictate to man terms of relationship in accordance with the instincts of her own inner nature. Economically independent of man, she could and would dictate her own terms, and a mighty change would result. But for ages she has occupied the position of a serf and a dependent, a state from which she is now slowly emerging. She has been taught that "wives should submit themselves unto their husbands," as a religious duty; from the pulpit she has been taught that it was God's will that she should so do. Nothing has been said to her of her right to herself. The husband had his "rights," which she has been taught to believe were the result of natural conditions. She has had no opportunity to live her own life, in her own way-she has been driven to marriage as "the woman's only profession," and was led to believe that the words of wedlock once uttered, there could be no immorality in the wedded state. Naturally she has stifled the instinctive and intuitive revolt of her soul, and has habituated herself to the ordinary conditions.

And the man, himself, has many excuses. He does not understand the woman's nature or instincts. He believes in his "rights" for such they are held to be under divine and human laws-and he insists upon them and deems the woman unloving if she demurs. The public has been with him, and on all sides he is supported in his ingrained notions. Moreover, the influence of heredity is manifest in his case. Many generations of children have been brought into the world under "accidental" conditions, and in response not to the natural promptings of the two sexes, well-mated, and under the proper conditions, but to the mere selfish desire for sensation and gratification on the part of the male parent. And it would be strange if the influences so transmitted through the many generations from father to son, should not be powerful enough to lead man away from the natural path and normal practice.

There are two sources from which the reform must come—for it will come, either in our own civilization or that which will succeed it. It is in the line of Evolution, and the race is intuitively reaching for it through its highest evolved individuals. The first of these sources is the education of men to the realization of Nature's true intent and purpose in the Sex function. When the present conditions are seen to be unnatural, an effort will be made to avoid them and public opinion will begin to remould itself. The second source is the emancipation of women from control and mastery by man.

When woman attains her freedom, and realizes that she has a right to her own body, she too will study Nature's plans and purposes and will refuse to live unnaturally and abnormally. She will assert the natural right of refusal and choice just as the female animal does-she will refuse to submit for the mere purpose of gratification of the male's inordinate desires and appetites. And in the end it will be seen that this second source of reform—this assertion of woman's right to herself and her Sex— will be the principal cause of the ultimate reform and revolution along these lines. *The* Female is the original *sex-the male **was** an **after** product.* And in the Female is the only hope for the return to natural conditions of Sex relationship. And the change **will** come —it must come. Nature is slow to wrath, but inexorable in her punishments. She will destroy the race which defies her edicts, and will build up a new one in accordance with her true plans. The swing of the Cyclic Pendulum is now beginning its return. Nature is beginning to reassert herself.

IX. HIGHER PHASES OF SEX

In the preceding chapter we stated the true and only function of Sex on the physical plane —namely, the procreation and reproduction of the species. But we did not mean to imply that this particular plane was the only one upon which the Sex principle manifests. On the contrary, Sex manifests upon every plane of life and being, in countless variety of forms of expression. But upon whatever plane it may manifest, the principle of *creative activity*— generation or regeneration, production or reproduction, creation or recreation—is present and active.

There are many other purposes than that of the begetting of young, 'for which the male and female sex activities meet, combine, commingle and unite. On the vital, mental and spiritual planes the union of the two elements of Sex occurs, with the result of calling into being new activities, elements, and manifestations. Therefore those who, seeing the perverted conditions connected with the ordinary sex relations in our civilization, pronounce all Sex impure, and who lead the lives of ascetics and who avoid the company of the other sex, make a great mistake. The Man and the Woman have much to give to and receive from each other—many other planes of union than that ordinarily recognized.

In the first place there is unquestionably existent the peculiar vital force or energy, generally called Vital Magnetism, which has its features and phases of Sex. It is most difficult to describe the nature of Vital Magnetism, but its presence may be realized 'from actual experience and observation. It is a fact known to all occultists that each person has his or her individual personal atmosphere, or magnetism, which affects those coming in contact with the person. Some persons depress those with whom they come in contact, while others stimulate them. Some have a tendency to weaken physically those around them, while some are so full of vitality that others actually draw upon the surplus stock and absorb the vital energy of such persons. There are vital "vampires" as well as vital* "radiators/'' The phenomena of Vital Magnetism are well known to those who have made a general study of the subject, and we shall not attempt to go into the matter at length in this place.

It is not so well known, however, that there is a particular phase of this Vital Magnetism which has much to do with the relations of the two sexes. This may be called Sex Magnetism and its poles are found in the opposite sexes, the male being the positive and the female the negative. It is this activity of the Sex Magnetism that has much to do with drawing together the two sexes. * Each *sex* feels the desire to participate in the magnetism of the opposite sex, the individual magnetism of persons, of course, varying in their degree of attractiveness. Some persons are so charged with Sex Magnetism that they tend to attract and draw to them persons of the opposite sex. There are many men and women who do not possess particularly attractive features, form or manner, who nevertheless attract the other sex to them in a manner astonishing to those not in the secret. There have been men, such as the celebrated bigamists of police history, who have seemed to attract women as the flame does the moth. And there have been women who have exerted a strong attraction over nearly all men who came into their circle of influence. Nearly every reader of these lines will recall cases of this kind in his own acquaintance, or from his general experience.

While this Sex Magnetism in such exceptional instances may work harm, it is also a fact that it exerts a strong influence for good in the majority of cases in which its effects are not neutralized by sexual excesses on the physical plane, such as we have indicated in our preceding chapter. The union and combination of the two currents of Sex Magnetism of persons of the opposite sexes who are harmonious and congenial tends to invigorate and vitalize both persons. Sex is always creative, and the Sex Magnetism tends to create new vitality in the persons whose magnetism is harmonious. The ascetic, or the person of either sex who avoids the company of the opposite sex, is apt to become withered, devitalized and impoverished in nerve force and blood supply. Such people fly in the face of Nature, and suffer the consequence. It is a necessity of normal life for persons of opposite sexes to mingle in each other's company, and to receive and give the magnetic benefits resulting therefrom.

It is the union of the Sex Magnetism which draws the majority of married people together originally. Each feels a glow when in the presence of the other—each feels the revitalization that takes place when they are together. Each feels better, stronger, happier and more vital when in the other's company. No proof of this is needed, for the experience of nearly every person will corroborate the statement. Then why, you may ask, does this not continue with all married people? The answer is very simple: Married people too often dissipate and waste the Sex Magnetism by the unnatural sex indulgences of which we have spoken. Very often these practices or abuses of married life cause a depolarization, or reversal *of* the Sex Magnetism, which results in creating a condition of *repulsion* between the married pair, in place of the attraction which originally existed. This regrettable condition may be changed, however, and the normal conditions restored, if the couple will turn away from the perverted conditions which they have maintained, and replace them with natural, clean, wholesome relations of comradeship, companionship and mutual harmony.

Married men and women can be of the greatest use to each other if they will but maintain the proper kind of sex relationship. Instead of the attraction growing less, it will actually increase, and the "honeymoon" will last over their mutual lifetime. Each will strengthen and vitalize the other, instead of weakening and devitalizing one or the other, or even both, which latter deplorable condition we see in evidence in so many cases of people who have failed to grasp the true secret of the marriage relationship.

On the Mental plane we also find the manifestation of the Sex principle, not only in the direction we have indicated in the opening chapters of this book, but also in the direction of the inspiration and incitement to active thinking that two persons of opposite sexes exert upon each other if they be in proper harmony. It will be found in the majority of cases of successful men and women in the prominent fields of human endeavor, that the successful man or the successful woman is inspired by the love or mental sympathy, or both, of some person of the opposite sex. Too often, alas! this "person of the opposite sex" may be some one other than the married companion of the person in question, but this is because the original bond of unity has been allowed to become a burden and a hindrance, by reason of the Sack of understanding- of the true Sex relationship. The mental *rapport* of the two persons having been allowed to perish, one or both will instinctively seek for the "inspiration" or **rapport** of sympathy *of* some other person of the opposite sex.

We hear much of "affinities" in these days, and the majority of persons think that these attractions between persons of the opposite sexes always arise from pure lust or physical attraction. But such is not the case, for in many cases the parties to these entanglements are originally attracted by mental characteristics and qualities. There is a subtle attractive force attached to the quality of mental "understanding" of one person by another. Every mind instinctively seeks and reaches out 'for "understanding," and in too many cases there is none of this quality to be found in those in whom it should be quite in evidence. The result is that when the man or woman is brought in contact with one of the other sex who can and does "understand " there is sure to be an attraction and a desire for each other's company which often leads to wrecked homes and ruined lives. That so many of these "affinity" attachments afterward degenerate into purely physical or even lustful relationship, is only another proof of the fact that the prostitution of the natural Sex instinct to purposes other than its normal function is sure to work evil.

Let us quote a few lines from a writer in the magazines, whose words carry with them a sense of realization of the normal and desirable conditions which should exist between husband and wife, on the mental plane. The writer says: "The more things that a man and woman mutually love, the greater will be their love for each other. The more things in which they are mutually interested, the greater will be their interest in each other. The object of their mutual interest may be children, work, books, hobbies, other people, or what not -it matters not so much just what- the thing is that there should be outside things, many of them, in which the two should he mutually interested. There should be outside planes upon which the two minds should be able to meet. .. Heed this lesson, you men and women. Read between the lines of these hastily written pages.

For throughout it all runs a vein of truth that may bring happiness to many of you; that may tend to prevent a further breach between some of you who have already drawn apart while treading the path that God intended that you two people should tread together, if at all, side by side, shoulder to shoulder, eyes level with eyes, looking out upon the world together, and seeing together the same scenes of that wondrous land through which you are now journeying. Marriage—true marriage—means Comradeship above everything else. And unless this be had, then the essence of the thing is missing, and naught but the husk and unsatisfying outer materials remain. And this is a part of what *a* quarter-century of wifehood has taught me—a quarter-century of mingled prosperity and adversity; of pleasure and pain; of ups and downs; of sunshine and shadow; of storm and calm—all of which I have tried to face with confidence and faith, inspired *always* by the knowledge that by my side was one who both understood and was understood. And by reason of it all, I know that I have gained that without which all would have been lost, but which, gained, causes me to feel that all through which I have lived, yes, all, bitter and sweet .alike, was well lived and worth while — Comradeship in Marriage."

There is a plane still higher than that of mind, in which Sex is manifest—the Spiritual Plane. While it is impossible in a book of this kind to consider this phase of the matter in detail, we wish to say that Man and Woman mount the Ladder of Spiritual Attainment hand in hand, and by each other's help. Akin to the inspiration on the mental plane, is this higher source of help, sympathy and encouragement of this higher life. On the spiritual plane is to be found the highest form and phase of Love —Love which is concerned with the evolution and unfoldment of the soul of the loved one, rather than with the generation of the species, To many this form of love must of necessity seem as but *a* faint dream, or the idlest fancy. But to those who have caught even a faint glimpse of its reality and existence, it causes all else to fade into insignificance. But the higher the height, the greater the fall therefrom—and mortals must ever guard against allowing the perverted instincts of the physical plane from entering into the

Paradise of a love of this kind, and dragging down into the depths a love whose true home is On The Heights. IF such a love as this has come to you, treasure it carefully—guard it jealously from the encroachment of the lower senses—preserve it ever as the Pearl of Great Price.

It is not permitted to speak in general terms to the general public, about this manifestation of Sex on the Spiritual Plane. It dwells in a world of its own, sheltered from the profane gaze of the vulgar and materialistic crowd, As Emerson says: "Every man's words, who speaks from that life, must sound vain to those who do not dwell in the same thought on their own part. I dare not speak for it My words do not carry its august sense; they fall short and cold. Only itself can inspire whom it will,"

But it is Real—lo those who have experienced it, the one Real thing in a world of illusions.

X. REGENERATION

Nature devotes a great amount of energy to the task of reproducing living forms. Many of the lower forms of life seem to live merely for the purpose of reproducing life—of passing along the flame of life from torch to torch. Nature's reproductive energies are highly concentrated, and are wonderfully potent. The amount of creative energy concentrated and compressed into the mustard seed is equal to that diffused over a whole large plant—in fact the entire creative energy which is to serve the plant for its lifetime must be stored up within the seed itself, for the vital force cannot come from outside, although the outer nourishment is needed to build up the physical shape, form, and substance. The germ of the animal contains within itself enough stored-up energy to carry the animal through its normal period of life. In the processes of reproduction and procreation, Nature avails herself of her inner powers, and every minute she works miracles of concentration and conservation of energy.

The ancient occultists recognized the wonderful power stored in the reproductive organism, which is given out not only in the act of actual reproduction and procreation, but which may be also dissipated in the unnatural excesses and practices to which the race is addicted. They soon discovered that this wonderful concentrated power could be, and is, used not only for the purpose of generation but also for the purpose of *regeneration* of the life activities within one's own body, the exhaustion of which occurs if the vital forces be not given out in procreation or waste. In other words, that the wonderful concentrated forces of the sexual functions, if not otherwise used or dissipated, might be used by the individual himself or herself in re-energizing, re-charging, or regenerating the vital powers within his or her own organism. This was one of the reasons that continence was enjoined as a duty upon the members of the ancient esoteric and occult brotherhoods and sisterhoods.

A. R. Stockham, M. D., says: "Physicists have demonstrated with incontrovertible facts that it is eminently healthy to conserve the vital principle. The seminal secretion has a wonderfully imminent value; and, if retained, is absorbed into the system and adds enormously to man's magnetic, mental and spiritual force. In ordinary married life this force is constantly being wasted. Other things being equal, the man who wisely conserves is in concentrated mental and physical power and effectiveness, like a Daniel amid his companions. He builds and constructs, he is the organizer and executive head of industries, he is the orator and the inventor. He is the leader of great movements, because his power is drawn from an inexhaustible storage battery. . .. Although woman has not the semen to conserve, yet equally with man she has the thrilling potency of passion, that when well directed, heals sensitive nerves, vitalizes the blood and restores tissue,"

Newton says: "It is important to know that here are other uses for the procreative element than the generation of physical offspring, far better uses than its waste in momentary pleasure. It may, indeed, be better wasted than employed in imposing unwelcome burdens upon toiling and outraged women. Bat there should be no waste. This element when retained in the system may be coined into new thoughts, perhaps new inventions, grand conceptions of the true, the beautiful, the useful; or into fresh emotions of joy, and impulses of kindness and blessing to all around. This is, in fact, but another department of procreation. It is the procreation of thoughts, ideas, feelings of good-will, intuitions of truth—that is, it is procreation on the mental and spiritual planes, instead of physical, It is just as really a part of the generative function as is the begetting of physical offspring. It is by far the greater part, for physical procreation can ordinarily be participated in but seldom, while mental and spiritual procreation may and should go on through all our earthly lives—yea, through all our immortal existence."

J. H. Kellogg, M. D,, says: "It has been claimed by many, even by physicians, and though with but a slight show of reason, that absolute continence, after full development of the organs of reproduction, could not be maintained without great detriment to health. It is needless to enumerate all the different arguments employed to support this position, since they are, with a few exceptions, *too frivolous to deserve attention the popular notions upon this subject are wholly erroneous*. Their general acceptance has been due, without doubt, to the strong natural bias in their favor. It is an easy matter to believe what agrees well with one's predilections. A bare surmise, on the side of the prejudice, is more telling than the most powerful logic on the other side."

Prof. Mayer says: "It is determined, in our opinion, that the commerce of the sexes has no necessities that cannot be restrained without peril. . . .The contrary belief appears to us to be erroneous, without foundation and easily refuted,. . . Health does not absolutely require that there should ever be an emission of semen, from puberty to death, though the individual live a hundred years,"

Acton says : "There exists no greater error, nor one more opposed to physiological truth, than that which holds that continence produces impotence. In the first place, I may state that I have, after many years' experience, never seen *a* single instance of atrophy of the generative organs from this cause. I have, it is true, met the complaint; but in what class of cases does it occur? It arises, in all instances, from the exactly opposite cause, abuse; the organs become worn out, and hence arises atrophy.

Physiologically considered, it is not a fact that the power of secretion is annihilated in well- formed adults leading a healthy life, and yet remaining continent. No continent man need be deterred by this apocryphal fear of atrophy from leading a chaste life. It is a device of the unchaste, a lame excuse for their own incontinence, unfounded on any physiological law."

Dr. Kellogg makes the following important statement, which corroborates the theories of the ancient occult teachers : "Recent investigations have shown that the sexual glands are useful, not only as a means of race-perpetuation, *but for the physical well-being of the individual, through the vital stimulus exercised by them, through the influence of their peculiar secretion upon the processes of development and nutrition.* In view of this fact, it is evident that, so far as the individual is concerned, physical benefit is to be looked for, not in the loss of the secretion of the sexual glands, but in its retention and appropriation. In other words, reproduction is accomplished at the sacrifice of individual interests, a law which prevails throughout the whole organic world, being', in some instances, so pronounced that the development of progeny is accomplished only through the death of one or both parents. These discoveries afford thoroughly satisfactory and scientific explanation of two facts which heretofore have rested solely upon *a* basis of observation and experience:

1. That *continence is favorable* to physical vigor,

2. That sexual intemperance *is* productive of exhaustion and debility to a most extraordinary degree."

Dr. Nicholas says: "It is a medical and a physiological fact that the best blood in the body goes to form the elements of reproduction in both sexes. *In a pure and orderly life this matter is reabsorbed. It* goes back into the circulation ready to form the finest brain, nerve and muscular tissue. This life of man, carried back and diffused through his system, makes him manly, strong, brave, heroic...The suspension of the use of the generative organs is attended with a notable increase of bodily and mental vigor and spiritual life." And, as another writer has said: "Nature finds another use for the unexpended sexual energy in employing it for the building up of a keener brain and more vital and enduring nerves and muscles."

Outside of the list of the occult brotherhoods, all of whom were strictly continent, history gives us a long list of eminent men who followed the practice of continence, which indicates the correctness of the old occult teachings of regeneration. Newton, Kant, Paschal, Michelangelo, Plato, and many other eminent men were strictly continent. *All* the great occultists and mystics of ancient times observed strict continence.

The Greek athletes training for the great Olympic games were compelled to observe strict continence, the experience being that by this course they were able to conserve their vigor and strength much better. The prizefighters of to-day are compelled by their trainers to observe strict continence during the period of training-. Many of the former "champions" who "went to pieces" suddenly, owe their downfall to a violation of this rule. Dr. Henderson, after years of experience in tropical countries, has said : "I have seen many suffer severely, destroying their strength, health, happiness and life, by following the promptings of their unbridled passions. Need I say *that I have never seen a man suffer from keeping himself pure?*

Dr. Kellogg well states the philosophy of continence as follows: "The sexual function is double in its purpose; first, the sexual organs are always active, even when not exited to such a degree as to obtrude their activity upon the *consciousness*, as they supply the body with a needed vital stimulus and regulator; *secondly*, they furnish the only means by which the physical life of the individual and the perpetuation of the race may be accomplished. In neither of these important functions is the personal gratification of the individual the primary consideration. The exercise of the sexual function with a purely selfish purpose would seem to be a debasement of the sacred function in which man approaches most nearly to the creative power of which he is the image."

But there is quite a difference, however, between the intelligent practice of continence on the one hand, and the practice of an unnatural asceticism on the other. In intelligent continence, the sexual power, function and organism is respected as one of the highest pieces of Nature's handiwork—the symbol of the great creative force of the universe—to be used either for the purpose of procreation and reproduction, or else for the equally high purpose of regeneration, of self-strengthening and development. On the other hand the unnatural view of certain schools of asceticism regards the sexual power, function and organism as something impure and vile.

The continent occultist or mystic does not revile his sexual power, nor does he despise it —on the contrary he rejoices in its possession, but instead of wasting and dissipating it in excesses or unnatural indulgences, he *transmutes* it in Regeneration, and builds up his physical, mental and spiritual nature. Those who despise the sexual nature, and who fear and loathe it, bring upon themselves the inevitable reaction which always accompanies the unnatural practice of opposing any of Nature's plans and processes as evil. They bring upon themselves the negative condition by which their creative forces are neutralized and inhibited, and they suffer in health, mind and spirit. *There is nothing impure about Sex—the impurity lies in the abuse and unnatural use of the sexual functions.* Continence is a *positive* process—Asceticism is a *negative* process. There is a difference as wide as the poles between the two. Do not make the mistake of trying to "kill out" the sexual nature—instead, strive to strengthen and develop it, but *transmute* its energies scientifically, intelligently and naturally, in accordance with the world-old occult and mystic teachings of Regeneration.

This, then, is the Ancient Wisdom regarding Regeneration, stated in a few pages. Consider it carefully and you will be richly rewarded. The Ascetic places himself in opposition to the currents of Nature's Creative Forces—the Continent individual places himself in full accord with the great Life Forces of Nature. Instead of neutralizing his force he conserves and transmutes it. Grasp the inner meaning' of the Paradox of Sex, and you will have in your hand the control of many of the Finer Forces of the Cosmos. We can but hint at the whole truth here. The time is not come for the full teaching—neither is this the place. But he who practices the teachings contained herein will place himself well upon the road to attainment, and the further truth will come to him as he progresses. Such is the Law of the Path of Attainment.

FINIS

Printed in Great Britain
by Amazon